JAPAN

CHINA

Shanghai

FORMOSA
(TAIWAN)

Hongkong

Hanoi

HAINAN

PHILIPPINE
ISLANDS

NDO-

VIETNAM

LAOS

Manila

CHINA

CAMBODIA

Saigon

NORTH
BORNEO

BRUNEI

la Lumpur

ALAYA

SARAWAK

MOLUCCAS

NEW
GUINEA

BORNEO

CELEBES

Singapore

INDONESIA

Jakarta JAVA

AUSTRALIA

MACMILLAN & CO. LTD.

SOUTH-EAST ASIA

SOUTH-EAST ASIA

A Short History

BY

BRIAN HARRISON

*Professor of History in the University of Hong Kong
Formerly Senior Lecturer in History in the
University of Malaya*

Second Edition

LONDON
MACMILLAN & CO LTD

NEW YORK · ST MARTIN'S PRESS

1964

MACMILLAN AND COMPANY LIMITED
St Martin's Street London WC 2
also Bombay Calcutta Madras Melbourne

THE MACMILLAN COMPANY OF CANADA LIMITED
70 Bond Street Toronto 2

ST MARTIN'S PRESS INC
175 Fifth Avenue New York 10 NY

PRINTED IN GREAT BRITAIN

PREFACE

This is a book for the general reader and the student of history, not for the specialist scholar. But whatever interest and value it may have for the ordinary reader is due to those scholars of various nationalities who have worked in different parts of the whole historical field, and without whose labours a work of synthesis such as this could not have been attempted. To them the author is deeply indebted, and as deeply grateful. Special acknowledgement is due to Professor George Coedès, whose distinguished researches have thrown brilliant light into the dark places of early South-east Asian history. There is a real fascination in the study of the early history of South-east Asia, but it is at times the fascination of an especially difficult crossword puzzle in which many of the clues are horribly obscure, if indeed they are not entirely missing.

The author also gladly acknowledges a debt of gratitude to all those friends, both students and colleagues, with whom he has worked in the University of Malaya.

It is particularly hoped that this book may contribute in some way towards stimulating a wider and deeper interest in the history of their own countries among students in South-east Asia itself.

HONG KONG   B.H.

February, 1954

v

CONTENTS

LIST OF ILLUSTRATIONS

PLATES

MAPS

INTRODUCTION

THE term 'South-east Asia' is a convenient one. Although the area to which it refers forms neither a political nor a cultural entity, it contains a group of countries whose social structures have much in common, and whose past history and present politics show many similarities.

Geographically, the region is fairly well defined, though again it does not form a natural unit. It really comprises two broad geographical groupings : mainland South-east Asia, or the Indo-Chinese peninsula, containing the countries of Burma, Siam, Laos, Cambodia, Vietnam and Malaya ; and island South-east Asia, or the Malaysian archipelago, stretching from Sumatra eastward and north-eastward to the Philippines. Mainland and island South-east Asia together form a great wall, with a few narrow gateways, between the Indian and Pacific Oceans ; at the same time they provide a causeway—partly a series of stepping-stones—from Asia to Australia. A sea and land cross-roads is thus formed by the north-to-south sweep of the peninsula and archipelago, and by the east-to-west sea-lane that runs between them.

On the north, the limits of the region are well defined by the mountain barriers that stand between the Indo-Chinese peninsula and the continental mainland of Asia. At the south-eastern end, however, where the archipelago stretches down towards Australia, no such clear definition is immediately apparent. But a closer view of the structure of the archipelago enables us to draw a boundary-line between the Moluccas and New Guinea, for structurally New Guinea belongs to the Australian continent and was once joined to it. On the other hand, the western islands of the archipelago— Sumatra, Java, Bali, Borneo, and other islands lying west of a line drawn through the Strait of Macassar and the Strait of Lombok— stand in a shallow sea on the Asiatic continental shelf and were once joined to Asia. The islands between them and New Guinea— the Lesser Sundas from Lombok eastward across to Timor Laut,

Celebes, the Philippines—form a transitional zone which may properly be included in island South-east Asia.

Almost the whole of this great region has a tropical climate, and consequently the mass of its 180 million inhabitants share broadly similar methods of food-production and ways of living. Rice is their basic food; the peasant family and the village community are the mainstays of their social structure.

The majority of these people are of Indonesian stock, but the external influences of two thousand years—Indian, Chinese, Islamic, European—have produced considerable linguistic, religious and cultural differentiation among them. South-east Asia has never been in any sense an isolated or self-contained unit. Because of its crossroads situation on the map of Asia it has always been peculiarly exposed to external influences; it has been a meeting-ground of commerce, cultures and civilizations. In a sense South-east Asia has always been part of something bigger than itself; it has generally played a passive role in history, one which has meaning and significance only against the background of the history of Asia as a whole. The really vital theme of its history is the theme of 'culture-contact'—the story of the successive waves of cultural and commercial influence which have swept over it in a dual process of destruction and creation, and of the repeated challenge to the peoples of South-east Asia to relearn, to readapt and to reinterpret.

Culture, commerce and religion have in past times been closely interrelated intrusive forces with which South-east Asia has had to reckon. The first introduction of Hinduism, Buddhism, Islam and Christianity was in each case associated with commercial enterprise. Each of these retains its adherents in South-east Asia, which is therefore far from forming a religious unit. About half the total population of the region is Moslem, the main concentrations being in Indonesia and Malaya. The people of Burma, Siam, Laos, Cambodia and Vietnam, and most Chinese in all parts of the region, are Buddhists. Most Indians throughout the region (mainly in Burma and Malaya) are Hindus. In the Philippines 95 per cent of the inhabitants are Christian.

Linguistically, South-east Africa again does not form a natural unit. Three of the great linguistic groups or families of Asia are represented in the region : Malayo-Polynesian, Austro-Asiatic, and Tibeto-Chinese. Languages of the Malayo-Polynesian family —one of the most widespread linguistic families in the world—are spoken in the Malay Peninsula and throughout island South-east Asia including the Philippines. Languages with a common Austro-Asiatic basis are spoken in parts of Burma, Siam, Cambodia, Vietnam and Malaya. Burmese and Siamese are included in the Tibeto-Chinese family.

One result of South-east Asia's exposed position is that it now contains fairly large minority groups of non-indigenous Asians. Chinese and Indian immigration into such countries as Burma, Malaya, Sumatra and Java has created similar social and political problems in each, the problems of the 'plural society', a society in which 'distinct social orders live side by side, but separately, within the same political unit'.[1] But these are really old problems in a new and enlarged form. It is hardly an exaggeration to say that for the last two thousand years South-east Asia has been occupied with working out the consequences of problems presented to it either by the rest of Asia or by Europe.

In modern times almost all the countries of South-east Asia have shared the common status of colonial or dependent territories, and during this period the region has been exposed more than ever before to the influences of the outside world, a world that was itself changing rapidly. In their South-east Asian colonies the European powers, though without a common policy and without co-ordination, had to attempt to solve common problems of political administration and economic development, and, in recent times, the common problem of emergent nationalism. South-east Asian nationalism, on its side, in its various forms and stages, has had to seek solutions of the common problem of winning and working self-government.

[1] J. S. Furnivall : *Netherlands, India,* 1939, p. xv.

Chapter One

THE HUMAN TEXTURE OF SOUTH-EAST ASIA

HISTORY proper begins with written records; it begins, in fact, with the alphabet. The material of history is the written word; writing on stone, clay, papyrus, parchment or paper. But for the prehistoric period we have no such records and so must look for other sources of information. This is largely a matter of spade-work, a question of digging at the right places for evidence of prehistoric man—his bones, his tools and his dwellings—and of piecing this evidence together in the light of our archaeological knowledge.

The decisive stage in the transition from earlier forms of life to human life may very likely have been reached in a tropical climate. At any rate, South-east Asia provides us with the earliest evidence of the way in which this transition took place. In central Java, near the village of Trinil on the Solo river, the upper part of the skull of a very early form of human being was found in 1891. It seemed to belong to a large hominid at an intermediate stage of evolution between anthropoid ape and man. This earliest known individual in human history, commonly referred to as Java Man, was named *pithecanthropus* (Greek *pithékos*, ape; *anthropos*, man).

No further evidence of early man in Java came to light until 1936, when a skull was found at Mojokerto (west of Surabaya) which was of pithecanthropoid type in miniature, belonging prob-ably to an infant. Then in 1938 a series of further discoveries was begun in central Java. At Sangiran, on the Solo river, Van Koenigswald found in 1938 another *pithecanthropus* skull similar to the find of 1891; in 1939 a skull of the same type, but much larger and heavier-boned than the two earlier finds; and in 1941 a massive lower jaw-bone with three very large teeth in position—too large a bone to belong to *pithecanthropus* skulls of the size found earlier. It is possible that this last creature was an ancestor of the hominid *pithecanthropus*; in other words, that the human form has evolved from much larger forms with a very massive skull.

From all this it appears that there was a momentous evolution of certain anthropoid-ape forms into primitive human forms in tropical South-east Asia somewhere about the beginning of the pleistocene, or most recent, geological period. *Pithecanthropus*, the product of this evolution, is a representative of the first human inhabitants of South-east Asia. Indeed it is probable that men of this type were at one time spread over the whole area from Java through the Indo-Chinese peninsula up to north China, where the remains of a very similar, though rather more 'advanced', type have been found—*sinanthropus* or Peking Man. A number of teeth belonging to a hominid similar to *sinanthropus* have been

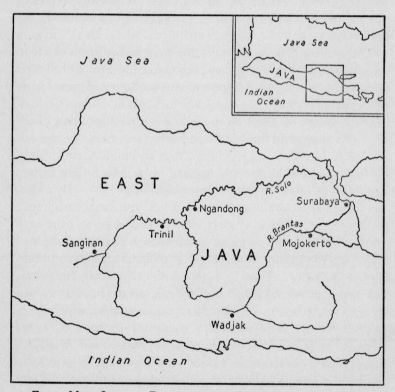

EARLY MAN: SITES OF DISCOVERIES IN CENTRAL AND EAST JAVA

unearthed in northern Vietnam. We may perhaps assume that pithecanthropoid man spread gradually northwards into China from tropical South-east Asia, undergoing further evolution along the way.

The two types, Java Man and Peking Man, lived long before any representative of human evolution so far discovered elsewhere in the world. Both probably—*sinanthropus* certainly—stood more or less upright in a biped posture; they had reached the real starting-point in human history after which it was possible for man to use his arms and hands, to make tools, to draw pictures, and thereby to develop a human brain. Ever since that starting-point man has gained mastery over the world around him mainly by making tools and by improving them. And throughout 98 per cent of human history the best tools that man has had were made of stone. The pithecanthropoid man of South-east Asia probably used the coarse chopping and scraping tools of palaeolithic, or Old Stone, type which have been unearthed in Java, Malaya, Burma and north China, as well as the chopping tools of petrified wood which have been found in Malaya and Burma. With such tools he gradually learnt to shape other instruments of wood and bone.

For thousands of years these pithecanthropoid men and their more human descendants were wandering among the jungles of South-east Asia and along its rivers and coasts, hunting or gathering their food, resting in cave dwellings or in rough shelters, as some of the primitive peoples of the area still do.

Central Java again provides evidence of the further physical evolution of early human types in the direction of modern man or *homo sapiens*. A collection of skulls and skull-fragments excavated from the terraces of the Solo river at Ngandong gives us a partial picture of a more advanced type, named Solo Man. His skull and brain case are much larger than those of *pithecanthropus*, but otherwise he retains a fairly close affinity to the pithecanthropoid type, and he is not yet *homo sapiens*. The earliest examples of *homo sapiens* in South-east Asia, called Wadjak Man, were also found in Java, near the south coast. The Wadjak skulls are believed to belong to the late pleistocene or post-pleistocene period; that is, to about twelve thousand years ago.

A skull known as the Keilor skull, found near Melbourne in Australia in 1942, bears a close resemblance to one of the Wadjak skulls, and this suggests that the Wadjak-Keilor type of man was ancestral to the Australoid type, which survives in the Australian aborigines of today as well as in some of the hill-tribes of Malaya, and which must have been the earliest fully human type to form a widespread population of South-east Asia.

As far as our present knowledge goes, then, we may picture the evolution of early human forms in South-east Asia as having moved along the line : pithecanthropoid form through Solo Man form and Wadjak form to Australoid form.

From the time when *homo sapiens* finally emerged, and for a period of thousands of years, a succession of different human types followed one another down from continental Asia through mainland South-east Asia and the islands. This 'drive to the south' is a recurrent theme in South-east Asian history. The succession of broad human groups which moved down into the region in prehistoric times seems to have been : Australoid, Negrito, Melanesoid and Indonesian (or Austronesian).

The *Australoid* and the very similar *Veddoid* people were probably the first widespread human inhabitants of South-east Asia. The Australoid type survives in the aborigines of Australia and in the Senoi and Sakai hill-tribes of Malaya. The Veddoid type (though generally with a Proto-Malay admixture) is seen in certain groups in the southern parts of Celebes, and on the Engano and Mentawei Islands off the west coast of Sumatra. There are also Veddoid types in Ceylon, and the peoples of southern India show a strong Veddoid admixture. The Australoid-Veddoid type is dark-skinned, with a depressed nose, and curly but not woolly hair.

The next oldest group of people to move down into South-east Asia were the small woolly-haired *Negritos*, surviving nowadays in Malaya as the Semang people of Kedah and Perak and the Pangan in Kelantan, and in the Philippines as the Aetas. Both Australoid and Negrito peoples spread southward as far as Australia.

Following these two groups probably came the *Melanesoid* people, a type no longer surviving in South-east Asia, but numerous in the Pacific islands to the east of New Guinea and Australia. Ancient skulls of Melanesoid type have been unearthed in north China and in Indo-China.

These three groups of peoples were at the mesolithic stage of culture, a transitional stage between the Old and New Stone cultures, at which some advance had been made in the quality and variety of stone tools and other implements and weapons, and also in invention of such equipment as fishing tackle and the dugout canoe with paddles. Examples of mesolithic industry have been found in Vietnam, Siam and Malaya, and in the larger islands from Sumatra to the Philippines. In the caves of northern Vietnam (Tonkin) a number of imperfectly polished or ground celts (chisel-edged stone tools) were discovered. This industry has been named Bacsonian, and there is another slightly different type known as Hoabhinian. Stone tools of a generally similar type to the Bacsonian have been found in Siam and, in the form of flaked hand-axes or scrapers, in Malaya and Sumatra.

The last great group of peoples to move down into South-east Asia in prehistoric times, probably between 2500 and 1500 B.C., was the group of the physical type called *Indonesian* or *Austronesian*. The descendants of these people form the basic population of Malaya and island South-east Asia today, and are essentially of the same human variety as the basic population of the rest of the Indo-Chinese peninsula and southern China. The mass of the southern Chinese are of the Indonesian physical type with a Mongoloid admixture, and it is very probable that the dispersal centre of the Indonesian people was in south-west China. The Indonesian physical type may be divided into two : Proto-Malay and Deutero-Malay. The Proto-Malay, which shows a clear Mongoloid admixture, probably formed the first basic Indonesian population of South-east Asia. It survives for the most part in mainland South-east Asia (e.g. the Jakun of Malaya), though in the islands the Bataks of Sumatra, the islanders of Nias, the Torajas of Celebes and most of the Dayaks of Borneo are Proto-Malay. The Deutero-Malay, a more mixed type—known also as the Coastal Malay—which must have followed the Proto-Malay very closely into South-east Asia, is represented by the Peninsular Malays, the Coastal Malays of Sumatra, the Javanese, Sundanese,

B

Madurese, Balinese, etc. ; in fact it is the normal Malay type of South-east Asia.

With the coming of the Indonesian people begins the neolithic, or New Stone, age in South-east Asia, when the majority of the inhabitants of the region used a variety of stone tools of advanced workmanship, well finished or polished, but had not yet begun to use metal implements. In the Malay Peninsula, Sumatra and Java the most typical neolithic implements were the quadrangular adzes. These were made of a very hard stone, beautifully finished by grinding and polishing, and square or quadrangular in cross-section. At one end was a bevelled cutting edge like that of an adze or chisel. These implements were probably used for cutting and shaping wood, the small ones for carving and the largest ones for building boats and houses. A large number of finished and half-finished quadrangular adzes have been found in Java, where there seem to have been well-organized production centres supplying other parts of the archipelago. The large quantity and the fine quality of these adzes, which were often made from semi-precious stones, suggest that Java already had a fairly dense population, and one that had reached a relatively high level of civilization, at any rate during the later phase of the neolithic period.

The Indonesian also showed a certain sense of artistry in the clay pots that he made for cooking or food storage. The Malayan neolithic pottery, for example, although roughly finished and unimaginatively decorated, reveals a real spirit of artistic enterprise in the remarkable variety of its shapes and designs.

It was in the neolithic age, reached at different times in different parts of the world, that man carried through the first 'industrial revolution' in history. It was then that he began to turn from hunting and gathering his food to cultivating it, and thus learnt the new ways of living that made civilization possible. History really begins with agriculture and the techniques and ways of living associated with it. The cultivation of food-crops, the domestication of animals, and the making of pottery were the great social-economic achievements of the neolithic age.

The Indonesian people still obtained their food partly by hunting and fishing, but they were also agriculturists. They cultivated rice and millet, either by the method of shifting cultivation (the *ladang* system), clearing a temporary field every year or so, or in permanent irrigated fields (the *sawah* system). They used these crops to brew a kind of beer as well as for food. They lived in wooden houses raised above the ground by bamboo or wooden piles. Their domesticated animals were buffalo and pig. They made cloth from the bark of trees. They were animists, believing that a life-force or soul-substance (*semangat*) was contained in all natural objects, and above all in their food plants. The life-force of the rice-field was personified as a goddess, the rice-mother, and a complex ritual made up of numerous prescriptions and prohibitions surrounded the cultivation and harvesting of the crop so that its life-force should be preserved and captured; for example, loud noise was to be avoided in the rice-field, and the grain had to be harvested with a small knife concealed in the hand. For the same reason the Indonesians were head-hunters, cherishing the head for its soul-substance.

Agriculture made possible a settled community life and the development of social custom and behaviour. The peasant village community became and remained the basic social unit under the guidance of its priest- or priestess-chief, who was the guardian of traditional religious and social custom (*adat*), regulations governing individual and group rights and duties, agricultural ritual, social privileges and penalties, all of which were handed down by word of mouth from generation to generation.

One aspect of early Indonesian community life is represented by megalithic or large stone monuments—tall upright stones (menhirs), raised horizontal stone slabs (dolmens), stone pyramids and terraces; all probably connected with ancestor worship or sacrificial ceremonies. On some of these monuments are carved simple magical symbols such as circles and rosettes. This megalithic culture is still alive in the Nias Islands off the west coast of Sumatra, and in the islands of Flores and Sumba; and even in parts of Java, Bali and Sumatra megalithic monuments are still used for ceremonial purposes.

The neolithic age in South-east Asia lasted from roughly 1500 to 300 B.C., when a new age began with the introduction of metals for utilitarian and artistic purposes, although polished stone implements naturally continued in use and were only gradually superseded. A bronze and iron culture, named *Dong-son* from the village in Vietnam where evidence of the bronze industry was first discovered, passed down into South-east Asia from China. The early Dong-son style of art appears to have been closely related to that of central China in the fourth to third centuries B.C. The use of bronze was thus introduced—the most distinctive product of Dong-son culture being the large bronze drum, decorated with ornamental patterns and sometimes with stylized representations of animals and men ; and iron seems to have been used at any rate during the later Dong-son phase, though its wide use was probably delayed until the later spread of Indian trade and settlement. The custom of urn-burial also seems to have been introduced during the Dong-son period.

Associated with this metal culture of the last three centuries B.C. was a new megalithic culture represented by sculpture in the round (e.g. the warrior figures of the Pasumah highlands in southern Sumatra) as well as bas-relief, and by monumental structures of smaller dimensions than those of the earlier Indonesian megalithic, such as the stone slab graves and tombs of Sumatra, Java, and the Bernam river area of Perak in Malaya. The decorative *motifs* common to Dong-son bronze and stone objects —double spirals, circles linked by tangents, patterns of wavy interlaced lines—were much freer and more complicated than the simple designs of the earlier megalithic. Traditional decorative designs of the Dong-son type are still found among certain peoples of southern China and among Bataks, Dayaks and other Proto-Malay groups.

Paintings were found on the inner walls of Dong-son stone chamber graves in Sumatra, and many such graves in various parts of the Malay Peninsula and the archipelago contained glass and cornelian beads, some of local origin but many of Mediterranean manufacture—an indication that trade connections between Europe, India and South-east Asia had already been established.

Chapter Two

EARLY CHINESE AND INDIAN INFLUENCES

WITH the neolithic and earlier megalithic, and then with the Dong-son and later megalithic, South-east Asia had already entered upon its long history as an area of successive culture-contact. From the earliest times the pattern of South-east Asian cultural history is woven upon the background of the history of cultural forces in the surrounding areas of Asia. And as those cultural forces become more integrated and articulated, they begin to exercise a correspondingly stronger and more easily defined influence.

We have already noticed the close affinity between early Dong-son art style and that of central China. In China the establishment of the Ch'in empire in 221 B.C. was followed by a short period of territorial expansion beyond the original state of Ch'in (which extended over what is now Shensi and part of Kansu), bringing the whole south-east coastal region of China under nominal Ch'in control. This region was at that time the country of the Yüeh people, distinct in race and in customs from the people of the Ch'in states to the north; and it may have been from the Yüeh that the Dong-son culture of South-east Asia was derived. Ch'in control extended for a time as far as Vietnam (Tonkin); but with the death of the first emperor in 210 B.C. this new imperial structure collapsed.

Out of the chaos that followed, there arose the Western Han empire, 206 B.C.–A.D. 9, with its capital at Ch'angan (Sian) on the plain of the Wei river. The zenith of Western Han influence was reached under the emperor Wu Ti, 140–87 B.C., when commercial and cultural contacts were established with central Asia and also with South-east Asia. The southern coastal region of China was again subdued and colonies of Chinese settlers were planted there, especially in the Canton delta; and the island of Hainan was brought within the Han sphere of influence. This expansion was perhaps part of Han trade policy, aimed at opening

up a south-west route to India as an alternative to the long and
difficult route by central Asia. Certainly Chinese goods were being
carried by caravan through Yunnan and Upper Burma and by the
Brahmaputra and Ganges rivers as far as the Hellenistic kingdom of
Bactria before 126 B.C. Han control of the southern coast of China
also led to the opening up of the sea-route to island South-east Asia.
Annals of a later dynasty record that a Chinese fleet was sent to the
southern seas between 116 and 110 B.C., and that the countries of
the south had sent embassies with tribute to the Chinese emperor's
court since that time. Envoys described in the Chinese annals as
'Romans' and Indians arrived between 73 and 49 B.C.

From South-east Asia itself comes clear evidence of direct
contact with China in the numerous specimens of Han pottery
found in east Borneo, in West Java and in south Sumatra (where
one sepulchral pottery vessel was found with an inscription dating
it 45 B.C.). From these finds we may be fairly certain that the
beginnings of Chinese trade and settlement in South-east Asia go
back to the first century B.C., even perhaps to the start of the
Dong-son period about 300 B.C.

The first definite Indian settlements that we know of were
established in the first century A.D., but references to South-east
Asia appear in Indian literature as early as the sixth century B.C.
The *Ramayana*, which dates mostly from the latter century, refers
to Suvarna-dvipa and Yava-dvipa ; *dvipa* being the Sanskrit for
'land with water on two sides', i.e. peninsula or island ; while
suvarna means gold, and *yava* barley. The *Puranas* mention
Malaya-dvipa and Yava-dvipa. It is impossible to be dogmatic
about the exact location of such place-names, but we may be
certain that they refer to parts of South-east Asia which attracted
Indian traders, on the peninsular mainland and in the islands.
Among the sea-faring people of the east coast of India the countries
of Lower Burma and the Malay Peninsula were known as lands of
gold, and it seems certain that from at least the sixth century B.C.
onwards Indian traders were sailing to those lands, and down
through the islands, in search of gold and tin. In the third century
B.C. the emperor Asoka sent Buddhist missionaries to Suvarna-
bhumi, 'land of gold'—perhaps the present Lower Burma.

If commercial contacts between South-east Asia and India were being made for hundreds of years before we have any definite record of them, the same is true of trade relations between India, the Middle East and the Mediterranean area. In the Dong-son period we may picture the whole overseas trade between the Mediterranean and South-east Asia as one single system, in which the eastward trade from India to South-east Asia was closely linked with the trade between India and the Mediterranean. Some of the goods reaching the Middle East from India would have come originally from further east; similarly, some of those exported from the Mediterranean to India would pass on to South-east Asia and China. Beads and glassware, for example, were exported in quantity from west to east, and collections of glass beads of Mediterranean origin are a characteristic feature of South-east Asia's Dong-son culture of the last three centuries B.C. A most remarkable collection of beads was unearthed along the Johore river in the southern tip of the Malay Peninsula. Nearly a quarter of these were Roman beads manufactured during the first two centuries A.D., but the collection also included a Hittite stone bead of about 700 B.C., a glass bead similar to those made in Italy about the same date, and glass beads of Phoenician or early Cypriot type. Another striking example of the wide movement of manufactures in these ancient times is a Roman lamp found in Siam, at P'ong Tük, which is considered to be almost certainly an import from the Mediterranean of about the first century A.D.

In the first two centuries A.D. there was a general expansion of commerce all along the Asian sea-route. With this there came an increase in geographical knowledge. A Graeco-Roman geographer named Ptolemy, who published a geography and atlas of the known world at Alexandria in about A.D. 150, provides the first real documentary evidence about South-east Asia. His map shows a number of ports dotted along the coasts of mainland and island South-east Asia. The Malay Peninsula, which is drawn with remarkable accuracy, he calls the Golden Chersonese, or Peninsula, which corresponds to the Suvarna-dvipa of the *Ramayana*. He also mentions, in South-east Asia, Iabadiou, or 'Island of Barley', which is exactly the Prakrit version of the Sanskrit Yava-dvipa. This has hitherto been generally taken to mean Sumatra-Java, but more recent research identifies it with Borneo.[1] It is impossible to identify all Ptolemy's place-names with certainty, but his map shows that he had access to fairly full information about the geography of South-east Asia, and this information must have come directly or indirectly from Indian traders who had been active in that region.

Indian trading activity in South-east Asia was greatly intensified during the first three centuries A.D., and the early settlements of traders, founded at convenient trading centres, gradually developed in wealth and cohesion until in the fourth and fifth centuries they formed separate areas of Indian rule and centres of Indian cultural, religious and artistic influence. Indian influence in South-east Asia was in origin a commercial influence, as was that of Arabs, Indian Moslems and Europeans in later times. Indian culture took root in various parts of the region because of the comparative wealth and prestige of Indian traders.

Direct evidence of the spread of Indian influence in South-east Asia during the first four centuries is rather scanty. We have the indirect evidence of the Chinese dynastic chronicles. According to them there was an 'Indianized' kingdom in Cambodia from the first century A.D., though the Chinese themselves did not enter into diplomatic relations with it until the third century. This is the kingdom which they called Funan (a name connected with the Khmer word *phnom*, mountain), and which they say was founded by a Brahman named Kaundinya (King of the Mountain). The state of Champa, situated along the coast of present Indo-China above Cambodia, enters history at the end of the second century. The Chinese records place its foundation (as the kingdom of Lin-yi) in about A.D. 190. Sanskrit inscriptions which are earlier than A.D. 400 show that Champa had become an Indianized state under a Hindu ruler.

Indians who voyaged overseas to South-east Asia naturally brought with them the ideas and practices of Hinduism and Buddhism. A way of life rather than an organized religion,

---

[1] *See* Braddell, Roland : 'An Introduction to the Study of Ancient Times in the Malay Peninsula and the Straits of Malacca,' in the *Journal of the Malayan Branch of the Royal Asiatic Society*, Vol. XIX, Part I (1941), pp. 21–74.

Hinduism was closely associated—as it is today—with the caste system of Indian society; its priests were *brahmans*, members of the highest caste. Its religious philosophy centred in the idea of a unifying principle of the universe, called the *Brahman*; for that reason, when considered in the somewhat restricted sense of a set of religious ideas and practices, it is referred to in these pages as *Brahmanism*. In practice, although the principle of a single ultimate reality was stressed by Brahmanist teaching, the worship of a number of individual or personal gods formed an important part of Indian everyday life, and Brahmanism found a place for them. It was these popular gods of Brahmanism, such as Siva and Vishnu, who were most likely to appeal to the unsophisticated peoples of

EARLY STATES OF THE IST TO 5TH CENTURIES

South-east Asia. Siva was the god of destruction, change and reproduction ; he was frequently worshipped in the form of a *linga* (the phallus, or male reproductive organ), represented usually in stone. The god Vishnu embodied the principle of preservation and permanence.

Buddhism arose partly as a challenge to the predominance of the Brahman caste as well as to the polytheism of ordinary Indian life. It had monks but no priests ; it was not linked to the caste system ; and at first it offered a practical philosophy of life rather than a system of religious worship. Later it divided into two schools, the Hinayana (the Little Vehicle of Salvation) which retained the simplicity of early Buddhism, and the more elaborate Mahayana (the Great Vehicle) in which the Buddha came to be worshipped as a central godhead surrounded by numerous *bodhisattvas*, temporary embodiments of the eternal spirit of the Buddha.[1]

Another Indianized state named Langkasuka was founded in the northern part of the present Malay Peninsula, according to the Chinese records, about the beginning of the second century ; though again the earliest actual contact between the Chinese court and Langkasuka is not recorded until much later, in the annals of the Liang dynasty under the year 515, where 'Langga-siu' is mentioned as having been founded over four hundred years before. In Malaya itself the tradition of the Kedah Annals (*Hikayat Marong Mahawangsa*) is that in ancient times a settlement was founded near Kedah, in the north-west of the Malay Peninsula, by a prince named Mahawangsa, who gave the place the name of Langkasuka ; but it seems that in fact Langkasuka and ancient Kedah were two separate settlements, the one on the north-east side of the peninsula and the other around the estuary of the Merbok river below Kedah Peak on the north-west side. North of Langkasuka, on the Gulf of Siam, was a kingdom called by the Chinese P'an-p'an. It sent an embassy to China about the year 450, and the Chinese annalist remarks that at the court of its king there were many Brahmans from India.

More direct evidence of Indian influence during the first four centuries is found in the images of the Buddha, belonging to about

[1] For glossaries of Indian and South-east Asian terms, and for general reference, see the *Handbook of Oriental History*, edited by C. H. Philips, M.A., Ph.D., and published by the Royal Historical Society, London.

the second and third centuries, which have been discovered in various places throughout South-east Asia; in Siam, Champa, Sumatra, Java and Celebes.[1] Buddhism seems to have opened the door to Indian cultural penetration of South-east Asia. These images are of the Indian art style known as Amaravati, from the town at the mouth of the Kistna river on the east coast of India, an important centre for the overseas spread of Buddhism during the second and third centuries. The Amaravati style is characterized by elaborately folded garments, showing Greek influence.

More positive record of Indian settlement and rule in South-east Asia begins with Sanskrit inscriptions. Some of these show that the Hindu cult of Siva had soon taken its place beside Buddhism in the Indianized states; the cult of Vishnu, however, does not seem to have begun before the fifth century. The earliest inscription in Cambodia (Funan) belongs to the first half of the third century; it is the rock-inscription of Vocanh, a Buddhist record in the Sanskrit language but in a script of south Indian origin. In Champa the Sanskrit inscriptions of the king Bhadravarman, dating from the second half of the fourth century, show that Siva-worship had been officially adopted there. In Malaya the earliest inscriptions, found in Kedah, are Buddhist and are not earlier than the fourth century. The inscriptions of Mulavarman in the region of Kutei, east Borneo, date from the beginning, and those of Purnavarman in West Java from the middle, of the fifth century. In Burma the earliest inscription, at the ancient site of Prome, belongs to the end of the fifth century.

Evidence of this kind gives a picture of the spread of Indian trade throughout South-east Asia and the establishment of Indian settlement and rule in several separate areas. Traders, adventurers and craftsmen were followed by Brahman and Buddhist priests and teachers, carrying the civilizing influence of Indian cultural and spiritual life and implanting it in these new lands by introducing the art of writing and the classical Sanskrit language and literature; bringing as well their own vernacular languages to enrich the

---

[1] In Siam, the bronze Buddha found at P'ong Tük; in Champa, the Buddha of Dong-duong (Quang-nam); in Sumatra, at Bukit Seguntang near Palembang; in East Java, in the south of the province of Jember; in Celebes, at Sempaga.

vocabularies of South-east Asia. Throughout the region generally, Brahmanism and Buddhism continued to exist side by side in mutual toleration. From time to time there was a change of emphasis, when one or the other would become temporarily predominant ; but in the Indianized states of South-east Asia they were simply two different aspects of a single Indian civilization.

The use of the Grantha script of southern India in most of the Sanskrit inscriptions gives a clue to the main homeland of the overseas Indians of South-east Asia in this early period. The Cholas of southern India had a major share in the trade with South-east Asia during the second and third centuries, and from the fourth century onwards the Pallavas of the Coromandel coast came to the fore as the Indians of greatest influence in the region. The rising power of the Pallavas suffered only a temporary setback in India itself from Samudragupta (c. 330–75), the ruler of the Gupta dynasty who conquered most of northern India and raided far into the south, and the importance of the Gupta period for our story is that it was one of great literary and artistic activity in India, when the literary use of Sanskrit became general and a new art style was evolved. Statues of the Buddha in Gupta style (characterized by transparent garments instead of the Greek folds of the Amaravati style) were exported to South-east Asia in about the fifth century, and several examples have been found in Siam, Malaya, Borneo and elsewhere. The establishment of a great Hinayana Buddhist centre at Conjeveram (Kanji) in the Pallava country in the fifth century must have given a fresh impetus to the spread of Buddhism across the Bay of Bengal. The Pallavas retained their commercial and political pre-eminence in South-east Asia until about A.D. 750.

We may ask what all this process of 'Indianization' meant for the peoples of South-east Asia and their 'Indonesian' culture. Those peoples who were to be affected were already distinguishable as a number of different groups by about the beginning of the first century A.D. Within the islands of the archipelago the basic population was proto-Malay, but all around the coasts lived the more mixed Deutero-Malay type, with whom Indian traders would first come into contact. On the Malay Peninsula the coastal people were probably still the Proto-Malay type. On the coast of the present central Vietnam, in Indo-China, were the Cham people, speaking a language belonging to the Malayo-Polynesian family. In the present southern Vietnam and Cambodia, and in the basin of the middle Mekong river, were the Khmer people, whose language was of the Austro-Asiatic group. In the valley of the Menam river (in modern Siam) and in Lower Burma were the Mon people, closely related in every way to the Khmers. In the Irrawaddy and Sittang river-basins (in the present Burma) was a group

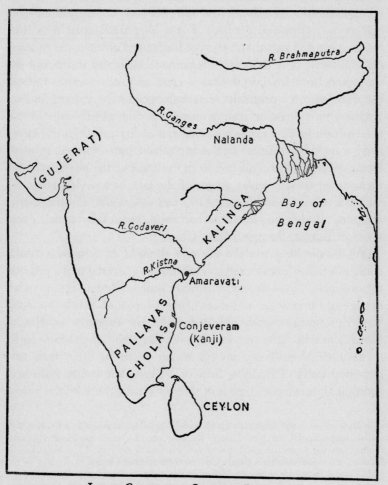

INDIA: CENTRES OF OVERSEAS INFLUENCE

which formed the spearhead of a southward drive of Tibeto-Burman peoples, the most important element in which was the Pyus.

To these peoples Indian influence meant the introduction of a developed culture based upon the art of writing,[1] the Sanskrit language and literature, the cults of Brahmanism and Buddhism, Hindu mythology, and distinctive artistic styles and techniques; and, where they came under direct 'Indianized' rule, upon the Hindu conception of monarchy, codes of law and methods of administration. No doubt the introduction and spread of this culture was slow and gradual. For a long time, apart from the royal courts and a small minority of Indianized officials, the peoples of South-east Asia must have remained essentially unaffected by the new culture, holding to their ancient ways of thought. Indeed the vast majority probably remained outside the pale of Indian culture and civilization throughout the period which lasted to the fifteenth century. Certainly during the earlier centuries the king, nobles and high officials in the Indianized states formed an aristocracy sharply distinguished from the mass of the people. Brahmanism, in the particular aspect of the cult of a divine kingship which it took in South-east Asia, was essentially an aristocratic religion. Buddhism, on the other hand, eventually struck deep roots in Burma, Siam and Indo-China.[2]

Yet in the long run the life and thought of South-east Asia could not fail to be coloured by Indianization, even if in the process the original colours were considerably watered down. If in general the age-old practices and beliefs of the peoples of South-east Asia were not fundamentally changed under the influence of Hindu culture, and if animism, ancestor-worship and their own agricultural ritual probably always meant more to them than the imported cults of Buddha, Siva or Vishnu, yet Indian influence brought about an enrichment of their original culture by the intro-

---

[1] The earliest extant example of a Malayo-Polynesian language in writing is the rock-inscription of Dong-yen-Chau in the province of Quang-nam, in the present Annam, dating from the third quarter of the fourth century. The language is Cham; the alphabet used is clearly derived from southern India.

[2] 'Viewed from one aspect Buddhism is Hinduism enlarged and divested of its social and institutional framework (caste and sacrificial ritual) and so adapted for export purposes' (Bouquet: *Hinduism*).

duction of new religious and artistic ideas, and a new mythology and folklore.

Meanwhile the relations between China and South-east Asia since Western Han times seem to have been commercial and diplomatic rather than cultural, and such Chinese as had settled in the region probably confined their interests to trade ; there was no export brand of Confucianism. The emperors in China assumed the status of paramount patrons and protectors of the rulers in South-east Asia, a status which was acknowledged by the despatch of occasional diplomatic envoys to the Chinese court. The Eastern Han dynasty with its capital at Loyang, which lasted from A.D. 23 to 221, extended Chinese authority across central Asia as far as the borders of Parthia, beyond which was Ta Ch'in, the Roman empire ; and a flourishing trade, especially in silk, between China and the Roman empire reached its height in the second century A.D. The trade followed not only the long trans-continental route to Parthia but also subsidiary land-routes such as those through the present Siam and Burma and then down the Salween and Irrawaddy rivers, for transhipment to the Mediterranean. The long sea-route from south China ports to South-east Asia, India and Europe was also followed, but the Chinese themselves did not take readily to overseas navigation and so left the initiative in the sea trade largely to others, as they were to do throughout most of their history. The seaports of the Indianized states of South-east Asia were ports of call and entrepôts for the China trade, and those states must have derived much of their wealth from the sea trade and also, on the north, from the trade passing along the subsidiary land-routes. Hence the diplomatic and trade missions from South-east Asia, and from India and the Middle East, which are recorded in the Chinese chronicles. The Eastern Han emperor received a mission in A.D. 132 from a country called 'Ye-tiao', which is thought to represent the name Yava-dvipa. A group of merchants arriving at the capital, Loyang, in 166 claimed to have come from some part of the Roman empire. Other merchants are mentioned as having passed through Tonkin to China.

Bordering on China itself, Tonkin (in the northern area of present Vietnam) felt Chinese power and influence more directly

than any other part of South-east Asia. Successive regimes in
China had brought Tonkin under control, and the Eastern Han
followed the example about the middle of the first century A.D.
Again in 226 Tonkin submitted to the kingdom of Wu, one of the
successor-states to the Eastern Han. The Wu kingdom followed
this up in 231 by sending expeditions further south to obtain the
nominal submission of Champa (Lin-yi) and Funan, and, some
fifteen or twenty years later, by the despatch of two envoys on a
diplomatic tour of South-east Asia.

China's door was open to foreign ideas as well as trade. Like
South-east Asia, she was a missionary field for Buddhism. After
its introduction into China by way of central Asia before or soon
after the beginning of the first century A.D., Buddhism was mainly
confined to the emperor's court until the fall of the Eastern Han in
221, but from then on it spread rapidly, and between the third and
sixth centuries it was adopted by the majority of the Chinese
people. Buddhist scriptures were brought in and translated by
Indian missionaries, and Chinese converts went on pilgrimage to
the great centres of Buddhist teaching and devotion in India.

One such pilgrim was Fa-sien, who left China in 399 and
travelled overland to India, where he remained, collecting and
copying the sacred texts of various Buddhist schools, until 411.
He then returned by sea from Ceylon by way of 'Ye-po-ti' (which
corresponds to the name Yava-dvipa and is identified with
Borneo),[1] where he stayed for several months before continuing
to China. After him there seems to have been a regular interchange
of Buddhist pilgrims and priests between China and India by the
sea-route. In 424 a Buddhist priest named Gunavarman was at
'Cho-po' (which again corresponds to Yava-dvipa) on his way
from Ceylon to China, and as a result of his teaching the ruler of
Cho-po was said to have been converted to Buddhism. The
Chinese records say that a number of embassies arrived from a
place called Ho-lo-tan in Cho-po during the first half of the fifth
century. The spread of Buddhism in China thus helped to reinforce its position in South-east Asia.

[1] See footnote on p. 12.

Chapter Three

EARLY INDIANIZED STATES: FUNAN AND SRIVIJAYA

The kingdom of Funan in present Cambodia was founded, according to the Chinese records, in the first century A.D. The Chinese account says that an Indian Brahman prince named Kaundinya arrived in Funan from the south by sea, and married the local chieftainess, named Willow-Leaf, after subduing her people. But Funan's earliest record is the rock-inscription of Vocanh, a Buddhist document in Sanskrit and a south Indian script, belonging to the first half of the third century. About the same time Funan sent the first of many embassies to China. Funan was certainly a most important centre of Indian rule and influence. Starting from a settlement on the southern tip of present Vietnam, it moved to the delta of the Mekong river and extended gradually over the present Cambodia and central Vietnam, along the valley of the Menam river, and down into the Malay Peninsula. For five hundred years it was the dominant power of the Indo-Chinese peninsula and by far the most important Indianized state in Southeast Asia. It held a commanding position on the Gulf of Siam, and its ports must have had a large share in the transit trade to China.

Somewhere about A.D. 400 a second Kaundinya arrived in Funan and became ruler; he came from a country which the Chinese annals call P'an-p'an, south of Funan on the Gulf of Siam, where Indian Brahmans were influential at the royal court. These early Brahman rulers must have introduced the Hindu cult of Siva, which was certainly well established in Funan in the fifth century; but Buddhism was also strong there in the fifth and sixth centuries.

Funan was at the height of its power at the end of the fifth century; the 'Indonesian' tradition of locating holy places on hills or mountains had accorded its rulers a divine status as 'Kings of the Mountain' (*phnom*, Funan). But the power of Funan

weakened in the course of the sixth century, and supremacy in the
Cambodian region was gained by the Khmer people of the state
called by the Chinese Chen-la, which centred in the high country
of the middle Mekong river. The Chinese sources say that Chen-la
overthrew Funan some time after 539. This conquest of Funan by
Chen-la is an example of the recurrent 'drive to the south' in the
history of the Indo-Chinese peninsula, the tendency on the part of
the peoples in the north to press down upon those in the south,
causing recurrent tension and conflict between the highlands of the
middle Mekong plateau and the alluvial plains of Cambodia, and
between the upper and lower valleys of both the Menam and
Irrawaddy rivers.[1]

With the conquest of Funan begins the Pre-Angkor period of
the Khmer kingdom, which lasted until 802. The seventh century
saw the steady extension of Khmer rule over the former Cambodian
territory of Funan. Funan had thus prepared the ground for the
flowering of Khmer civilization, which was to be one of the most
successful results of the transplanting of Indian culture to the soil
of South-east Asia. The Khmers entered into the cultural inheri-
tance of Funan, and their rulers adopted the dynastic legend of the
'Kings of the Mountain'.

The glory that was Funan lived on in the memory of Cambodia
and of South-east Asia in general. In central Java, where a powerful
dynasty established itself in the seventh century,[2] the rulers were
to assume the title of Sailendra or 'King of the Mountain', probably to signify their claim to be the imperial successors to the kings
of Funan. And that claim was to be made good when, in the
middle of the ninth century, the Sailendra dynasty placed itself at
the head of a new great Indianized power of South-east Asia, the
imperial power of Srivijaya.

The kingdom of Srivijaya, with its river-port capital at Palembang in southern Sumatra, was the real successor to Funan as the
predominant political and commercial power in South-east Asia.
Its more commanding position on the sea-route between India and
China gave it greater advantages than Funan had possessed, and

---

[1] Coedès, G.: *Les Etats Hindouisés*, p. 117.
[2] *See* de Casparis: *Inscripties uit Sailendra-tijd* (Bandung, 1950).

made it the first in the succession of great seaports, such as Malacca, Achin, Batavia, Penang and Singapore, that were to derive their strength from a prominent situation alongside the Straits of Malacca.

The prosperity of a commercial power situated on the Straits naturally depended to a large extent upon the flow of trade to and from the Middle East, India and China. Close trade relations between the Coromandel coast of India and the Straits area had already been firmly established. Since the third or fourth century Persian ships had been regularly engaged in the carrying trade between the Middle and Far East. In the Chinese annals from the end of the fourth to the beginning of the seventh century, imports from East Africa, Arabia, India and South-east Asia are normally referred to as products of 'Po-sse' or Persia, because that was the home country of the majority of the merchants importing those goods into China. In the seventh and eighth centuries, the time when Srivijaya fully emerged as the dominant commercial power on the Straits, there was also a marked revival of China's export trade as a result of conditions of production and commercial policy under the T'ang dynasty. Renewed Chinese interest in overseas trade had already been displayed early in the seventh century by the despatch of a trade mission to South-east Asia in 607. Under T'ang rule (618–907), when the land frontiers of the Chinese empire were advanced to the Caspian Sea and the borders of Persia, China's tolerant and cosmopolitan policy opened her doors wide to foreigners and to foreign ideas and trade ; and at the same time her industrial productivity in pottery, bronze and silk, itself stimulated by this policy, gave an added stimulus to trade and travel along the overland and oversea routes. In 750 the river at Canton, which had become a flourishing port with a large foreign community, was described as crowded with ships belonging to traders from Persia, India and South-east Asia. T'ang pottery was in demand in many parts of Asia ; broken pieces have been unearthed at a number of scattered sites in India and the Middle East. It was upon these general conditions of Asian trade, as well as upon her own position on a main highway of that trade, that the growth of Srivijaya's commercial power was based.

For some glimmer of light on the origin of Srivijaya we must turn, as usual, to the Chinese annals. They contain reference to a mid-fifth-century state called Kan-to-li, which they say was later named San-fo-ts'i, a Chinese equivalent to Srivijaya. The Kan-to-li of the annals was certainly an Indianized state whose rulers and envoys had Sanskrit names, but there is no clear evidence of the existence of Srivijaya itself prior to A.D. 670 when its first embassy to China was recorded. Soon afterwards Srivijaya recorded events in its own history between 683 and 686 in a group of four stone inscriptions. These are in the Old Malay language—a mixture of Sanskrit and Malay—and in south Indian script. Two inscriptions were found near Palembang, one of which describes how the king led an army of twenty thousand men against some enemy, while the other commemorates his founding and dedication of a public park. A third was found near a tributary of the river Jambi (north of Palembang), and another on the island of Banka, recording an invasion of Java. Taken together, the inscriptions seem to show that the kingdom of Srivijaya, with its capital at or near Palembang, had extended its supremacy over the southern part of Sumatra, including the island of Banka, and had invaded Java.[1] North of Palembang, in the region of the present Jambi, there was a state called Malayu. It sent an independent embassy to China in 644, but it was absorbed by Srivijaya between 689 and 692.

A visitor to Srivijaya in the late seventh century was the Chinese Buddhist pilgrim I-tsing. He arrived in a Persian ship in 672 and stayed for six months to study Sanskrit grammar before going on to India. On his return from India he stayed in Srivijaya for four years, and later returned there again from China to write his memoirs. Buddhism, as well as trade, still gave a strong impetus to travel, and Srivijaya seems to have been in regular communication with India and China. I-tsing notes that there were over a thousand Buddhist priests in Srivijaya; and soon afterwards (717) a fleet of thirty-five Persian merchant ships arrived at Srivijaya from Ceylon. From 670 to 740 Srivijaya was sending regular envoys to China, and in 724 a Chinese title was conferred upon its ruler.

---

[1] Perhaps West Java, the location of a mid-fifth-century Sanskrit inscription (see *ante*), and of a kingdom of Taruma of which nothing more is heard after its embassy to China in 666–9.

The eighth-century rulers of Srivijaya combined commercial enterprise with an enthusiasm for Buddhism of the elaborate Mahayana school. Because some control of the Malay Peninsula was necessary for the continued command of the trade-route through the Straits of Malacca, Srivijayan interests and Mahayana Buddhism were both fostered in that region. A Sanskrit inscription of A.D. 775 found in Ligor, in the northern Malay Peninsula, praises the great king of Srivijaya and commemorates his erection of a Mahayana Buddhist sanctuary. The general extension of

INDIANIZED STATES OF THE 7TH TO 9TH CENTURIES

Mahayana Buddhism in the Malay Peninsula,[1] Cambodia and island
South-east Asia at this time was a reflection of the influence of the
new Pala dynasty in northern India and, more specifically, of that
of the Nalanda university in east Bengal.

In central Java the introduction of Mahayana Buddhism is
associated with the rise of a powerful dynasty, the Sailendras, and
a great age of cultural renaissance in that region. The origin of this
new dynasty remains a matter of much speculation. It may have
sprung from a state which appears in the Chinese annals from 640
onwards as Ho-ling (an equivalent of Kalinga), founded perhaps
by émigrés from the Kalinga country in eastern India. Ho-ling
was a centre of Buddhist culture in the middle of the seventh
century, but its exact location is doubtful. There is documentary
evidence from central Java itself in the form of a stone inscription
of 732, which records the erection by a King Sanjaya of a Siva
monument (a stone *linga*) in the island of Yava, 'rich in grain and
gold-mines'.[2] This King Sanjaya, a patron of the cult of Siva,
may have laid the foundations of Sailendra rule in central Java ;
and the Brahmanist temples on the Dieng plateau, in which the
Siva cult seems to have predominated, may be associated with the
Sanjaya regime on the reasonable view that they belong to the first
half of the eighth century.

It was from about the year 750 that central Java began to respond
to the new influence of Mahayana Buddhism. This sect of Buddhism was to show, in Java and elsewhere, a strong tendency
towards assimilation with the Brahmanist cults, especially with
that of Siva. However, it is not unlikely that an immediate result of
the acceptance of Mahayana Buddhism, and perhaps of the appointment of Mahayanist teachers from Bengal to the royal household,
would be the disestablishment of conservative Brahmanist interests
associated with the previous regime in central Java. This, at any
rate, is a possible interpretation of the Chinese sources which
mention the removal of Ho-ling to the east by a king named Ki-yen
between 742 and 755 ; and it is an interpretation which gains

---

[1] *See* Winstedt : *Cultural History*, p. 20.
[2] Ho-ling and King Sanjaya may be associated with a Hindu power which ruled
in both Borneo and Java.

THE BOROBODUR SHRINE, CENTRAL JAVA, INDONESIA

support from the presence of a Sanskrit inscription of the year 760 at Dinaya, near Malang; this inscription, the oldest that can be dated in East Java, records the foundation of a sanctuary in honour of Agastya (the great teacher of Brahmanism in southern India) by a Prince Gajayana—a name which may be represented by the Chinese Ki-yen.

At any rate Buddhism now becomes predominant in its central Javanese setting at the same time as the Sailendra rule is being fully consolidated. The Maharajah Panangkaran, who was ruling in 778, definitely carried the title of Sailendra. It was this combination of new political power with new religious impulse that produced the great Buddhist monuments of central Java. At Kalasan, in the Prambanan valley, there stands a temple built in honour of the Buddhist goddess Tara by the Sailendra king Panangkaran in 778. At Kelurak, in the same area, a Bodhisattva image was consecrated in 782 by a Mahayanist teacher from Bengal. The influence of Bengal is evident in the use of a Pre-Nagari script in both cases.[1] Apart from these examples, fixed dates cannot be assigned to the Buddhist monuments of the Prambanan valley, but they certainly belong to the Sailendra period. To that period also belong the Buddhist monuments of the Kedu plain, including the supreme achievement of this age of renaissance in central Java, the Borobodur.

Along with these political, religious and artistic developments in Java itself there went an expansion of Sailendra political influence into mainland South-east Asia—along the east coast of the Malay Peninsula and into Cambodia. The real extent of this Sailendra 'imperialism' is uncertain. Later tradition credited King Sanjaya with wide conquests as far as Cambodia and China. According to Vietnamese sources, Tonkin was invaded in 767 by forces from Cho-po and K'un-lun (the latter a general term for the coastlands of the south); in 774 and again in 787 the coast of Vietnam was raided, apparently from Java in both instances. The Sailendras are linked with the northern part of the Malay Peninsula by an incomplete inscription on one side of a *stele* (upright stone slab) in Ligor, which refers to a king 'who bears the title of Maharajah because he belongs

---

[1] The Nagari script developed in northern India out of a variety of the Gupta script.

to the Sailendra family'. This inscription probably belongs to about the year 775 (which is the date of a separate inscription on the other side of the *stele*, belauding the great king of Srivijaya). As for the Khmer kingdom of Cambodia, there is a tradition of Sailendra domination there during the second half of the eighth century, which is supported to some extent by later Arabic sources. It may have been due to Sailendra influence that Mahayana Buddhism spread to Cambodia, as a Bodhisattva image of 791 found there indicates. The title of Sailendra (King of the Mountain) may very well have expressed the claim of the central Javanese rulers to be the political successors to the Cambodian imperial dynasty of Funan 'Kings of the Mountain', a claim likely to be substantiated by some control over Cambodia itself. Certainly when Jayavarman II founded the new Angkor dynasty shortly after 800 he repre-

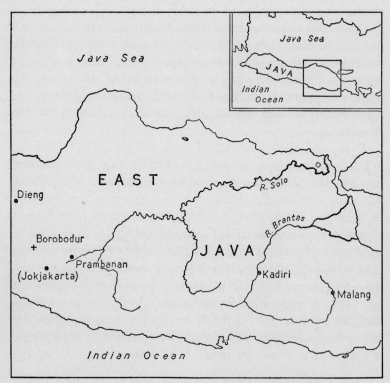

CENTRAL AND EAST JAVA IN THE SAILENDRA PERIOD

sented himself as the liberator of Cambodia from Javanese suzerainty. Again, the evolution of Khmer art from 800 onwards appears
to have owed much to the stimulus of central Javanese influence.

But of far greater political significance was the extension of
Sailendra influence into southern Sumatra, the heart of the Srivijayan empire, whose rulers, as we have seen, also cultivated Mahayana Buddhism. At some date about the middle of the ninth
century the Sailendras obtained a controlling influence in Sumatra,
possibly as a result of a royal marriage. Evidence is provided by a
royal charter of 850–60 from Nalanda in east Bengal, which shows
that Suvarna-dvipa (i.e. the Malay Peninsula and Sumatra) was at
that time governed by a Sailendra prince. He is described as
balaputra, or younger son, of King Samaragravira, who was himself
son of a king of Yava-bhumi (Java), 'ornament of the Sailendra
dynasty'—the latter probably being the king Panangkaran of the
Kalasan temple of 778.

This union of Sailendra energy and prestige with the imperial
power of Srivijaya, which took place about the year 850, was the
outstanding event in the history of South-east Asia in the ninth
century. The Sailendras, now installed as Maharajahs of Srivijaya,
continued to direct the fortunes of that empire down to the time
of its fall in the fourteenth century. From about 850 onwards there
was an unprecedented concentration of political and commercial
power in the Srivijaya empire.

This great change involved the transfer of the seat of Sailendra
power from central Java to its new home in southern Sumatra. For
Java it meant the end of the Mahayanist interregnum and the return
of the Brahmanists. The first indication of this restoration is a Siva-
inscription of 863 in the Prambanan district, where later, at the
beginning of the tenth century, the full resurgence of Brahmanism
was to be signalized by the construction of the Lara-Jongrang
group of Hindu temples. Yet Buddhism was not eliminated from
Java ; on the contrary, the normal assimilative tendency reasserted
itself between Brahmanism (especially in its Saivitic form) and
Buddhism, and indeed was to culminate in the cult of Siva-Buddha.

The revival of Brahmanism and Siva-worship in central Java
marks the rise of the new kingdom of Mataram, a name which

first appears in inscriptions between the years 898 and 910. After 929 Mataram moved its centre to East Java, where it began to develop overseas trade and sea power, and to build up a political and commercial sphere of influence which rivalled that of Srivijaya. The adjacent island of Bali, where Buddhism and Siva-worship coexisted, remained an independent state during most of the tenth century, but came under the authority of Mataram between *c.* 985 and *c.* 1006. In the last years of the tenth century Mataram seems to have decided to challenge the supremacy of Srivijaya and there were continued hostilities between the two, but in 1006 Srivijaya invaded Java and destroyed the Mataram capital. Thus at the beginning of the eleventh century Srivijaya remained master of the Straits region. The dual basis of her power in Sumatra and the northern Malay Peninsula was indicated in the description of her ruler as 'king of Kadaram and Srivijaya'.

But Srivijaya was not to be allowed to retain her dominant position on the Straits without challenge from other quarters. Early in the eleventh century she had to face a new challenge from India itself. The Cholas of Tanjore in southern India were developing a strong naval power, and were extending their commercial activities along the sea-route eastward to South-east Asia and China. Their relations with Srivijaya seem to have been friendly at the beginning of the eleventh century, for the king of Srivijaya had a Buddhist temple built at Negapatam, on the Coromandel coast, in *c.* 1005. But commercial rivalry between the two powers developed soon afterwards. Srivijaya may have attempted to restrict or impede Chola commerce on its way through the Straits ; it may have made exorbitant demands for transit and port dues. Commercial monopoly has a long history in the Straits of Malacca. At any rate a large invasion fleet was sent eastward against the Srivijaya empire in 1025, and a Chola inscription (the Tanjore inscription of 1030) claims the capture of the 'king of Kadaram and Srivijaya', the conquest of Srivijaya itself, and other victories. The Malay Annals (*Sejarah Melayu*) record that the Cholas destroyed Ganganagara on the Dinding coast and a fort on a tributary of the Johore river, and captured Temasek, the site of the future Singapore. The Chola conquest, however, does not seem to have had lasting results. It would not be easy to keep such distant lands under

permanent control from southern India. Srivijaya, having probably been forced to acknowledge Chola suzerainty and to concede
favourable commercial terms, was left independent, and there was
no displacement of Mahayana Buddhism. But there appears to
have been renewed aggression from the Cholas in 1068–9, when
they claimed to have conquered Kadaram on behalf of a ruler who
had appealed for their intervention, and to have handed the kingdom over to him.

Meanwhile the Mataram kingdom in East Java, under King
Airlangga (1019–42), was recovering from Srivijaya's onslaught
of 1006. In about 1050 dynastic rivalry split the kingdom into two
parts ; but one of these, the state of Kadiri, rapidly developed into
a strong maritime power, its sphere of influence extending outwards over the eastern parts of island South-east Asia.

Chapter Four

INDIANIZED STATES OF THE INDO-CHINESE PENINSULA

By its conquest of Funan the Khmer kingdom known to the Chinese as Chen-la had entered into a heritage of Indian cultural and religious tradition. In the early, or Pre-Angkor, period of the new Khmer Cambodia, which lasted until 802, Buddhism seems to have been almost as prominent as in Funan times, while Siva-worship became virtually the state religion. Indian models were followed very closely in the Khmer art style of this period, for the Khmer had not yet begun to translate the Indian tradition into his own art language.

In 802, after an uncertain period during which, as we have seen, Cambodia appears to have been brought to some degree under Sailendra influence, the country was reunited by the 'liberator' Jayavarman II, founder of the Angkor dynasty. This Angkor kingdom flourished from the beginning of the ninth to the end of the twelfth century. The civilization which the Khmers evolved in this period was to have a powerful influence on the later Thai kingdoms of the Mekong and Menam river-basins.

Our knowledge of Khmer civilization is mainly derived from the great group of buildings of the ancient Khmer capital at Angkor, near Siemreap in present Cambodia. Here we have a pattern of Indianized rule in South-east Asia and the clearest example of the adaptation of Indian ideas to local tradition. Although the monuments of Angkor are Khmer in style, they are essentially Indian in spirit. The whole plan of the main buildings is based upon the ancient Indian conception of the structure of the universe. The essential features of this cosmology, common to Brahmanism and Buddhism, were a central mountain called Meru, above which was the home of the gods ; a surrounding ocean ; and an enclosing wall of rock. The plan of the royal capital at Angkor was designed as a model of this world-structure, as an image of the world in miniature, with the essentially religious purpose of inducing sympathy and harmony between the human community and the divine world, between the microcosm and the macrocosm, and more particularly between the ruler and the gods. Closely linked with this ideal of exact correspondence between the royal city and the divine world was the conception of the king as being himself a god, a living link between heaven and earth. This tradition of divine kingship, supported by both Brahmanism and Mahayana Buddhism, had passed down to the Khmer rulers through the Funan and Sailendra 'Kings of the Mountain'. It was apparently reintroduced into Cambodia from Java by the first Angkor ruler, Jayavarman II.

Although both Brahmanism and Mahayana Buddhism were patronized by the Angkor kings, Brahmanism enjoyed special favour from the foundation of the dynasty early in the ninth century down to the second half of the twelfth century, and for most of that period the cult of the god-king was closely bound up with the worship of Siva. Siva, it was believed, had endowed the founder of the dynasty with the 'essence' of kingship in a ceremony that had taken place on a holy mountain in the centre of the kingdom. The 'essence' of kingship was embodied in an image of Siva himself, in the shape of the *linga*, and thereafter this was housed in a pyramid temple—an artificial holy mountain—built by the king at the centre of the capital city. This mountain-temple could then be regarded both as the centre of the world and as a symbol of the essential union of god and king. Moreover, the temple was the final destination of the king himself; for although during his lifetime he resided in a wooden palace, on his death, having abandoned his earthly kingship and become completely divine, he was transferred to a temple built of stone, where he could be worshipped as a god of one substance with Siva.

The magico-religious symbolism which lay behind the Khmer royal cities and temples was the governing force in the lives of its rulers and officials. The Khmer king was worshipped as a god in his own person; and after his death he became Siva or Vishnu or even the Buddha, according to his preference. The numerous stone images of the period were intended to represent not only the gods but also the actual god-kings who had been or would be united with the gods at death. The various temples were primarily funerary structures or mausoleums, where the god-kings would reside after death and where they would be worshipped in the appropriate form.[1] Thus the whole politico-religious life of the Khmer state revolved about the god-king. To his people he was both king and god of their whole world; his earthly residence, the royal capital of Angkor, with its surrounding wall and moat, symbolized the great universe within its encircling wall of rock and ocean; and on the highest point of the Meru mountain-temple which marked the centre of this world-city stood an image of the god-king in the shape of Siva, Vishnu or Buddha. The Khmer city, with its cosmic pattern and its god-king, sought to mirror the great universe and its presiding godhead, and in that reflection to capture prosperity, power and permanence.

The politico-religious ideas reflected in the buildings of Angkor, and in the numerous stone inscriptions found elsewhere in ancient Cambodian territory, were essentially those of the Khmer court and hierarchy. The monuments and inscriptions throw no direct light on the life of the people, beyond indicating the immense labour that must have been directed to the task of construction. The religion of Angkor was a religion of the court and the aristocratic oligarchy; its civilization was essentially their civilization. Court and aristocracy, although they did not represent a separate racial element—for the dominant Indian aristocracy of the earliest period of Indianization in South-east Asia had now become infused with local blood through intermarriage—still stood above and apart from the mass of the people. The great Khmer temples, then, did not rise out of a popular faith, as did the cathedrals of Europe. They were not places of public worship, but primarily royal or princely foundations constructed to house the personal worship of the founder or his ancestors in the form of one of the gods of the Brahmanist or Buddhist pantheon. Yet the Khmer monarchy itself was doubtless 'popular' in so far as it was regarded as the agent of prosperity, i.e. good rice harvests.

[1] The same is probably true also of the images and temples of the 'Hindu' period in Java.

The whole spirit of Angkor Wat, the greatest of the Khmer funerary mountain-temples, is one of aloof majesty, but the labour and artistic skill dedicated to its construction have made it the noblest example, rivalled only by the Sailendra mountain-temple of Borobodur in Java, of the flowering of the Indian cultural and artistic tradition in South-east Asian soil. Angkor Wat was the funerary temple of King Suryavarman II, a great conqueror ; although it is to all appearances a sanctuary of the Hindu god Vishnu, the deity worshipped there was in fact the Khmer king identified as Vishnu after death. This great building dates from the first half of the twelfth century.

As successor-state to Funan, Khmer Cambodia also inherited territorial ambitions and the urge to expansion over the former Funan dominions in the Indo-Chinese peninsula. On the western side, in the Menam river-basin, the Khmers subdued the Mon people, closely related to themselves, during the first half of the eleventh century. On the eastern side they reduced Champa to subjection for a time during the twelfth century. Champa, although at one time a dependency of Funan, had itself formed a distinct area of Indianized rule since about the end of the second century A.D., but from the ninth century onwards, sandwiched between two powerful and frequently aggressive neighbours—the Khmers of Cambodia and the Vietnamese of Tonkin—it had to fight hard for survival. The Khmers invaded in 945 ; pressure from the Vietnamese increased after 980, and forced Champa (about the middle of the eleventh century) to surrender the northern parts of her territory. Then in the first half of the twelfth century, under their god-king Suryavarman II, founder of Angkor Wat, the Khmers swept northwards as far as Tonkin, and part of Champa was annexed. Now, however, Champa fought back. Having first obtained a non-intervention agreement from Tonkin, she attacked Cambodia in 1177, captured the god-king's capital of Angkor, and devastated it. But the Chams were soon expelled, and the restoration of the Khmer capital in the form in which it has survived— Angkor Thom with the mountain-temple of Bayon at its centre— was carried out under King Jayavarman VII during the last twenty years of the twelfth century. Indeed the Khmers re-established control over Champa, installed a puppet ruler in 1190, and virtually annexed the whole kingdom from 1203 to 1220.

Khmer expansion had also followed the earlier pattern of Funan in other directions. In the twelfth century, according to Chinese sources, the territory under Khmer domination extended from Cambodia across the Menam river-basin and north-westward to the border of the present Burma, and also southward down the Kra Isthmus as far as the Bay of Bandon—that is, to the northern outpost of the Srivijaya empire.

While the Khmers thus dominated the central part of the Indo-Chinese peninsula, Vietnamese power was expanding outward from the Red River delta over the eastern part of the peninsula. Tonkin, which had been under Chinese provincial government since the first century A.D., gained political independence in the tenth century, and from then on the Vietnamese, with their strongly Sinicized culture, exerted increasing political and cultural pressure southward upon the Indianized people of Champa.

The story of the transmission of Indian culture to the peoples of Burma is linked with the history of the Mons, a group of Indo-nesian stock closely related to the Khmers, who from the earliest times inhabited the coastal region of Lower Burma as well as the valley of the Menam river. Lower Burma—perhaps the Suvarna-bhumi or 'Land of gold' to which Buddhist missionaries were sent by Asoka in the third century B.C.—must have been one of the first parts of South-east Asia to be visited by Indian traders and teachers when they began to follow the coastline of the Bay of Bengal eastward. The Mons of Lower Burma were certainly the earliest 'Indianized' people of that country. At the same time this area was subject to intermittent pressure from Upper Burma as a result of the southward drive of Tibeto-Burman peoples, who eventually became part of the modern Burmese population. The first wave of Tibeto-Burman immigration was represented by the Pyus, northern neighbours of the Mons, and those people also owed their first civilization to the Indian influences that entered Burma from the sea. Indeed our first positive evidence of the penetration of Indian culture in Burma comes from the ancient site of Prome, at the head of the Irrawaddy delta, in the old Pyu country. This evidence, which belongs to about A.D. 500, consists of fragmentary inscriptions containing extracts from the Pali canon of the Buddhist scripture—the Tripitaka. Besides this there is considerable evidence from Old Prome, in sculptures and in bronzes, of the influence of the Gupta art of India. Chinese Buddhist pilgrims of the seventh century describe Prome as a centre of Hinayana Buddhism, the form which finally prevailed in Burma.

Meanwhile the Mons of Lower Burma had proved apt pupils of their Indian teachers. They learnt the art of writing and adapted south Indian script to their vernacular Austro-Asiatic language. The shapes of the letters in the earliest Mon inscriptions (belonging to the late eleventh and early twelfth centuries) are almost identical with those of earlier inscriptions of Champa and Java, and are apparently derived from the Grantha alphabet of southern India. The Mons accepted Hinayana Buddhism and retained close contact with Hinayana centres in southern India and Ceylon. Their cities of Pegu and Thaton became important seats of Buddhist culture.

The Pyus of Prome now proved to be merely the forerunners of other less cultured Tibeto-Burman immigrants into the lower Irrawaddy valley, who were finally to dominate the whole of Burma. For some two centuries before A.D. 800 the Burmans had been pressing southwards from eastern Tibet into the Irrawaddy plain, gradually subduing and absorbing the Pyus. The Burmans overthrew the old Pyu capital at Prome about the middle of the eighth century and founded a new capital of their own at Pagan in the ninth. Then, after a period of consolidation, from 1044 onward they began to extend their power southwards to the coast, conquering the kingdom of the Mons. This period of Burman expansion began with their king Anauratha (1044–77), under whom an earlier Mon irrigation system was reconstructed to the east of Pagan on the rice-plain of Kyaukse, which became the granary of northern Burma.

The Burmans had almost certainly come under Mon cultural influences well before this time, but according to tradition King Anauratha was converted to Buddhism by a priest who came from the Mon city of Thaton to the Burman capital of Pagan in 1056. The king then sent one of his ministers to Thaton to obtain a collection of scriptures of the Pali canon, but this request was

D

refused, whereupon Anauratha organized an expedition which captured Thaton in 1057 after a three-months siege. Thirty collections of the Pali canon, as well as the Mon king, his ministers, priests and numerous skilled workers, were transported to Pagan. Politically, the conquest of the Mon country marked a further stage in Burman expansion and opened a window to the sea. On the cultural side it brought the Burmans fully within the orbit of 'Indianized' civilization ; along with Hinayana Buddhism they now accepted and assimilated the writing, literature and art of the people they had conquered. The Mon script became the main vehicle of Mon-Burmese culture and the ancestor of the modern Burmese form of writing. The Pagan period of Burmese history, beginning with King Anauratha in 1044 and lasting until the Mongol invasion of Burma in 1287, is therefore one of great importance in the cultural history of the Burmese people. Two centuries of unified rule, during which the whole territory corresponding to modern Burma was under the control of the Burman rulers of Pagan, made possible an easy and natural process of cultural assimilation between Mons and Burmans.

Meanwhile a new phase in the southward drive of peoples into the Indo-Chinese peninsula had begun. The Thai or Shan people (Shan being a Burmese term, and Thai the indigenous name) seem to have been originally scattered through central and southern China ; the population of present-day southern China contains a high proportion of this strain. They were united after about A.D. 650 in a kingdom known to the Chinese as Nan Chao or 'the Country of the Southern Lord', with its capital (after 750) at Tali in the province of Yunnan. But Chinese pressure continued to drive the Thai gradually further southward. They moved naturally down the river valleys ; down the Mekong, the Menam, the Salween and the Irrawaddy. They entered the 'Shan states' of the upper Irrawaddy valley about the middle of the eighth century, conquering the Pyus of that area. In northern Siam itself the first Thai settlement of importance is traditionally ascribed to about the year A.D. 860. In Laos the Thai were strongly entrenched by the early eleventh century.[1]

[1] To the Chinese the Shan or Thai were known as Ai-lao or Lao. The last name is still applied to the Shans of Upper Siam and to the people of Laos.

A.D.	BURMA (Pyus)	SIAM (Mons)	CAMBODIA (Khmers)	VIETNAM (Chams)(Vietnamese)	MALAY PENINSULA (Proto- and Deutero-Malays)	SUMATRA	JAVA
100			FUNAN	TONKIN (UNDER CHINA)			
200					KEDAH LANGKASUKA		
300				CHAMPA			
400							
500	SOUTHWARD DRIVE OF BURMANS		FUNAN CONQUERED BY KHMERS				
600			PRE-ANGKOR KHMER KINGDOM				
700	PROME (PYU CAPITAL) CONQUERED SOUTHWARD DRIVE OF THAIS					SRIVIJAYA	SAILENDRAS
800	PAGAN (BURMAN CAPITAL) FOUNDED PAGAN DYNASTY	SOUTHWARD DRIVE OF THAIS	ANGKOR KINGDOM				
900				TONKIN GAINS INDEPENDENCE	UNION OF SAILENDRAS & SRIVIJAYA		MATARAM
1000		THATON (MON CAPITAL) TAKEN	WARS BETWEEN KHMERS & CHAMS				
1100							KADIRI
1200	MONGOL INVASION— END OF PAGAN DYNASTY	THAI ESTABLISHED IN CHIENGMAI	THAI ATTACKS	MONGOL INVASION	TAMBRA-LINGA	INVASION	SINGHASARI MAJAPAHIT
1300	PEGU (INDEPENDENT MON KINGDOM)	THAI ESTABLISHED IN AYUTHIA		MING CONQUEST	MALACCA	CONQUEST OF SRIVIJAYA	
1400			ANGKOR ABANDONED	VIETNAM GAINS INDEPENDENCE	SIAMESE INVASIONS		
1500							END OF MAJAPAHIT

CHART TO ILLUSTRATE THE MAIN LINES OF POLITICAL CHANGE IN SOUTH-EAST ASIA TO 1500

In the thirteenth century the disturbance caused by the Mongol invasion of Sung China, and the actual conquest of Yunnan province by the army of the Mongol Kubilai in 1253–4, gave a final impetus to the Thai drive to the south and west; while the Mongol invasion of Burma in 1287, by overthrowing the Pagan dynasty and leaving nothing in its place, facilitated the Thai advance in that direction. Northern Burma was overrun by the 'Shans'; and in the south the Mons, freed from the domination of Burman Pagan, re-established an independent kingdom with its centre at Pegu. Burma remained thus disunited until the middle of the sixteenth century, by which time the Burmans had regained a measure of control in the middle and lower parts of the Irrawaddy basin and had reconquered the Mon country.

Passing down into the Menam valley and overthrowing the Khmer imperial regime in that area, the Thai established first the kingdom of Chiengmai in the upper valley (c. 1275), and later the kingdom of Siam proper with its capital at Ayuthia in the Menam delta (1350). After a long struggle with the advancing Thai, the Khmers were thus forced to withdraw eastward within their territory of Cambodia proper. A Chinese envoy who visited the country in 1296 found it sadly impoverished as a result of the campaigns against the Thai. Renewed pressure from the Thai finally compelled the Khmer kings, before the middle of the fifteenth century (1431), to abandon their great city of Angkor.

ANGKOR WAT, CAMBODIA

Chapter Five

INDIANIZED STATES OF SUMATRA AND JAVA

THE Straits of Malacca and island South-east Asia enjoyed a marked revival of commerce in the twelfth century, and Srivijaya, having survived the Chola challenge of the previous century, was now able to recover her former strength. Just as the trade of island South-east Asia, and particularly that of Srivijaya, had been invigorated by economic conditions and policy in T'ang China from the seventh to the ninth century, so the commercial revival of the twelfth century was in part a reflection of a new expansion of Chinese foreign trade under the Southern Sung dynasty (1127–1276). The Chinese were now themselves taking an active part in overseas trade. The increased concentration of population and capital on the south China coast under the Southern Sung was an important factor in this development, which was accompanied by advances in ship building and design, and in the science of navigation. The Sung porcelain industry was another factor of equal importance, for Sung ware was in demand in many parts of Asia as far as India and the Middle East, and on the east coast of Africa. The South-east Asian countries, and especially Srivijaya because of her position on the sea-route across Asia, naturally stood to gain by participation in this movement of trade. Production of pottery was stimulated in the area itself; high-quality 'celadon' ware characteristic of the Sung period was manufactured by immigrant Chinese potters in Siam from about 1300 or earlier, and probably also in other parts of the Indo-Chinese peninsula.

But the major economic assets of South-east Asia consisted of natural products, and it was these that enabled the whole area, and the islands especially, to gain a considerable share of the trans-Asian sea trade. The gold and tin which in ancient times had drawn Indian traders eastward were still important products, but to these had been added others for which there was a steadily increasing demand both in Asia and Europe, such as ivory, ebony and camphorwood, and above all spices—pepper, nutmeg and cloves. Although from very early times the pepper-vine of the Malabar coast of India had constituted a source of supply which for centuries was rich enough to meet the demands of western Asian and Mediterranean markets, the gradually expanding commerce of Asia had increasingly drawn on the supplies of another species of pepper —long pepper—which in one form was indigenous in island Southeast Asia. Pepper therefore formed a commercial asset of growing importance for much of South-east Asia, and the increasing demand for this commodity in the world market was to have a powerful influence on the future history of the whole area. Of even greater potential value, however, were those spices—nutmeg and cloves— which were the exclusive products of South-east Asia. Nutmeg, and its by-product mace, grew on the tiny island group of the Bandas and nowhere else in the world ; while cloves could be obtained only from a tree that was a native of the Moluccas or Spice Islands. The scarcity-value which these spices possessed was eventually to draw the merchant-adventurers of Europe across the seas to those remote islands of South-east Asia.

Already, however, the predecessors of the Europeans were at work on the exploitation of the produce markets of South-east Asia. From the third or fourth century Persian traders had visited Southeast Asian ports, transacted business with Indian and local merchants, and carried the products of the area to other countries of Asia. Arab and Chinese merchants had also had a share in this trade, and from the ninth century Arab geographers included in their works a description of the Malay Peninsula and the islands, usually in rather confused and romantic terms, with a smattering of factual information which was reproduced by one writer after another. They mention the tin and bamboo exports of Kalah (usually understood to be Kedah in the north of the Malay Peninsula), a port which was a dependency of Zabag or Srivijaya, and a busy entrepôt centre for Arab and Chinese traders in camphor, ivory, amber and spices, as well as in the various products of the *Selat* or Straits area known in modern times as 'Straits produce'. They describe the island of Rami (Sumatra) with its gold and camphor, its rhinoceroses and elephants. They point out the difficulties and dangers of trading in the Straits area on account of widespread piracy.

The founder of Islam had been a member of the trading community of Mecca, and the expansion of Islam beyond Arabia itself was an economic movement as well as a religious and political one. Once their military conquests were over the Arabs settled down to administration and trade, and the unified regime which they established over the Middle East after the conquest of the two great commercial centres of Damascus and Alexandria (A.D. 635 and 642) had made possible a vast expansion of trade between the Mediterranean and the Indian Ocean, and so provided a stimulus to the commerce of Asia as a whole. Islam also moved eastward after the conquest of Persia in the seventh century; Arabs established themselves in Baluchistan about A.D. 650 and conquered the coastal region of that country in 710; soon afterwards they entered India, conquering Sind and the whole of the lower valley and delta of the Indus in 712, and thus establishing a Moslem pocket in north-west India. Islam was on the move across Asia, and Moslem merchants were carrying the faith along with their merchandise wherever they travelled.

Yet it was not until seven hundred years after the foundation of Islam that the faith succeeded in taking permanent root within South-east Asia. Persian and Arab merchants continued to visit its ports during all that time, and knowledge of Islam came with them, but it was not until the faith was presented by Indian Moslems that it became acceptable. It was not to Persia or Arabia but to India that South-east Asia had always looked for cultural inspiration combined with commercial prestige. The acceptance of Islam among the islands and in the Malay Peninsula had therefore to await its acceptance by Indians who were prominently engaged in the overseas trade between India and South-east Asia. It was not until the thirteenth century that this condition was fulfilled, when Islam began to entrench itself in north-west and north-east India under the rule of the Turkish sultanate of Delhi; and it was mainly from Gujerat (south of Sind), and by the Moslem mercantile community of its port of Cambay, that Islam was then transplanted.

Meanwhile Gujerati trading vessels were already appearing in South-east Asian ports in the twelfth century, along with others

from the east coast of India, from Persia and Arabia, and from the
south coast of China, all sharing in the commercial revival of the
time. Reference has been made to the stimulating effect on Asian
sea trade of developments in south China in the twelfth and
thirteenth centuries. Another notable factor in the trade revival of
this period was the general stimulus to trade between Asia and
Europe created by the Crusades (*c.* 1100–1300), which affected the
Indian Ocean especially. Here the Moslem Gujeratis were beginning to assert themselves as leading agents in India's overseas
trade, both with the Far East and with the Middle East and the
Mediterranean. They acted as direct exporters of Indian goods and
also as intermediaries between Far Eastern, Indian and Middle
Eastern markets, and they were well equipped to do so by the
existence of a growing textile industry in Gujerat itself, which
provided them at once with a commodity of high intrinsic value
and with a medium of exchange in other Asian markets, as, for
example, in the spice markets of South-east Asia. From this time
onwards there was a growing demand in Europe as well as Asia
for the spice products of island South-east Asia, and these formed
a valuable proportion of the goods which flowed from Asia through
Egypt and Syria into the Mediterranean area, producing important
effects there in the enrichment of the Italian commercial cities, the
development of European trade routes, and the growth of credit
and financial organization. The products of South-east Asia, in
other words, were helping to build up those energies and resources
in Europe which were destined to recoil upon Asia itself when,
from the sixteenth century onwards, they began to seek new outlet
in a wider world.

The play of these larger economic forces was to induce changes
in the balance of power in South-east Asia right down to our own
day, and in the twelfth and thirteenth centuries we may discern
new shifts of power in the island area which suggest that this
process had already begun. In East Java the kingdom of Kadiri,
well placed for domination of the produce markets of southern
Celebes and the spice islands of the eastern archipelago, had
developed by the twelfth century into a great commercial power
which was also a strong centre of Hindu culture and of a politico-

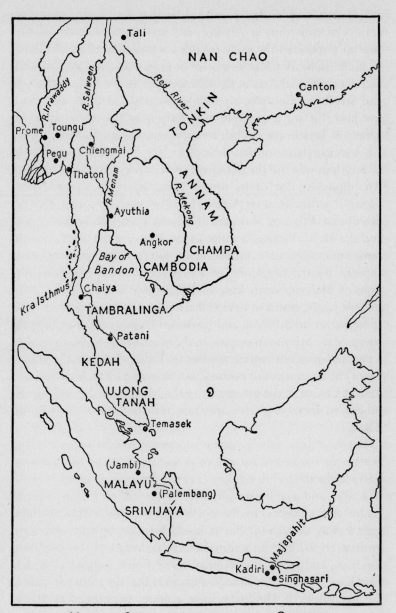

MEDIEVAL STATES OF THE 9TH TO 14TH CENTURIES

religious cult of Vishnu paralleled by that which was flourishing
about the same time at Angkor, and which, like that of Angkor,
probably reflected the early twelfth-century revival of Vishnuism
in India itself. A Chinese writer[1] in 1178 places the leading commercial powers of Asia in the following order : Arabia,[2] Chö-p'o,
and Srivijaya. Chö-p'o, a puzzling geographical term, may stand
for Java ; if so, it is likely that Kadiri, as the one commercial
power of Java in the twelfth century, represented Chö-p'o for the
Chinese merchants of that time.

Srivijaya was still the dominant power on the Straits of Malacca.
An impressive list of its fifteen vassal states is provided by a
Chinese writer in 1225,[3] covering the western zone of island
South-east Asia and also part of present Lower Siamese territory
and the Malay Peninsula south of the Bay of Bandon. But at the
same time signs of a relaxation of Srivijaya's control begin to
appear. By the beginning of the twelfth century the Sumatran
state of Malayu, north-west of Palembang in the region of the
present Jambi, seems to have ended a period of four hundred years'
subservience to Srivijaya and reasserted its independence. On the
fringe of the Srivijayan empire, to the north of the Malay Peninsula,
a new independent regime appears in Tambralinga (in the area of
Ligor) in the thirteenth century, as evidenced by an inscription of
1230 at Chaiya in the present Kra isthmus. This whole region was
subject to increasing pressure from the southward drive of the
Thais.

But East Java was the scene of changes of the greatest significance for the future balance of power in island South-east Asia.
Early in the thirteenth century (1222) a revolution ousted the ruler
of Kadiri, and a new East Javanese regime was established with its
centre at Singhasari, to the north of the present Malang. This
regime was shortlived, but it lasted long enough to produce a
great warrior-king, to accomplish the downfall of the empire of
Srivijaya, and to lay the foundations of future imperial power in
East Java. At the same time Singhasari represents a further stage in
the evolution of Hindu-Javanese culture, in which the Indian

---

[1] Chou Ch'u Fei.
[2] Meaning probably the Moslem peoples of South-west Asia generally.
[3] Chao Ju Kua. See Coedès : Les Etats Hindouisés, p. 308.

contribution has become more fully assimilated and Javanese elements and attitudes begin clearly to assert themselves. This is seen in architecture, where the simplicity, dignity and harmony of line of the earlier Javanese temples is replaced by greater richness and elaboration of texture, and by a greater concentration on decorative detail—in which may be seen perhaps a revival of the Indonesian Dong-son tradition ; and also in religious ideas, where both Siva and Buddha have now become as it were naturalized to the point of synthesis as Siva-Buddha.

The great warrior-king of the Singhasari epoch was Kertanagara (1268–92). His armies established his sovereignty over most of Java and gradually carried his authority into the overseas dominions of Srivijaya. The Srivijaya capital itself was outflanked on the north by an expeditionary force which invaded Sumatra and, about the year 1286, conquered the kingdom of Malayu, which now became a puppet state of Singhasari. Javanese forces remained in Sumatra for some seventeen years, penetrating far into the interior and jolting the Menangkabau people of the hills out of their ancient isolation. Srivijaya itself still stood, but bereft of its overseas prestige, encircled by Javanese power, and overshadowed by the Javanese-protected state of Malayu. In the outer islands, in south-west Borneo and the Moluccas, and on the eastern side of the Malay Peninsula (Pahang), Kertanagara claimed acknowledgment of his imperial suzerainty.

At this time the armies of the new Mongol dynasty of China were spreading outward as if to complete the conquest of the whole of the Far East. They conquered Korea and invaded Japan ; driving down into the Indo-Chinese peninsula, they overran Annam (central Vietnam) (1257–8) and invaded Burma (1287). When ambassadors from Mongol China appeared at Singhasari in 1289 Kertanagara promptly had them arrested and expelled. This brought a punitive expedition from China to East Java in 1292, but when it arrived it found the country in a state of turmoil. An uprising against Kertanagara had been engineered by a prince of the displaced house of Kadiri, the king had been killed, and his son Vijaya had been forced to flee to a village on the river Brantas named Majapahit (Bitter Fruit). Vijaya now enlisted the support of the newly-arrived Chinese forces to drive the Kadiri usurper out of Singhasari and retrieve the throne. Having succeeded in this, he then turned on his Chinese supporters, compelled them to withdraw to their fleet, and saw them depart homeward. The village of Majapahit held Vijaya's affection as the starting-point of his career, and it became his new capital. Thus began the history of the last of the Hindu-Javanese kingdoms.

Majapahit was to succeed before long to the imperial status and prestige of Singhasari, but for the first sixty years or so of its history (c. 1293–1353) it was sufficiently occupied with the rehabilitation of the East Javanese state. West Java was outside its control, and indeed was to remain so ; and apart from the coast of south-west Borneo, the overseas territories, including Malayu in Sumatra, over which Singhasari had exerted or claimed suzerainty, were left to go their own way. But a new period of East Javanese expansion began about the middle of the fourteenth century. In 1331 Gajah Mada was appointed Pateh or Prime Minister of Majapahit, and under the direction of this statesman, who has been described as the first conscious empire-builder of Indonesia, the predominance of Majapahit was rapidly established over a large part of island South-east Asia and the Malay Peninsula during the early years of the reign of King Hayam Wuruk (1350–89), grandson of Vijaya.

The task that Gajah Mada had undertaken amounted to the restoration and extension of the framework of Kertanagara's empire, and before his death in 1364 it had involved the southern countries of South-east Asia in a series of 'Majapahit wars'. In Sumatra a new puppet regime was set up with its centre at Malayu, which soon extended its authority over the coastal ports to the north and south, and inland over the hill country of Menangkabau. The ghost of Srivijaya that lived on in the ancient district of Palembang was now finally laid, and a dependent ruler was installed there. Elsewhere Majapahit seems to have found little difficulty in filling the political vacuum created by the downfall of the empire of Srivijaya and the dissolution of its temporary successor Singhasari, and as early as 1365 she could claim domination over most of Sumatra and the Malay Peninsula as far north as Kedah, Langkasuka and Patani ; over the south and west coasts of Borneo ; and over southern Celebes and the Moluccas. She even claimed a protectorate over the countries of the Indo-Chinese peninsula, including Siam, Cambodia, Champa and Annam.

But this attempt to centralize imperial power in East Java was destined to collapse before the new political and cultural forces that were coming into play in South-east Asia. In the north the Thai kingdom of Siam, centred since 1350 in the Menam delta, was emerging as the most powerful state of the Indo-Chinese peninsula, with a leaning towards further expansion southward and consequent claims to suzerainty, which it was in a strong position to enforce, over the loosely-organized states of the Malay Peninsula. In the south, commercial prosperity was giving to Malayu and other river and coastal ports on the east coast of Sumatra—now no longer overshadowed by Srivijaya's monopolist control of trade and shipping—a new sense of power and a new independence of outlook. At the same time a fresh cultural force was making itself felt in the Straits of Malacca. Islam, closely associated with commercial progress, had by now taken root in influential quarters among the coastal states of Sumatra, and was beginning to fan outwards across the Malay Peninsula and the islands, undermining as it went—or at any rate greatly modifying—the traditional concepts upon which the Hindu-Javanese culture of Majapahit was based. East Java was to become a fading power on the fringe of a changing world. The future commercial and cultural centres of southern South-east Asia would lie on or near the Straits of Malacca.

Chapter Six

THE COMING OF ISLAM

ONE of the Sumatran seaports over which Majapahit claimed dominion in 1365 was Perlak, situated at the north-eastern end of the island near the present Diamond Point. This town had been visited in 1292 by Marco Polo, the merchant of Venice, on his return voyage to Europe via the Straits of Malacca after a stay of seventeen years in China. Later he found time in an Italian prison to write the story of his travels, and he is the first European to describe the countries of South-east Asia, though his references to place-names are not easy to elucidate. He makes very general observations on Champa and Java, but describes various ports on the east coast of Sumatra in rather more detail; and in writing of Perlak (which he calls Felech) he remarks that many of its inhabitants had been converted to Islam by the foreign merchants who frequently called there. Slightly earlier evidence of the rise of Islam in Sumatra is provided by Chinese sources, which record an embassy led by two Moslems from Malayu to the Mongol or Yuan court of China in 1281. Pasai, another seaport on the north-east coast, also provided a foothold—possibly the earliest one—for Islam in Sumatra ; its first Moslem ruler died in 1297.

Islam gained a sure foothold once it was adopted, just as Hinduism or Buddhism had been adopted in earlier centuries, by the rulers and chiefs of the coastal areas. Once they had set the seal of their authority on the new faith it became acceptable to a people who were accustomed to direction in such matters from above, accustomed, in fact, to acknowledging a system of religious worship and ritual that was essentially *provided* by rulers and aristocracy, while retaining in their own fields and villages an older but less sophisticated set of religious customs and beliefs which we may term 'Indonesian'. In the same way, the spread of Islam along the Straits of Malacca was largely due in the first instance to marriages between members of royal or merchant families—as, for example, the marriage of the first Moslem Sultan of Pasai to a daughter of the ruler of Perlak—which gave it prestige value and an authoritarian aspect in the eyes of the ordinary man. In the early days, even where royal families or educated groups were converted to Islam, conservative instincts tended to reconcile the new belief with the old forms of Hinduism. This was especially true in Java, where some of the early mosques were built in the traditional style and with many of the decorative motifs of the old Hindu-Javanese temples, and where Moslem tombs were carved with emblems of Hinduism.

THE SPREAD OF ISLAM IN THE 14TH AND 15TH CENTURIES

The conversions to Islam on the east coast of Sumatra and the north coast of Java were the missionary work of Gujerati and Bengali merchants engaged in overseas trade between India and island South-east Asia, and the acceptance of Islam by the local rulers of those coastal areas must have been largely inspired by the

wealth, commercial success and good business which those merchants represented. Some of the first Moslem tombstones in
Sumatra and Java were actually imported from Cambay, the port
of Gujerat, where they had been manufactured and engraved. The
best-known examples are those which stand at each end of the
grave of one Malik Ibrahim who was buried at Grisek, north-west
of Surabaya, in 1419. This is the earliest known Moslem grave in
Java, and romantic tradition has visualized Malik Ibrahim as a
saintly apostle of Islam in that country, but modern scholarship
prefers to regard him as a wealthy Persian merchant who probably
made good money in the spice trade. Grisek, on the north-east
coast of Java behind the island of Madura, was the Majapahit
entrepôt port for the prized spices of the Molucca and Banda
Islands further east, and as such it attracted traders from India in
search of the most favourable terms of exchange for their cloth
goods with the island spices. Up to 1400 or soon afterwards the
normal route followed by Gujerati trading vessels bound for
Grisek, according to the Portuguese traveller Pires, was by the
west coast of Sumatra, up through the Sunda Strait, and so along
the north coast of Java. This suggests that at first the Gujeratis
confined their activities in Sumatra to the ports of the north-east
tip of the island—Achin, Pedir and Pasai; and if they wished to
proceed further eastward they would not carry on down the Straits
of Malacca but, doubtless preferring to avoid the difficulties of
navigation and the dangers of piracy in the Strait of Singapore and
the Riau Archipelago, would turn to the more open sea-route via
the Sunda Strait. But gradually, in the course of the fifteenth
century, the Straits of Malacca were opened to Gujerati and Bengali
trading and missionary activity.

The door to South-east Asia had been opened for Islam, and a
new phase in the process of culture-change had begun. Although
motives for the acceptance of Islam were mixed, it was a voluntary
acceptance by Asian people of an Asian religion and culture.
Already, however, the seeds of more violent change were being
sown for South-east Asia and for Asia as a whole. Marco Polo
had brought back to Europe news of the rich spice markets of the
islands; the story of his 'Travels' became known among mer-

chants long before it was first printed in 1477, and it provided an
incentive to others to follow in his steps. Mongol rule had established settled conditions right across central Asia, and for the fifty
years or so following Polo's return to Europe (c. 1290–1340) there
was a steady stream of merchants and missionaries travelling across
the ancient overland caravan routes to the Far East. But although
the overland route was considered to be much safer and shorter in
the political conditions of the time, it was also now possible for
European merchants to travel through Mongol Persia (until the
conversion of the Ilkhanate to Islam) and continue by sea to India,
thus bypassing the middlemen of Egypt and the eastern Mediterranean. This brought them so much closer to the production
areas of spices, adding greatly to their knowledge of prices in the
produce markets, and of the potentialities of the spice trade
generally.

But the carrying trade of the Indian Ocean was still firmly held
in Moslem hands. Arab, Persian and Indian Moslem ships supplied
Europe with the products of the Far East, South-east Asia and
India, which were collected at the various main entrepôts in Asia,
shipped to the Persian Gulf or to the Red Sea, and forwarded to
Alexandria and other centres of distribution in the Middle East.
From these centres eastern goods were distributed throughout
Europe, mainly—from the fourteenth century onwards—by the
merchants of Venice, who had numerous trading stations in the
eastern Mediterranean controlling the routes by which eastern
goods entered Europe. The products of Asia therefore passed
through many different hands and through many processes of
loading, unloading and transhipment before they reached the
various markets of Europe, and because of this their final costs were
high. It would clearly be of great advantage to Europe if eastern
goods could be carried direct to European ports in an uninterrupted
shipment. Direct access by sea to the centres of production in
Asia was still beyond the knowledge and the skill of Europe, but
the travels of Marco Polo, by throwing a beam of light across the
world upon the 'Spice Islands' of South-east Asia, helped to fire
the imagination and arouse the commercial instincts of Europe to
the point where they would be satisfied by nothing less than the
'discovery' of those lands. Both Prince Henry the Navigator and

E

Christopher Columbus were inspired by the 'Travels' of Marco
Polo, and the spice islands of the Indies were the magnets which
were to draw European mercantile ambition across the oceans in
the great Age of Discovery.

Meanwhile in South-east Asia the process of Islamization went
forward, during the fourteenth century, as the faith was dissemi-
nated from its first lodgement in Sumatran soil, and became planted
here and there along the coasts of the islands—nominally if not
actually subject to Majapahit from about the middle of the century
—and on the coast of the Malay Peninsula—over which Majapahit
and the new kingdom of Siam contended from time to time for
suzerainty, which, translated into material terms, meant the
exaction of tribute in gold or tin. In the Malay Peninsula Islam
makes its first historical appearance at a spot twenty miles up the
Trengganu river on the north-east coast, where a stone inscribed
with Arabic letters was set up in 1386 (or perhaps 1326). But it
was in Malacca, a new centre of commerce on the west coast of the
peninsula, facing the Sumatran coast across the Straits, that Islam
was to find the powerful patronage that would carry it forward
with renewed prestige and vigour through the whole island area.

The origin of Malacca is linked in tradition with the story of Old
Singapore—thus early in their history were the two Straits settlements in a sense associated—and with the now diminished state of
Palembang. The Malay tradition is contained in the *Sejarah
Melayu* or Malay Annals, apparently written for the most part
before 1536; and the earliest Portuguese version of the story—
based, of course, on second-hand information obtained in Malacca
and thereabouts—is given by Tomé Pires in his *Suma Oriental*,
written between 1512 and 1515. With the coming of the Portuguese to South-east Asia at the beginning of the sixteenth century
the first serious attempts were made to carry out what we might
call regional surveys of the area. These surveys had their limi-
tations; they were somewhat hasty and superficial, and rather
coloured by prejudice; but on the whole they were extremely
informative, generally honest, and as scientific as could be expected
of European travellers coming for the first time face to face with the
strange peoples and civilizations of another continent over four

hundred years ago. Pires's work presents a valuable account of the origin and early history of Malacca, forming part of what is the first comprehensive and detailed survey of the whole South-east Asian region.

As for the origin of Singapore itself, we can only say that at the point in our history which we have now reached it had probably been the long-established but insignificant headquarters of a small fishing and seafaring community which, whenever possible, exploited the strategic position of the southern end of the island for purposes of piracy in the neighbouring straits. According to the Malay tradition, Temasek—generally understood to be the name of this Old Singapore—was founded by a prince from Palembang, and certainly Temasek seems to have formed part of the reduced empire of Srivijaya in the fourteenth century. As that century wore on, however, Temasek became involved in the struggles between the new expansionist powers of Siam and Majapahit for domination of the Malay Peninsula, being forced now by one and then by the other to acknowledge its suzerainty. The Siamese attacked Temasek by sea shortly before 1349 (according to a Chinese account), and a Siamese record mentions Ujong Tanah (the extreme south of the Malay Peninsula) as being subject to Siam in 1360. In 1365, however, the Javanese *Nagarakritagama* claims Temasek as subject to Majapahit,[1] and at the time of its final onslaught on Palembang, the heart of the shattered Srivijayan empire, Majapahit attacked and devastated Temasek about the year 1376.

Singapore remained quite insignificant until the nineteenth century, but the old connection between Palembang and Temasek led, according to tradition, to the foundation of Malacca about the end of the fourteenth century—though it is possible, indeed likely, that there had been an earlier Indian trading centre somewhere in the region of that port. The story as recounted by Pires is that a prince of Palembang named Parameswara, 'a great knight and a very warlike man', threw off his allegiance to Majapahit and as a result was driven out of his kingdom by the Javanese. He fled to Singapore, where he soon had the local ruler assassinated, and himself then ruled over that and the neighbouring islands as a kind of

[1] *See* Ferrand : *Rélations de voyages et textes géographiques* ... II, pp. 651 *et seq.*

pirate king. But five years later a Siamese force was sent against him, and he had to flee to the Muar river ; there he and his followers settled down as an agricultural community, with occasional piracy as a sideline, for six years. Meanwhile a body of *orang selat* or Straits fisherfolk-cum-pirates, who had left Palembang along with Parameswara, had arrived at the Malacca river and penetrated a few miles inland, where they found spacious country well suited to agricultural settlement. These people now sent to the Muar river and invited Parameswara to become their ruler. After an examination of the country, 'a plain surrounded by beautiful mountain ranges and abundant waters', he accepted the invitation.

With its rapid rise as a commercial port during the first quarter of the fifteenth century, Malacca became a natural magnet for the Moslem influences that had already been installed in the ports of north-east Sumatra. Its ruler—either Parameswara himself or, if we follow the Portuguese version, his son—was converted to Islam as a result of pressure from Pasai. He had approached the Sultan of Pasai, says Pires, for recognition of Malacca as a trading port that could pay for imports in gold, but official recognition would not be granted unless he agreed to become a Moslem. He was unwilling to do so at that time, but nonetheless Gujerati and other Moslem merchants who saw new openings for business in Malacca were quite prepared to grant it practical recognition by calling there. The combined result for Malacca was commercial expansion and the increase of Moslem influence, so that when later its ruler was again urged to become a Moslem—and was at the same time offered a Pasai princess in marriage—he agreed, taking the title of Iskandar Shah. This did not mean that the royal house of Malacca had been finally won over to Islam, for the immediate successors of Iskandar Shah (who died in 1424) bore Hindu titles. But with the accession of Muzaffar Shah (c. 1445) Malacca became a spearhead of the further advance of Islam, an advance achieved by growing commercial power and consolidated by judicious royal marriages. Both Muzaffar Shah, who assumed the title of Sultan, and his successor Mansur Shah, made good use of the marriage value of Malacca princesses to carry Islam northwards to the rulers of Pahang and Kedah, and southwards to those of the Sumatran river-ports of Siak, Kampar, Indragiri and Jambi. But apart from the direct missionary work of its royal house, Malacca as an entrepôt port with widening trade relations carried the influence of Islam outward from the Straits of Malacca into island South-east Asia, sponsoring or reinforcing the faith by its prestige in the ports of the north coast of Java, whence it would be spread still further eastward as far as the Moluccas.

Although Majapahit was a fading power, unable to prevent the infiltration of Islam into the territories over which she had claimed suzerainty during the previous century, or to hinder the growth of a new commercial and political power on the Straits of Malacca, her name was still respected in the southern regions of South-east Asia, and as long as she continued to exercise a general overlordship over the north coast of Java it was good diplomacy for Malacca to maintain the fiction of a formal subservience to her. As an entrepôt centre Malacca was concerned to cultivate good trading relations with such Javanese ports as Demak, Japara and Tuban ; besides, her growing population depended on Java to a large degree for imported supplies of rice. But gradually Majapahit lost her grip on the Javanese north coast ports, as Islam and commercial prosperity together developed in them the desire for political separation. In 1478 the Moslem coastal state of Demak was strong enough to lead an invasion of Majapahit itself, and by the end of the fifteenth century Majapahit had been reduced to an East Javanese state with a glory that was past ; it had become the lingering ghost of the last of the medieval Hindu-Javanese empires.

As well as the nominal imperial status of Majapahit, the diplomacy of the young kingdom of Malacca had to respect the expansionist tendencies of the new kingdom of Siam on its north, and also, for a time, China's traditional suzerainty over the whole South-east Asian region. In China the Mongol dynasty had been overthrown in 1368 when Ming forces captured Peking, and in 1381 the Mongols were driven out of Yunnan. The establishment of the Ming dynasty released the full force of Chinese reaction against the foreign rule and methods of the Mongols ; there was a strong revival of Confucianism and a triumphant restoration of traditional Chinese methods of government. More than ever China now regarded herself as the one enlightened and civilized state of the whole world, a Middle Kingdom surrounded by inferior and dependent peoples. And along with this renewed sense of superiority, Ming rule displayed for a time a tendency towards imperialism, inherited by the early Ming emperors from the regime they had displaced.

These political changes in China soon had repercussions in South-east Asia. Ming land forces drove down into the Indo-Chinese peninsula and conquered Vietnam. A series of seven naval expeditions was sent across the China Sea and into the Indian Ocean during the first thirty years of the fifteenth century to assert Chinese suzerainty, which was acknowledged by the despatch of embassies and tribute to Nanking or Peking from as far as Aden and the East African port of Magadoxo. Siam, Java, Sumatra and Malacca were each visited by these roving diplomatic fleets, and were persuaded to send official missions as tributary states to China in return. Malacca sent missions in 1405 and 1407, and its rulers themselves went to pay homage to the Ming emperor on several occasions between 1411 and 1433.

But this forward policy on China's part soon ceased as suddenly as it had begun. The capital had been moved from Nanking to Peking in 1421, and the renewed pressure of nomadic tribes on her northern frontier turned China's energy inland in that direction. She abandoned her sudden interest in overseas territories and turned to the policy of seclusion. Soon after 1430 the coastal doors to China closed ; Chinese subjects were forbidden to go overseas without licence ; maritime trade was restricted mainly to Canton, and was there fettered with the strict regulation that was to surprise and irritate European traders in the centuries to come. In South-east Asia Vietnam regained her independence in 1431, and the other countries in the area were left alone to achieve a political balance among themselves—and to see that balance overturned by a new force from the West.

But while Malacca was impelled to admit Chinese suzerainty during the first half of the fifteenth century (and in fact, in the traditional manner of South-east Asian states, continued to do so afterwards), it was with the kingdom of Siam that she had to reckon as a more immediate overlord in that period ; indeed the tribute sent from Malacca to the Chinese court was partly in the nature of protection-money against Siam. The Ming chronicles themselves describe Malacca as subject to Siam in 1403, and this is confirmed by Ma Huan, who visited the port in 1412–13. An appeal to China for intervention against the threat of Siamese aggression in 1419 suggests that Siam had been demanding heavier tribute from Malacca as her trade increased. But the expansion of Malacca's commerce, and of her political influence on the Malay Peninsula and across to southern Sumatra, while provoking repeated Siamese demands and attacks by land and sea, provided Malacca at the same time with the resources which enabled her to withstand them. Costly as they doubtless were, she was able to survive Siamese inroads into her territory by way of Pahang (*c.* 1445) and an attempted invasion by sea (1456) ; and after 1460 she was strong enough to take the offensive and assert her authority northwards into Kedah (whose ruler acknowledged Islam *c.* 1474) and into Patani.

In the southern parts of the Malay Peninsula and Sumatra, Malacca had a freer hand to exercise her own particular brand of aggression, to extend her control by a mixture of force, missionary endeavour and diplomatic marriages. Under her last four Sultans (1445–1511) she asserted her authority southwards to Singapore, the Riau Archipelago and the island of Lingga, and across the Straits to the Rokan, Siak, Kampar and Indragiri river-states in Sumatra. There was no finality in this process, however ; no stable balance was achieved ; indeed Malacca seems to have been involved in almost perpetual warfare with subject states, and they with one another. Islam certainly did not bring peace to the Straits of Malacca or a sense of unity to the various Moslem states and ports on its shores. Commercial relations between the various trading centres on the Straits were dictated largely by the force of the strongest, and they had always to be protected against parasitic pirate fleets, whose methods all parties were compelled to adopt. For these reasons, Malacca's wars were essentially commercial wars ; they were fought either to control key sources of supply or to eradicate the island bases of the pirate fleets that interfered with the flow of supplies. Control of Selangor, Perak and Kedah, for example, ensured supplies of tin ; command of the river-ports of Kampar and Indragiri ensured supplies of gold from the Menang-kabau hinterland of Sumatra ; while the flow of trade through the Straits and the Java Sea was protected from the predatory activities of pirates by control of the island of Rokan (opposite Malacca) on the one hand, and of the main islands of the Riau and Lingga archipelagos on the other. South of the Lingga Archipelago a limit to Malacca's ambitions was set by the north Javanese coastal state of Demak, which dominated the Javanese ports as far east as Cheri-bon and had a controlling influence over the southern end of Sumatra as far north as Jambi.

By the close of the fifteenth century Malacca had fully established herself as the leading commercial power of South-east Asia. But the fact that she was a Moslem power did not mean that she had made a complete break with the past. The complex of traditions inherited from the earlier Indianized states could not be so easily shed. In many ways—in the Hindu features of her court ritual, in the mixture of war and commerce with which she dominated the Straits, in her continued diplomatic fidelity to China—she was but the latest vehicle of the curiously mixed traditions that had grown up in this cross-roads region of South-east Asia. 'No one but the King of Malacca,' says Pires, 'may wear yellow ; no one but him may wear a Chinese hat.' Malaya has always been a country of mixed customs and divided loyalties.

Chapter Seven

THE COMING OF THE WEST

WHEN the sixteenth century opened, the trade of South-east Asia was attuned more than ever before to the demands of world markets. But the fundamental basis of that trade remained, as it had been for centuries before, an exchange between the staple produce of island South-east Asia—pepper and spices—and the staple manufactures of India—textile fabrics. The exchange of goods with China, though a valuable branch of the trade, was essentially subsidiary.

The commercially strategic position of any port—such as Malacca or Srivijaya before it—that dominated the Straits of Malacca was bound to make it the natural pivot of the trade of the whole South-east Asian region. Such a port, standing at a point where the converging shipping routes from east and west could most conveniently meet, was sure to be the shop-window for South-east Asian produce. It stood on a natural cross-roads on the highway created by those monsoon winds which have always determined the routes of sailing vessels across the Indian Ocean and the China Sea. The south-west monsoon, blowing from May to October, carried merchant ships from the Red Sea and India out to the Straits of Malacca, and bore them on, with homeward-bound Chinese vessels, to the Far East. The north-east monsoon, between November and April, brought the Chinese junks down to the Straits and carried Indian and Arab traders back to their home ports. Malacca, as Pires put it, was 'the end of monsoons and the beginning of others'; adding, in his dry way, that 'there you find all you want—and sometimes more than you are looking for'.

The increasing demand for South-east Asian products concentrated an immense entrepôt trade in Malacca. She was at one and the same time the greatest single outlet for the pepper and spices that the kitchens of Europe as well as of Asia required in order to

make their food palatable, and the main inlet for the Indian cloth
that South-east Asia was so ready to purchase in exchange. In her
harbour and warehouses the products of South-east Asia were
collected and distributed, and Indian, Chinese and Mediterranean
goods exchanged and transhipped. She was the centre of a triangular system of trade between South-east Asia, India and China.
Further to the east there was a secondary focal point in the spice
trade system, in the Banda Islands. Here were collected for shipment to Malacca the nutmegs of which the Bandas were the main
source, as well as the cloves of the Molucca Islands. Within the
whole area were numerous ports carrying on a busy transit trade
as well as exporting pepper and other local products, as, for
example, Macassar in the Celebes, Bantam in the Sundanese
country of Java, Achin, Pedir and Pasai in Sumatra, Kedah in the
Malay Peninsula.

From China to Malacca came porcelain ware, pearls, silver,
silks, satins, damasks and brocades ; and in exchange for these the
Chinese junks took away large quantities of pepper and much
camphor—especially the Borneo kind which was valued highly as
a medicine, along with cloth from India and opium from Arabia.
From Cambay in Gujerat came the famous Cambay cloths which
Malacca distributed all over South-east Asia, and also the miscellaneous exports that came from the Mediterranean through
Alexandria and Aden—dyed woollens, hats, glass beads and
mirrors, copper and steel. In return for these the Gujeratis carried
spices, drugs and precious woods over the Indian Ocean as far as
the Red Sea. The entrepôt port of Cambay was Malacca's main
link with the Middle East and Europe ; and although merchants
from Egypt, Arabia and the east coast of Africa came themselves to
Malacca and some of them settled there, Cambay and Malacca were
interdependent ports. 'Malacca cannot live without Cambay, nor
Cambay without Malacca,' wrote Pires. The Gujeratis were to be
found in every seaport of South-east Asia, and their ships were the
largest and best equipped of any. In Malacca there were a thousand
Gujerati merchants, astute business men who had the cream of the
trade, and whom Pires compared in commercial acumen to the
Italians—as high a compliment as a European of those days could
pay.

India exported cloth to Malacca not only from Cambay but also from the Coromandel coast and Bengal, where there were well-organized weaving and dyeing industries in which production was largely geared to the requirements of South-east Asia. Bengal cottons were in especially high demand, and Bengali traders had a large share in the Malacca trade. Pasai in Sumatra had earlier been a great centre of theirs, but the bulk of the trade had shifted to Malacca, and numbers of Bengali merchants, with their womenfolk, had settled there.

In exchange for all types of Indian cloth, Malacca imported pepper from Sumatra and West Java, cloves and nutmeg from the Moluccas and Bandas (where Islam was now established along the coasts), gold from Sumatra, camphor from Sumatra and Borneo, sandalwood from Timor. For her food requirements she obtained supplies of rice, meat, fish and vegetables from north Java ports, Sumatra, Siam and Pegu (southern Burma). All kinds of fruits came from Java and Sumatra, including the durian, confidently described by Pires as 'certainly lovelier and more delicious than all the other fruits'.

The Sumatran ports naturally had close commercial relations with Malacca. The Sundanese ports of West Java (not yet Moslem) had a considerable export trade in rice and other foodstuffs, pepper, and slaves. The Moslem ports on Java's north coast, which were dominated by Demak, exported large quantities of rice. Further east was Grisek, a great exchange centre for cloth and spices, 'the jewel of Java in trading ports,' as Pires wrote, 'where the ships at anchor are safe from winds, with their bowsprits touching the houses'.

Malacca obtained tin from the mining areas in the Malay Peninsula northward to Kedah, and gold from Pahang. Rivalry for control of the tin areas was the root cause of continued wars between Malacca and Siam (a strong Siamese invasion fleet descended on Malacca in 1489, but was driven off); and although Malacca could obtain rice supplies from Siam, Siamese ships themselves never entered her harbour, but traded with the north Sumatran ports and also directly with Bengal and southern China. With southern Burma (Pegu) there was a steady trade, Malacca supplying Chinese goods and the produce of the Straits and islands in exchange for rice. Pegu's teak forests provided the material for a shipbuilding industry which supplied shipping to most of the coastal states of South-east Asia. Tin coinage was minted in Malacca, and some of the Sumatran ports—such as Achin—had gold, silver and tin coinage of their own. Doubtless a wide variety of coins was current in the South-east Asian ports.

Malacca was a well-administered port, with regulations and a system of duties and payments that afforded favourable conditions of trade. The chief administrative official was the Bendahara, who was Lord Chancellor and Lord Treasurer combined ; under him was the Temenggong or chief magistrate. The senior naval officer was the Laxamana or admiral. The executive port officers were the four Shahbandars, each responsible for the commercial trans-actions of all ships arriving at Malacca from a certain quarter : there was one Shahbandar for the ships from Gujerat alone ; one for those that came from the east coast of India (Coromandel and Bengal), from Pegu and from north Sumatran ports ; another to deal with shipping and cargoes from and to south Sumatra, Java and the Spice Islands ; and a fourth who was responsible for vessels from the coasts of Indo-China and China. Pires indicates that foreign Moslem merchants enjoyed extra-territorial privileges in the town.

It is not surprising that Malacca, as the headquarters of South-east Asian trade, should have created a deep impression on the minds of the Europeans who first sailed into her harbour in the early years of the sixteenth century. 'Men cannot estimate the worth of Malacca on account of its greatness and profit,' wrote Pires ; it 'is a city that was made for merchandise, fitter than any other in the world'. 'It is the richest seaport,' wrote Barbosa, 'with the greatest number of wholesale merchants and abundance of shipping and trade that can be found in the whole world.' And those words were echoed by Varthema : 'I believe that more ships arrive here than in any other place in the world.' But it was Pires who pointed to the wider significance of all this : 'Whoever is lord of Malacca has his hand on the throat of Venice.'

Political changes in the Middle East during the fourteenth and fifteenth centuries had disturbed and dislocated the trade between

Asia and Europe, thereby increasing the already high cost of eastern goods to the European consumer. The rising power of the Ottoman Turks in Asia Minor and the eastern Mediterranean seriously obstructed the trade-routes. The flow of trade was never completely stopped, and for half a century after the fall of Constantinople (1453) Venice was allowed to retain her commercial privileges in the eastern Mediterranean under Ottoman concessions. But the deterioration in trading conditions through the Middle East added new point and emphasis to Europe's need of an alternative route to India and the 'East Indies', a sea-route that would be unaffected by the political changes and chances on which the land-routes depended. And by the year 1478 Portuguese explorations southward along the west coast of Africa had in fact reached the point where a new sea-route to the East was about to be revealed. This was the inevitable culmination, though it had not been the conscious aim, of the Portuguese voyages of the fifteenth century. Under the inspiration of Prince Henry the Navigator, the ambitions of Portuguese exploration did not look beyond the exploitation of the wealth of West Africa (especially its gold), combined to some extent with the discovery of a supposed Christian kingdom that would make a new ally in the long war against the Moslem 'Moors' of North Africa. But after Prince Henry's death (1460) the southward drive along the African coast continued, and when in 1487 the Cape of Good Hope was rounded by Diaz, and the immense possibilities of an eastward advance were thus revealed, it was a natural and easy step for Portugal to transfer her quest for wealth and her war against Islam from Africa to Asia. Europe had now gained the knowledge she required to open a new door to Asia. And she had the power, in material resources and in equipment—in the ocean-going three-masted sailing ship with its navigational instruments, maps and charts—to pass through the doorway and on to the uttermost parts of this new world.

In 1497 a Portuguese squadron of four ships under the command of Vasco da Gama left Lisbon, rounded the Cape, and arrived at the port of Melinda on the east coast of Africa. There the services of an Indian pilot were obtained, and the squadron then sailed straight across the Indian Ocean to the port of Calicut, on the Malabar coast of India, arriving there in May 1498. It is related that when they dropped anchor in Calicut harbour the Portuguese were asked what they sought in those parts. 'Christians and spices,' was the answer. They failed to find the first object of their search—the fabled Christian kingdom of Prester John; but they loaded full cargoes of Malabar pepper. And in the year following da Gama's return to Lisbon, King Manoel of Portugal added a new title to his crown : 'Lord of the conquest, navigation and commerce of Ethiopia, Arabia, Persia and India.'

The arrival of Vasco da Gama at Calicut in 1498 marked the completion of the first stage in an eastward journey that brought the Portuguese to South-east Asia, China and Japan. Once the initial step of establishing a base in India had been achieved, it became possible for the Portuguese to pursue two aims : firstly, to divert the flow of eastern goods to Europe from the Moslem-controlled routes through the Middle East to the Portuguese-controlled long sea-route round the Cape ; and secondly, to advance eastward from India along the trade-route that led to South-east Asia and China. The achievement of the first aim necessitated a sea war between Portuguese and Moslems for the command of the Indian Ocean, fought primarily for commercial ends, but intensified by religious hatred and fear, and issuing in the establishment of a Portuguese coastal dominion in India. The achievement of the second aim required the capture of Malacca and the establishment of fortified bases in island South-east Asia, and it involved the Portuguese in a long series of mainly defensive battles in South-east Asian waters against local sea forces, and, in the end, against the forces of European rivals.

Between 1500 and 1509 the Portuguese fought their way to mastery of the Indian Ocean. By 1503 they possessed a fortified base at Cochin, from which the waters off the Malabar coast could be patrolled and rival shipping excluded from the pepper ports or compelled to trade only under Portuguese licence. In 1504 the permanent organization of Portuguese power in Asia began with the appointment of Francisco d'Almeida as first Viceroy with headquarters at Cochin. Then followed the decisive struggle with Moslem forces for control of the wider seas. Mercantile interests in Gujerat and in Egypt were quick to see in the coming of the

Portuguese a serious threat to their virtual monopoly of the export trade from Indian ports to Europe, but they were slow to move decisively against them. In 1507, however, an Egyptian fleet was despatched from the Red Sea, and it defeated a Portuguese squadron off Chaul in March 1508. But early in the following month the decisive battle took place when the Viceroy's fleet engaged combined Egyptian and Indian forces at Diu and gained a complete victory, a victory that gave Portugal command of the Indian Ocean for a hundred years. Regular sailings of merchant vessels between Portugal and India via the Cape were now possible, and Lisbon gradually displaced Venice as the greatest market in Europe for Eastern goods.

The Portuguese were now ready to take the next step forward in their eastward advance. Approval was given for an expedition to Malacca, and a squadron under the command of Lopes de Sequeira was ordered from Lisbon in 1508. After calling at Cochin, and assisting at the battle of Diu, four ships of the squadron reached Malacca in August or September 1509. Sequeira presented letters from the King of Portugal to the Sultan, and was granted permission to land and trade. But the merchants of Malacca, especially the Gujeratis, were naturally suspicious of Portuguese intentions, fearing a repetition of the tactics they had adopted on the Malabar coast; and they finally persuaded the Malay authorities to plan a surprise night attack on Sequeira's ships. News of the plan reached the ships, however, and they drew out of the harbour and bombarded the town. On the following day, after failing to secure the release of Portuguese factors who had been left ashore, the squadron sailed away. A return visit was inevitable.

Afonso d'Albuquerque, who succeeded Almeida as Viceroy in 1509, took vigorous measures to secure Portuguese domination of the whole maritime trade system of Asia. He had occupied the island of Socotra, commanding the entrance to the Red Sea, in 1508; he took Goa, the seaport of Bijapur on the west coast of India, in 1510, making it the capital of the Portuguese empire in Asia. In 1511 he turned to Malacca. Leaving Cochin in May with a fleet of eighteen ships, he proceeded first to Pasai and Pedir in Sumatra and thence to Malacca, where he arrived on 1 July.

According to a Dutch account written long afterwards, the day of
Albuquerque's arrival at Malacca was the wedding-day of the
Sultan of Pahang and a daughter of the Sultan of Malacca; as the
Portuguese ships entered the harbour, fully dressed, with trumpets
blowing and guns saluting, a number of Malay royal wedding-
guests were being driven round the town in a magnificent trium-
phal car on thirty wheels.

Albuquerque immediately demanded the surrender of the
Portuguese left behind by Sequeira, with compensation for confiscated goods. After some hesitation, the prisoners were handed
over and trade negotiations began; but these were clearly overshadowed by the threat of Portuguese guns, and before long they
were broken off. Refusing an offer of assistance from Chinese
ships in the harbour, Albuquerque bombarded the town and tested
its defences by a landing on 25 July. He now increased his demands, and would accept nothing less than the submission of
Malacca to the King of Portugal. Failing to obtain this, he ordered
the final attack. On 10 August Malacca was taken, with much loss
of life and destruction of property.

Thus rapidly had Albuquerque, the real architect of the Portuguese empire in Asia, carried out his broad design and laid down
the main lines of an imperial structure that needed only to be completed in detail by his successors. The foundation of this whole
structure was the naval command of the Indian Ocean already
achieved by Almeida; and the principles of Albuquerque's design
were the establishment of direct rule over a limited number of
main strategic bases so disposed as to secure Portugal's hold on the
maritime trade route across Asia, and the maintenance of such subsidiary fortresses as might be necessary to command supplies of
particular commodities such as spices. The whole design was
dictated by the essentially commercial aims of the Portuguese in
Asia. It was related primarily to trade-routes and produce-
markets, not to territorial conquest or colonial rule. And for
that reason the Portuguese empire was in essence a fortress
system; it hinged on the concentration of commercial and
naval power in a limited number of strategic bases which
looked outward to the high seas, not inward to the lands

and peoples of Asia. Only to a limited extent did Portuguese rule spread out beyond the main fortress centres ; and where it did, it did so reluctantly.

In several respects Portugal laid down the pattern of future European rule in Asia. In the sequence of steps by which she normally approached her objectives—a sequence which may be expressed in the formula : voyage, factory, fortress—she was followed by her European successors. In the essential basis of her rule—the fortress system—her example was again followed. European rule in Asia remained a fortress system, in principle, down to the nineteenth century. Its commercial aims restricted it generally to the fringes of Asian countries and societies (which for that reason remained for the most part unaffected by it), until the economic revolution which created modern European industrial organization had revised and widened those commercial aims and so broadened the basis of colonial rule. Again, in the distinctive features of the colonial fortress itself the Portuguese pattern was to be closely followed down to our own day. The colonial fortress town, the main centre of European rule, was made to reflect many of the visible features of the town in Europe. Though the vast majority of its inhabitants were Asians, it was in a sense a European reserve, an extension of the territory of the homeland, to which were transplanted the typical administrative, municipal, religious and social institutions of the home country.

Immediately after the capture of Malacca the Portuguese began the work of transforming it into a fortress town, the first model of a headquarters of European rule in South-east Asia. The mosque below the hill in the centre of the town was demolished, and the stones from it and from the tombs of Malacca's Sultans were used to construct, on the same site, a tall donjon tower or keep. The wooden palace of the Sultans on the hill-top was replaced by a stone church. A strong fortress wall was then built around the tower and the hill, following the line of the river mouth and the shore on its southern side. Within the fortress were erected in course of time the State Council Chambers, the Governor's palace or 'Government House', the Bishop's palace, a cathedral and several other churches, a monastery, a prison, barracks, hospitals, and, in 1548,

F

a school beside the church on the hill. Outside the walls other monasteries and numerous churches were built.

The invasion of South-east Asia by Portuguese commercial power in alliance with the Christian Church was accompanied by much violence. For South-east Asia there was nothing new in the association of commercial power with warfare, but the peculiar combination of commercial war and religious crusade that the Portuguese introduced was something with which the region had not been confronted before. For Portugal, the advance to the East was not simply an invasion along the main highway of Asian trade but also a great forward outflanking movement in the holy war between Christianity and Islam. Her commercial aims, and the means of achieving them—deeds of violence against Moslems, or the plunder of Moslem shipping—were therefore conveniently sanctified. Later, however, after the first onslaught of soldiers and merchants, when the Church itself was able to operate independently of immediate commercial interests, it performed good work in education and welfare as well as in spiritual guidance, though in general only among those who were prepared to accept conversion. Moreover, after the violence of the initial impact of the Portuguese upon the inhabitants of Malacca had subsided, it became apparent that their prejudices were religious rather than racial. Coming from a corridor country of Europe, in which East and West had met, fought and mingled for hundreds of years, and which had absorbed into its Christian population strong Middle Eastern and North African racial elements, they were accustomed as a people to the idea of racial admixture and to the practice of natural human relationships with other races. In Malacca they did not hold themselves aloof from the local population, but rather governed their relations with it by a combination of stern discipline and easy familiarity. The Portuguese soldier was disposed to marry the local woman, and indeed he was directly encouraged to do so. Portugal, with her very limited resources in manpower, could not afford to place large establishments of troops and officials in the colonial fortresses, and she looked for a solution of this problem in intermarriage between Portuguese soldiers and Asian women, and the creation of a local body of Eurasian government servants, troops and artisans who would be bound by ties of interest and blood to the fortunes of the Portuguese, and who at the same time would look upon Malacca as their true home. The normal Portuguese population of the Malacca fortress did not exceed two hundred troops and three hundred civilians, but within a hundred years of its capture the town had a Christian population of 7,400 living in suburbs outside the actual fortress. A number of the 'Malacca Portuguese' families have survived to the present day, having preserved their faith, their peculiar dialect, and their identity as a community ; and in most of the seaports of South-east Asia there are old Eurasian families with good Portuguese names.

But Malacca was after all a large colonial centre in which, once the Portuguese had settled down, fairly stable social conditions could be established and maintained under organized government. In the outlying parts of South-east Asia, however, the rapacity and violence of individuals and groups could not be so easily restrained, nor settled conditions introduced. In the Moluccas especially, where the chief rulers had accepted Islam and where the sources of the most highly valued spices were found, religious hatred and commercial greed sustained war and terrorism for many years. Warfare was already endemic in that area before the arrival of the Portuguese, for the Sultans of the two main islands of the group, Ternate and Tidore, were traditional enemies ; but it was Portuguese policy to keep this warfare alive, promising assistance to one side or the other—or to both—for the price of commercial concessions. The presence of the Spaniards in the Moluccas after 1521 only served to add fresh fuel to the flames of war and destruction in this area.

Chapter Eight

THE PORTUGUESE CENTURY

THE Moluccas, or Spice Islands, were the logical destination of the Portuguese eastward advance. Soon after the capture of Malacca a squadron of three ships under Antonio de Abreu was sent forward to reconnoitre the island area and to open up trade there. Leaving at the end of the year 1511, the squadron reached Amboyna in company, but between Amboyna and Banda it encountered bad weather conditions and broke up. One of the ships was lost, but its captain, Francisco Serrao, was picked up by local craft and carried to the clove island of Ternate in the heart of the Moluccas. Abreu managed to reach the Bandas, but was unable to proceed northwards to the Moluccas proper.[1] Serrao remained at Ternate for some nine years, and during that time established a great personal influence over the Sultan by advising and assisting him in his wars against the rival Sultan of Tidore. As it happened, however, it was his presence in the Moluccas that set in motion a series of events leading to the coming of the Spaniards to dispute Portugal's claim to supremacy in that area. For Serrao was a friend of Ferdinand Magellan, and to him he sent a full description of the Spice Islands.

Magellan had left Portugal in 1505 to serve as a volunteer in the Portuguese forces in Asia. He was a member of Sequeira's expedition to Malacca in 1509. In 1517, however, having obtained information on the Spice Islands from Serrao, he decided to approach the authorities in Spain with an offer to discover a Spanish route to the islands. The offer was eventually accepted, and in September 1519 Magellan sailed from San Lucar in Spain in command of a squadron of five ships, small craft of from 60 to 250 tons. After

---

[1] The term Moluccas originally referred to the five volcanic islands of Ternate, Tidore, Motir, Makian and Bachan (with their dependent islets), which lie along the west side of Halmahera or Gilolo; but in course of time it was extended to include Amboyna and the Bandas to the south.

crossing the Atlantic and spending some eight months in exploring the coast of South America, he passed through the straits at the southern tip of the American continent and entered the Pacific. Some three months later he reached a group of islands which he named the Ladrones or Robber Islands (afterwards renamed the Marianas), and in April 1521 he arrived at a larger group which was named St. Lazarus (renamed in 1542 the Philippines). Magellan landed at the island of Cebu and was well received. Like other European adventurers of his time and of later times, he was ready to intervene in local wars in order to increase his country's influence, while local rulers for their part were generally unable to assess the skill and equipment of the Europeans except in the light of their own immediate ambitions. It was while supporting the ruler of Cebu in an operation against a neighbouring island that Magellan met his death on the beach of Mactan in April 1521.

Command of the squadron, of which only two ships now remained, was taken over by Del Cano, and in November 1521 he arrived at Tidore in the Moluccas. Tidore and Ternate were permanently at feud, and so from the first the Spaniards and Portuguese in the Moluccas were ranged against each other in opposite camps. Del Cano obtained a cargo of spices at Tidore, but one of his ships was so unseaworthy that it had to be abandoned, and in the remaining ship, the *Vittoria*, he sailed for the Indian Ocean in December 1521. The Cape was rounded in the following April, and the *Vittoria* with her crew of eighteen finally reached Seville in September 1522. It was the first voyage round the world. Magellan, though he had not lived to complete the circumnavigation, had proved the contention of Columbus that there must be a westward sea-route to the Far East.

From the Spanish point of view the great achievement of the voyage was not so much the circumnavigation of the globe as the discovery of a new route to the Moluccas, and contemporary comment outside Spain was concerned with the commercial implications of Spanish access to the spice-producing islands rather than with the navigational achievement of Magellan and his comrades. Certainly the circumnavigation was not hailed in Europe as a refutation of the theory that the earth was flat, for in fact ever since the days of classical Greece the vast majority of educated people in Europe had believed the earth to be round. The Spanish view of the whole matter was well illustrated in the coat of arms granted to Del Cano by the emperor Charles V, in which nutmegs, cloves, cinnamon sticks and Moluccan rulers featured a good deal more prominently than the representation of a globe bearing the motto *Primus circumdedisti me*. The Moluccan rulers of Del Cano's arms are depicted as eminently venerable monarchs in the Western convention; their features are remarkably European; they are very correctly dressed in royal crowns, long beards, and flowing robes which reach to their ankles; and each holds aloft a spice branch.

Spain and Portugal, the great maritime powers of sixteenth-century Europe, had each found a sea-route to Asia—one westward across the Atlantic, the other eastward from the Cape of Good Hope—and had met at the other side of the world in South-east Asia. Although the Moluccas lay within the Portuguese sphere of world exploitation according to a line of demarcation agreed between Portugal and Spain in the Treaty of Tordesillas (1494), Spain considered that prior discovery of Tidore had given her rights in the Moluccas area. For some years Spaniards and Portuguese fought for supremacy there, supporting opposite sides in the local wars. A Portuguese expedition from Malacca had built a fort on Ternate in 1521, and this was used as a base of operations against Tidore, from which the Spaniards were finally expelled in 1527. Spain then decided to give up the struggle in the Moluccas, and Portugal obtained a free hand in the area by the terms of the Treaty of Saragossa in 1529.

The logic of the situation led Portugal on from commercial exploitation to annexation of territory as a form of commercial insurance. In 1530 Tidore was compelled to agree to an annual tribute of cloves, but by the following year the Governor of Malacca had been invested with royal authority to take possession of any territory 'discovered or arrived at' by the Portuguese. Gradually Ternate was reduced to the point of signing away its independence (1564), not so that the Portuguese might concern themselves with internal administration but so that they might hold a legal warrant for the exaction of increasingly heavy tribute.

But violence and cruelty, murder and reprisal, continued. At the same time, although the work of Catholic missionaries was in itself humane and sincere, Christianity was used by Portuguese administrators in the Moluccas as an added instrument of power, so that while the advance of Christianity was accompanied by commercial and political gains, for the inhabitants of island South-east Asia generally that religion tended to be regarded as a badge of servitude. Amboyna—used by the Portuguese mainly as a transit station between Malacca and the Moluccas proper—was presented by its ruler to the Portuguese commander at Ternate in 1562 in token of his conversion; but Christianity did not take real root in Amboyna until the period of Dutch rule. The Portuguese built their castle of New Victoria on Amboyna in 1580. After the beginning of actual Spanish settlement in the Philippines in 1565, Christianity began to take hold on the inhabitants of those islands. For the Spaniards, as for the Portuguese, overseas expansion in the sixteenth century was partly a Christian crusade; political annexation and religious conversion were interrelated aims.

The conquest of Mexico, with its great resources of silver, had provided a potential base on the Pacific for the renewal of Spanish operations in the Spice Islands after Magellan's voyage, but by the time the Spaniards in Mexico were ready to turn their attention in that direction the Portuguese had established themselves too firmly to be dislodged. This was demonstrated in 1545, when—in spite of the Saragossa agreement of 1529—a Spanish fleet from Mexico made an unsuccessful attempt to challenge Portuguese supremacy in the Moluccas. After this setback the Spaniards made no further attempt to gain a foothold in South-east Asia until 1565, when an expedition from Mexico, avoiding a direct clash with the Portuguese, conquered Cebu in the Philippines. From there Spanish power was extended northward to Luzon Island, making its headquarters in Manila in 1571. The Portuguese had meanwhile obtained permission to trade and settle in the Chinese port of Macao (1557), and now these two outposts of European expansion, Manila and Macao, faced each other across the South China Sea. In Macao the Portuguese built up a most valuable entrepôt trade between China, Japan and South-east Asia, and for over two centuries they acted as the main commercial agents between China

and the outside world. After 1571, however, shipping and commodities were attracted from southern Chinese ports to Manila,
which became the colonial entrepôt for a growing trans-Pacific
trade between south China, the Philippines, Mexico and Spain.
Mexican silver provided a great stimulus for this trade; Manila
paid for her imports mainly in silver, and consequently the Mexican
dollar became standard exchange currency in the ports of eastern Asia.

Once Malacca had become a Portuguese base, no time was lost
in establishing contact with China and Siam as well as with the
Moluccas. Indeed the first Portuguese envoy to Siam was sent off
in a Chinese junk which left Malacca between Albuquerque's
arrival and the capture of the town. The envoy, one of Sequeira's
men who had been imprisoned in Malacca, was well received at
Ayuthia and a Siamese envoy accompanied him on his return.
Other missions followed, and as a result the Portuguese obtained
formal permission to settle and trade in Ayuthia, Mergui, Tenasserim, Nakon on the Bay of Bandon, and Patani. Siam still laid
claim to a general suzerainty over the Malay Peninsula, but she was
not prepared to challenge Portugal's newly-won position in
Malacca, especially as this promised possibilities of a boost to
Siam's overseas trade. Besides, the Siamese of Ayuthia were pre-
occupied with the dangers that threatened from Chiengmai in the
north. Chiengmai was still a separate Thai kingdom in the upper
Menam valley, and for a long time a state of war had existed
between it and Ayuthia; a united state of Siam in the modern
sense had not yet begun to emerge. Ayuthia probably therefore
also hoped to be able to make use of Portuguese assistance against
Chiengmai.

But Siam's greatest potential danger lay in Burma. At the
opening of the sixteenth century that country was split up into
several separate states : the Shan or Burmese Thai country in the
north; the remnant of the old Pagan kingdom of the Burmans
with its centre at Ava (near the present Mandalay) ; other Burman
kingdoms of Prome and Toungu; and the Mon kingdom of
Pegu. Malacca had established trade relations with Pegu, a great
rice-growing area and a good market for the sale of island spices
and Indian textiles ; and when the Portuguese arrived they soon

followed up this trade. But now a new shift in the balance of power in Burma took place, leading to the beginning of a long series of wars between a partially reunited Burma and the Siamese of Ayuthia. Here the Portuguese were to find their opportunity to gain influence and obtain concessions by lending support to the rival powers. But unstable as these states of the Indo-Chinese peninsula were, they had sufficient strength and organization, as compared with the island kingdoms in the Moluccas, to be able to afford to employ Portuguese assistance without incurring the risk of having to pay for it with their independence. The activities of the Portuguese in these countries were essentially individualistic, and the concessions and influence they gained were mainly personal. Partly because the states of the Indo-Chinese peninsula had reached such a stage of political development that they could not easily be forced to submit to commercial control from outside, partly because they did not in any case offer anything like such scope for direct commercial exploitation as Malacca or the Spice Islands, and partly because they were situated too far from the main line of communication and trade between Goa and the Moluccas, Portugal made no sustained attempt to maintain commercial relations with those countries on a basis of official arrangement, but left whatever exploitation was possible to individual merchants and adventurers.

In the early years of the sixteenth century the kingdom of Toungu, on the Sittang river, was a rising power in Burma. By 1540 it had subdued Pegu, and in 1542 it conquered Prome. A new united Burmese state was beginning to emerge. But these developments had alarmed the Siamese, and when, as they alleged, their frontier was crossed by the Burmans in the course of the campaign against Pegu, they went to war. For this the Siamese had to suffer invasion after invasion by the aggressive Burmans of Toungu down to the last years of the sixteenth century. Striking eastward, the Burmans took Chiengmai in 1556 and so brought to an end the separate existence of that Thai kingdom. In a southward drive Ayuthia was taken in 1569, and for a time the whole of Siam was under Burman rule. But fifteen years later the Burmans were driven out; and although they returned to the attack again and again, by the end of the century the balance of this mutually exhausting contest had swung in favour of the Siamese, who first brought both Tenasserim and Tavoy under control, thereby securing access to the Indian Ocean, and then conquered the whole of Pegu.

During all this time the Siamese had been forced to fight on two fronts, for the Khmers of Cambodia, acting on the principle that Siam's difficulty was their opportunity, had repeatedly raided Siamese territory from the south-east. But in this direction, too, the end of the century saw the reassertion of Siamese authority. The Khmer capital of Lowek, which had replaced medieval Angkor soon after its fall to the Siamese in 1431, was itself captured in 1593. Yet this was not a conclusive victory for the Siamese; it provided merely an interval of peace in the wars against Cambodia which were carried over into the seventeenth century.

These wars and disturbed conditions in the heart of the Indo-Chinese peninsula provided favourable opportunities for Portuguese adventurers and mercenaries—Feringhi, as they were called. One hundred and twenty of them enlisted as a *corps d'élite* under the Siamese ruler of Ayuthia in 1538, and there was a corresponding *corps* on the Burmese side. A famous adventurer, Philip de Brito, established himself as ruler over Syriam (just south of the present Rangoon) for eleven years in the early part of the seventeenth century. Spaniards from the Philippines were trying their fortune in Siam about the same time, and a strong bodyguard of Japanese was employed by the Siamese king. The coastal region of Arakan, lying to the west of the Irrawaddy towards India, was a particularly favourite hunting-ground of the Portuguese freebooters of the sixteenth century. This area—linked to India by geographical proximity and by direct river communications, and separated from Burma proper by a long mountain range—must have formed one of the earliest fields of Indian commercial and cultural activity. Hinayana Buddhism had been established there before the arrival of the Burmans in the tenth century. Arakan was brought under Burman rule during the Pagan period (1044–1287), but thereafter it retained its independence until well on in the eighteenth century. In Portuguese times it had developed a considerable sea-power, specializing in piracy and coastal raids; it therefore offered splendid opportunities for the Portuguese adventurer.

The situation of the Portuguese on the Straits of Malacca was a very different one. Here they themselves were one of the main contestants in a commerce-war that hardly ceased during the whole period of their occupation of Malacca. The first phase of this war, from the capture of Malacca in 1511 to about 1526, was fought to establish Portuguese control of the Straits against the continued resistance of the Malays. A Malay squadron mustered by Malacca's former Laxamana or admiral in the Muar river was easily disposed of, but a Javanese fleet of over a hundred ships, sent in support of the Malays by the Sultan of Demak, was a tougher proposition for the dozen or so vessels that the Portuguese had at their disposal in 1513, although these were enough for victory. Meanwhile the ex-Sultan of Malacca had retreated to the island of Bintang, in the Riau group to the south-east of Singapore, which became for a time the headquarters of Malay resistance and the source of repeated attempts to dislodge the Portuguese from Malacca. But the fortress withstood the strong Malay assaults of 1518 and 1523; and by 1525 the Portuguese were able to take the offensive, invade Bintang, and instal a puppet Sultan there. The dispossessed Sultan of Malacca, having now apparently abandoned hope of recovering his former kingdom, retired to Kampar in Sumatra. His sons returned to rule in the Malay Peninsula, but over feeble and comparatively remote kingdoms which could be largely contained by Portuguese sea-power, and which dimly reflected the shattered power of Malay Malacca. The eldest son became the first Sultan of Perak; and the third son, leaving Kampar soon after his father's death in 1529, became the first Sultan of Johore.

The second phase of the commerce-war in the Straits began with a new challenge to Portuguese power from Sumatra. There the leading coastal sultanates in the early years of the sixteenth century were Achin, Pedir and Pasai, all situated in the north-eastern end of the island. Their seaport capitals, the first in South-east Asia to have been converted to Islam, had been busy exchange ports before the rise of Malay Malacca, as well as main outlets for such Sumatran exports as pepper, gold and camphor. Malacca had drawn much of the trade away from these ports in the fifteenth century, but with its downfall, and the violently anti-Moslem attitude displayed by the Portuguese on that occasion, the exchange trade naturally tended to shift back to the Sumatran ports. And equally naturally the Portuguese, once established in Malacca, began to turn their attention to these ports with a view to controlling, or if necessary suppressing, their trade in the interests of Malacca's commercial supremacy.

The Portuguese approach to Pasai was cautious at first. Although they gave a clear hint of what their commercial policy in the Straits was to be by stationing a blockade squadron off Pasai in order to divert shipping to Malacca, yet they managed to maintain friendly relations with the Sultan, supplying him with military assistance in local disputes and obtaining in exchange permission to build a factory or storehouse. Then in 1519 this tractable Sultan was expelled by a rival claimant to the throne, who had the support of the ex-Sultan of Malacca at Bintang. This was the signal for Portuguese intervention. They drove out the new Sultan in 1521 and put their own protégé in his place, in consideration for the monopoly of Pasai's pepper exports and the cost of a new wooden fort. Here was a pattern for future European diplomacy in Southeast Asia ; the prince with a claim to a valuable throne could be made to serve as a stepping-stone to power. The policy of intervening in—or if necessary fomenting—dynastic disputes and rivalries as a means of gaining concessions and control was one which different European interests were to adopt, as opportunity offered, down to modern times. Success in such a policy was made possible by the extremely personal nature of royal rule, and by the very limited political vision of the majority of the rulers, in the smaller states of South-east Asia.

So well had intervention succeeded in the case of Pasai that the Portuguese were tempted to try it again in the neighbouring state of Pedir immediately afterwards. But this time their calculations were upset by the third state in this area, Achin. From their first encounters with the Achinese the Portuguese had found them to be stubborn and intractable material ; wild and dangerous people, they defended themselves vigorously when attacked. They now made the first move against the threat of Portuguese encroachment from the direction of Pasai by invading and subduing Pedir in 1521, thus tempting the Portuguese to intervene on behalf of its dispossessed ruler. But the detachment of Portuguese and Malays that was sent to Pedir was driven back, and the Achinese now carried the war against Pasai itself. The town was taken in 1523; and although the besieged Portuguese fort held out until the arrival of ships to evacuate the garrison, it was then burned and abandoned. The Achinese succeeded in salvaging some cannon and military stores, which they afterwards used with effect against the Portuguese. Achin had fully established her supremacy in northern Sumatra. The Portuguese, abandoning all hope of maintaining a permanent settlement in that area, reverted to the less expensive, though also less effective, policy of commercial blockade.

After the expulsion of the Portuguese from Pasai a bitter enmity developed between them and the Achinese, an enmity that was intensified by merciless reprisals on both sides. Achin began to build up the naval and military forces with which she hoped to drive the Portuguese out of the Straits, and by 1537 the second phase in the operations against Malacca began with the first of a long series of Achinese attacks.

. The Portuguese of Malacca were in an unenviable position. Of all the Portuguese bases, Malacca found it most difficult to reconcile two fundamentally incompatible aims of Portugal's policy in Asia—to maintain control of the main trade routes at a minimum cost in personnel and material, and to derive from that control the maximum commercial profit. The permanent problem of the authorities in charge of Malacca was how to balance the demand for profitable commodities in Lisbon against the requirements of security in the Straits. The insistent demands of the home government for the largest possible annual shipments of spices and other products meant that the limited shipping resources of the Portuguese in Asia were strained to the utmost, especially during the period of the north-east monsoon, the favourable season for homeward voyages. Malacca was expected to despatch every available ship with full cargoes during the monsoon months between November and April, retaining only the bare minimum of vessels essential for the control of the Straits and the defence of Malacca itself. She had therefore to work on an extremely narrow margin of safety, and often to take grave risks, in an endeavour to strike a

balance between commercial policy and strategic requirements.
Even though the departure of the last homeward-bound convoys
might be delayed until the latest possible moment before the end
of the north-east monsoon, there was always an anxious interval
of weeks before relieving vessels could be expected to arrive from
Goa with the beginning of the south-west monsoon. This period
between the monsoons was the most dangerous time of the year
for Malacca, when her naval defences were at their weakest, and
her garrison of about 1,500 troops (of whom no more than two
hundred were Portuguese) was most liable to attack and siege by
Achinese and other hostile forces in the Straits. Time and time again
the besieged fortress was saved only by the eleventh-hour arrival
of a relief squadron from Goa.

But there was one factor in the situation in the Straits which
proved to be the salvation of Portuguese Malacca : her enemies
were divided among themselves. The Achinese might have been
expected to line up with the Malays of the peninsula in combined
operations against their common enemy in Malacca. But this did
not happen ; there was no united Moslem front against the
Portuguese. On the contrary, Achinese and Johore Malays carried
on a long war among themselves as rival Moslem powers. War
against Portuguese Malacca was not therefore primarily a religious
war from the Moslem point of view ; it was rather—and certainly
so from Achin's point of view—a war for commercial and maritime control of the Straits. Achin would attack the Portuguese
with all the forces she could muster, but she would not co-operate
with the Malays for that purpose ; she had no intention of driving
the Portuguese out of Malacca only to see Malay rule reinstated in
such a commercially strategic centre. Achin was rather concerned
to bring the Malays under her domination as the successor to the
commercial hegemony of Srivijaya, Majapahit and Malacca ; and
to that end she was prepared to carry on war against both Portuguese and Malays with equal enthusiasm.

The triangular contest between Portuguese, Achinese and
Malays lasted throughout the sixteenth century, with Javanese
forces from Japara occasionally coming to the support of the
Malays. Typical of the complexity of conflicting purposes was the
sequence of major operations that took place from 1550 onwards.

Combined Malay and Javanese forces in an amphibious operation of 1550–1 captured the suburbs of Malacca but failed to storm the fortress. Then in 1564 the Johore Malays were attacked by the Achinese, their town of Johore Lama was captured, and their Sultan carried off into captivity. In 1567–8 Achin organized a large-scale offensive against Portuguese Malacca, employing Turkish troops and guns; the town was taken, but again the fortress held out. Between 1571 and 1575 Achin and Japara, attacking in quick succession, delivered a series of sledgehammer blows against Malacca, but still the fortress stood. As Marsden wrote in his *History of Sumatra* : 'It is difficult to determine which of the two is the more astonishing—the vigorous stand made by such a handful of men as the whole strength of Malacca consisted of, or the prodigious resources and perseverance of the Achinese.'

The Portuguese policy of monopolist control of trade in the Straits followed the traditional lines laid down by their predecessors of Srivijaya and Majapahit. Commercial monopoly in the Straits was not a European invention ; what the Europeans introduced was an increased efficiency in the maintenance of monopoly, an efficiency derived from superior techniques and equipment. And yet in the case of the Portuguese the margin of superiority in those respects was a narrow one, and it was rather their greater powers of tenacity and endurance that kept them masters of the Straits. They certainly achieved great things with the limited resources at their disposal. At the same time, the continued sense of insecurity that resulted from the failure to establish a clear superiority over the enemies around them must have been one of the main factors contributing to an increasing demoralization of the official class in Malacca. When a colonial government was so insecure that it seemed likely to be overthrown at any moment, and when at the same time it felt itself to be inadequately supported or even virtually forgotten by the home government, its members soon tended to shoulder off the sanctions and discipline of service and to join in a more or less legalized scramble for personal gain. And for the Malacca administration this tendency was reinforced by the grossly inadequate rates of pay allowed by the home government. In this respect, as in so many others,

Portugal set the example for future administrative policy in Asia down to the nineteenth century. The later European Companies were disposed to pay their servants in the East only nominal salaries, being satisfied that their real salaries would be paid by the local merchants and others who could afford the costs of bribery.

The whole structure of Portugal's commercial empire in Asia was created and maintained by the State. Commerce with Asia was a royal monopoly which left no room for commercial organization independent of the State. Consequently the policy by which the Portuguese in Asia were directed was in general an uneasy and ineffective combination of commercial and feudal ideas. For a small initial outlay of capital and man-power the royal government of Portugal expected, and for a time secured, immense profits. The annual fleet of up to twenty royal ships carried home rich cargoes of pepper, spices, precious stones, porcelain and textiles ; and on the outward voyages they shipped silver, glass, metal manufactures, linens and woollens. Besides this direct trade with Asia, the State also controlled, in theory at any rate, the even more valuable inter-port trade of Asia. The Malacca administration, for example, attempted to maintain a permanent road-block across the sea-lane of the Straits, holding up all traffic and compelling it to turn in to the port of Malacca ; and although the resources at their disposal were not equal to the task of subjecting larger vessels from India and China to these methods, the Portuguese maintained them more or less effectively against the local shipping of South-east Asia. Again, the profits of the direct trade and of inter-port commerce were supplemented by piracy, directed mainly against Moslem shipping ; for the Portuguese 'carrack' was armed with cannon and fitted out for war as well as for commerce. Another source of profit was found in the direct tributes of spices and other commodities exacted from weaker rulers, such as those of the Moluccas, who were reduced to a status of feudal vassalage to the King of Portugal.

Clearly an empire run on such aggressive principles would need to be supported by well-sustained supplies of men and armaments. A good proportion of the profits of commerce would need to be put back into the organization. But the Lisbon government lacked the business foresight to adopt such a policy in the early stages, and as time went on it became increasingly incapable of doing so because earlier parsimony had resulted in a serious reduction in the profits themselves. No doubt Portugal was a poor country with very limited resources in man-power and wealth, but if her empire, essentially a commercial one, had been run on commercial lines from the start, and if she had poured back into Asia a higher proportion of the new wealth derived therefrom, she would have had a better chance of providing the necessary equipment, the honest and efficient administration, and the loyal forces of Portuguese and Asian troops, with which the empire might have been maintained.

Lisbon's feudal attitude towards the Asiatic possessions, and her reluctance to reinvest sufficient capital in them, meant for Portuguese officials in Asia inadequate salaries and inadequate protection. The results of this were soon seen in Malacca, where officials began to engage in private trading, turning the monopoly, priority and other special rights claimed for the royal trade to their own account. Lisbon's policy had led to a permanent conflict of interest between the royal trade and the officials as private traders, and the home government began to lose control of its administrative machinery in the East. It was reported from Malacca to the King of Portugal in 1530 that 'the whole trade is being lost which afforded the revenues of your factory; your Highness has not, nor will have from Malacca any profit as long as the trade is being done by the Captains', who 'buy and sell their own goods, and not for the King'. It was a vicious circle. The inadequacy of salaries and the absence of sufficient controls led to the development of a wholesale system of corruption and competitive private trading, which in turn deprived the Crown of those funds which might have enabled it to reform and reinvigorate the administration. Thus the financial difficulties of Lisbon resulted only in increasing inefficiency and corruption. Lack of funds prevented the proper maintenance and defence of the fortress of Malacca and other subsidiary outposts in South-east Asia. In its desperate need of money the Crown was driven to accept the standards of its servants in the East and sell lucrative posts to the highest bidder. Thus by the end of the sixteenth century, when the Portuguese in Malacca

G

were beginning to need greater support than ever before, when new European rivals, Dutch and English, were about to be added to their enemies in the Straits, Portugal's financial resources were at their weakest, and there were insufficient funds, men and ships to meet the requirements of an increasingly dangerous situation.

Without powerful naval forces the Portuguese could not hope to maintain their position in South-east Asia indefinitely. With Malacca as their main base they had concentrated on the exploitation of the Moluccas, neglecting Java and failing to overcome Achinese opposition in Sumatra. Portuguese power in South-east Asia was thus constructed on a strategically unsound basis, one which could only be supported by strong naval superiority. For it left open a door to the Moluccas for any other European power that could establish a footing in Sumatra or Java. This the Dutch were able to do; and once they had consolidated a base within island South-east Asia they were in a position to drive a wedge into the Portuguese dominion, to intercept their trade, undermine their power, and attack them in the Moluccas and at Malacca in turn.

Chapter Nine

DUTCH AND ENGLISH BEGINNINGS

In the middle of the sixteenth century merchant ships from the Netherlands were calling regularly at Lisbon and loading cargoes of Eastern goods for distribution to the ports of northern Europe. The Portuguese, who needed all their heavy-tonnage shipping for transoceanic trade, could not afford to concern themselves directly with reshipment of their bulk imports from overseas. It was here that Netherlands enterprise stepped in and began to lay the foundations of a world-wide carrying trade. Antwerp developed close commercial ties with Lisbon. But after the middle of the century, disturbed political conditions in the southern Netherlands under the government of the Spanish king Philip II brought about the commercial decline of Antwerp, with a corresponding rise in the importance of the seaports of the northern provinces of Zeeland and Holland. When Antwerp was plundered by Spanish troops in 1576, and again when it fell to Spanish forces in 1585, much of its commercial organization was evacuated to Amsterdam, which thus became the new headquarters of overseas trade for the Netherlands. Meanwhile Philip II in 1580 had become the ruler of a united kingdom of Spain and Portugal, and when the Dutch of the northern United Provinces of the Netherlands revolted against his rule he was able to reply by closing the port of Lisbon to their ships, thus cutting them off from the distribution-centre of Eastern goods.

The Dutch at this time were exploring the possibility of a northeast passage from Europe to the Far East, and some of their sailors had already been to the 'East Indies' in Portuguese ships. It is probable that the developing maritime commerce of the Dutch must have brought them sooner or later into conflict with the Portuguese in the East. But the closure of the port of Lisbon, and the national struggle against Spanish-Portuguese rule, provided

87

immediate incentives for the Dutch to seek direct access to the spice-producing islands and the valuable markets of South-east Asia. For the Dutch, every inch of ground won in South-east Asia, every extension of their influence there, would represent at once a commercial and a political victory against Spain, and would at the same time furnish them with the material resources with which to carry on the struggle. They would wage their war for national independence not only in Europe but also on the oceans and, with greatest intensity, among the islands of South-east Asia, where they would outflank and eventually overwhelm the bases of Portuguese power.

To the Portuguese in Asia, for whom political changes in Europe meant less than the traditional and personal rivalries of the East, the issue did not at first appear in such clearly defined terms. The Dutch voyager van Linschoten was able to spend five or six years at Goa and to travel extensively throughout the Portuguese sphere in eastern Asia, collecting detailed information which, after his return to Holland in 1592, he published in the form of a manual of sailing directions for the Eastern seas (*Reysgeschrift*, 1595), and a general account of his travels and observations in the Portuguese East (*Itinerario*, 1596). These works, part of which appeared in an English translation in 1598, made detailed information about South-east Asia, hitherto confined almost exclusively to the Portuguese, the common property of western Europe. An immediate outcome of the application of this new knowledge to Holland's political and commercial purposes was the first Dutch expedition to South-east Asia, which set out from Amsterdam in April 1595. Four ships under the command of de Houtman, with van Linschoten's sailing directions to guide them, reached Bantam, the pepper and general exchange port on the north-west coast of Java, in June 1596. They were well received not only by the local authorities but also by Portuguese merchants. Leaving Bantam, the expedition visited Jacarta (or *Jacatra* as it was called in all European accounts of the time) and the islands of Madura and Bali, and then returned by the south coast of Java to the Indian Ocean and Europe.

The success of de Houtman's expedition immediately directed Dutch commercial organization to the development of trade with island South-east Asia. Companies were formed in Amsterdam, Rotterdam and Middelburg to finance a series of separate voyages to Sumatra, Java and the Moluccas. With characteristic thoroughness, some of these early Dutch companies minted coins specially for currency in the East, hoping to drive the Mexican dollar out of circulation. In the year 1598 alone twenty-two ships left Dutch ports for the East, and between 1595 and 1601 a total of sixty-five ships sailed in fifteen separate expeditions. The Dutch thus began their trade with a series of separate voyages organized by independent and competing syndicates ; on arrival in island South-east Asia each expedition sought favourable terms of trade for itself and concluded separate agreements with local rulers. Bantam was the usual port of arrival, and the Dutch developed a steady trade there, but there was no delay in pushing on to the spice-markets of the Moluccas ; an expedition visited Amboyna and Banda as early as 1599 and obtained cargoes of mace, nutmeg and cloves.

But the Dutch were in South-east Asia for war as well as for trade, and they were soon working to build up a system of local alliances, offering protection and the toleration of Islam in return for trading concessions and co-operation against the Portuguese. Amboyna agreed to an alliance in 1600, and Banda accepted Dutch protection in return for a monopoly of the nutmeg export trade in 1602 ; but agreements with such minor states presumed stronger support and better organization than the Dutch could as yet provide. The Achinese, with powerful resources of their own and with long experience of warfare against the Portuguese in the Straits, were clearly the most hopeful material from the Dutch point of view ; and although the first contacts with Achin in 1600 were not promising, the Dutch persisted in their approaches and obtained permission to establish an agency there. Two Achinese envoys were taken to Holland in 1601. At the same time direct action against the Portuguese had already begun ; the first blows had been struck in the struggle for the command of South-east Asian waters. The Dutch attacked the defence squadron off Malacca in 1597 ; and the year 1602 opened with a decisive naval victory over the Portuguese off Bantam which secured the Dutch position in that port, established command of the Sunda Strait, and laid open the road to the Moluccas, where Dutch activities had so far been tentative and sporadic.

It soon became apparent, however, that the successful pursuit of war and trade in the East demanded something more than the uneven organization and the limited resources of separate companies ; that, in fact, a pooling of capital and a unification of organization and policy were called for. Accordingly in 1602 the States General of the United Provinces effected an amalgamation of all the groups concerned into a united East India Company, with a subscribed capital of $6\frac{1}{2}$ million guilders, for ten years. The governing body of the Company was a board of sixty directors, closely linked in personnel and in policy with the States General, which retained a careful supervision over administration and finance. The direct management of the Company's affairs was entrusted to an executive committee, or Board of Control, of seventeen.

England, like other European countries, had for many centuries purchased a share of the Eastern goods that were shipped to the Mediterranean. Spices, especially pepper and cloves, were always in demand because they helped to make salted meat palatable in the winter months. In those days it was extremely difficult to keep sheep and cattle alive during the winter, for the cultivation of roots and artificial grasses for winter feeding was still unknown. Fresh meat was therefore practically unobtainable in winter, and the flavour of dry salted meat was unappetizing without the addition of spices. Until the sixteenth century these and other products of Asia were carried to English ports almost entirely in Italian, especially Venetian, ships, or in ships belonging to the Hanseatic ports of north Germany and the Baltic. English exports of wool and cloth were also largely carried by such foreign shipping. England's share in her overseas trade was, on the whole, a passive one.

Before the sixteenth century England was in no position to challenge this foreign control of her overseas trade. She lacked the shipping and the commercial organization necessary to do so, and she was far away from the focus of European trade in the Mediterranean. It was not until her shipping had been developed, and the Indian and Atlantic Oceans opened up, that England's position in relation to transoceanic trade-routes gave her an advantage that she was able to take. Even then the initial advantage lay with Portugal and Spain, who had the benefit of readier access to Italian geographical knowledge and commercial technique, and were prepared to reap the immediate profits of their position on the edge of the ocean. Yet although England was far behind Portugal and Spain on the road to world trade, she made some progress in that direction during the sixteenth century. The Portuguese reached India by sea in 1498, the English not until 1608, but during the years between Englishmen made many attempts to open up trade relations, directly or indirectly, with Asia. Since Portugal and Spain between them monopolized the ocean routes of the world, it seemed at first that England's only hope of reaching Eastern markets was to develop alternative routes outside the Portuguese and Spanish spheres of control. This was the motive behind the English search for a north-west or north-east passage to the East, and behind the various attempts to develop trade relations with Russia and the Levant.

England's interest in Eastern trade in the sixteenth century was not merely that of an importer. She wished to obtain oriental products as cheaply as possible, but she also hoped to expand her exports and to find markets in Asia for her woollen cloth. In this respect her motives differed from those of both Dutch and Portuguese, who were not concerned with building up a national export trade. The Dutch aimed at capturing the carrying trade between Asia and Europe from the Portuguese. The English in the sixteenth century had no such ambitions, and although they were to find, when they followed the Dutch along the old Portuguese sea-route to the East in the seventeenth century, that Indian and not English cloth was the acceptable exchange commodity in South-east Asia, and that trade with the East required the export not of cloth but of silver, yet their original motives for entering Asia derived from the national policy of broadening the real basis of England's wealth—the export trade in woollen cloth.

But, as with the Dutch, the final impetus that brought the English to Asia was hostility to Spain. From 1577 onwards

England pursued an aggressive anti-Spanish policy overseas, and in November of that year Francis Drake sailed from Plymouth across the Atlantic to begin operations. Drake's original instructions were to go and return by the Straits of Magellan, but at the last moment the plan was changed and he was directed to push on across the Pacific to the Spice Islands. In November 1579 Drake anchored off the island of Ternate in the Moluccas. The Sultan, welcoming the arrival of the representative of a new power to play off against the Portuguese, concluded an informal agreement for protection and trade, and gave permission to load a cargo of cloves. Drake then sailed by the south coast of Java across the Indian Ocean to the Cape of Good Hope, and so home to England. His circumnavigation showed that a light, fast ship could safely cross the oceans. His success in gaining direct contact with the Moluccas, and establishing friendly relations there, greatly stimulated the interest of English merchants in trade with South-east Asia. Queen Elizabeth's ministers were also anxious to follow up Drake's achievement by organizing further efforts to establish English trade along the Portuguese route via the Cape to island South-east Asia, but the queen herself regarded the proposal as too dangerous, and the beginnings of a national effort to develop trade in that direction had to wait another twenty years.

The first Englishman to visit mainland South-east Asia was Ralph Fitch. With three companions he arrived in 1583 at Ormuz, the Portuguese base at the entrance to the Persian Gulf, where he was arrested and sent to Goa. Released on parole, he escaped from Goa to Hoogly in the Ganges delta region. Although there was a Portuguese settlement at Hoogly, the Goa government's writ did not run there, and Fitch was able to sail in a Portuguese ship to Pegu. From there he travelled overland to Chiengmai and then in 1588 sailed to Malacca, where he stayed for seven weeks. The information that Fitch brought back to London in 1591 helped to stimulate further interest in the prospects of trade with South-east Asian countries.

Meanwhile events had been occurring which were to provide the final drive to the English approach to South-east Asia. In 1585 war broke out between England and Spain, and in the same year an Anglo-Dutch alliance was formed. The ensuing war encouraged English and Dutch ambitions by exposing the weakness of Spain and Portugal overseas. In 1586 Thomas Cavendish, following Drake's example, set out with three ships on a Pacific expedition via the Straits of Magellan. After touching at Guam and the Philippines, he sailed through the Philippine archipelago to the south of Luzon, and then turned southward to Java. His exact course is uncertain, but he seems to have passed through the Macassar Strait between Borneo and Celebes, and then by either Bali Strait or Sunda Strait to the south-west coast of Java, where he anchored and obtained provisions. On his return to England in 1588 Cavendish claimed to have established the fact that trade could be carried on in the Moluccas without hindrance from Spaniards or Portuguese. Meanwhile Drake in 1587 had captured a homeward-bound Portuguese carrack off the Azores, with a cargo valued at over £108,000 and documents containing valuable information on Portuguese organization in the East.

The defeat of the Spanish Armada in 1588 gave a powerful new impulse to England's developing interest in Eastern trade, and in the following year a group of London merchants began to work on a scheme for an organized reconnaissance expedition by the Cape route to South-east Asia. But although three ships procured and equipped by this group sailed eastward in 1591, only one, captained by James Lancaster, reached its destination, and in the event it engaged in commerce-raiding rather than direct trade. Reaching a small island off the north-west tip of Sumatra in June 1592, Lancaster crossed to Penang Island and remained there for several months, using it as a base for piracy in the Straits. Then, after calling at the island of Ujong Salang (Junk Ceylon to the English sailor; the present Puket) off the coast to the north of Penang, he sailed westward and reached England in 1594. The London merchants had little to show for the capital they had invested in this enterprise. The proceeds of Lancaster's piracy were insignificant and had been obtained at great cost of life; twenty-six of his crew had died at Penang.

In 1592 the imagination of Englishmen had been fired once again by the capture of a Portuguese carrack, the *Madre de Dios*, off the Azores, with a cargo worth over £140,000. With the carrack were captured a description of China printed at Macao in 1590, and a general account of Portuguese administration and trade in the East. But English effort to establish a footing in South-east Asia was confined for some time longer to small-scale group enterprise, which met with little success. The Dutch, by contrast, achieved a striking initial success in de Houtman's expedition of 1595–7. This example, together with the appearance of an English translation of van Linschoten's *Itinerario* in 1598, and the conclusion of an Anglo-Dutch agreement for co-operation in the same year, brought the English government and the London merchants, in December 1600, to the final step of forming an East India Company.

James Lancaster was chosen to command the English Company's first expedition to South-east Asia, and in June 1602 his fleet arrived at the port of Achin. The Dutch, who had already succeeded in obtaining permission for a trading depot there, seemed ready to co-operate, and helped to arrange an audience with the Sultan at which Lancaster presented a letter and gifts from the English queen. The queen's letter emphasized the mutual benefits to be derived from trade, since it had been 'so ordained that no place should enjoy all things appertaining to man's use, but that one country should have need of another'. Trading facilities were granted, and at Bantam, which Lancaster visited several months later, negotiations were equally successful. A million pounds of pepper were shipped to England in 1603. English agents were permitted to remain, with their Dutch opposite numbers, in the Chinese suburb on the western side of Bantam, preparing a cargo for future shipment.

The Portuguese were now confronted by a second rival European power in South-east Asia, but in fact the English presented a much less serious threat than did the Dutch. The English carried out isolated attacks on Portuguese shipping in the Straits, but the Dutch were waging a more systematic war of attrition against the bases of Portuguese power. In 1603 they cut off the main bulk of Malacca's food supplies from Java, and threatened Goa itself. They cultivated the friendship of the Johore Malays, whose attack on

Malacca in 1585–6 had been answered by heavy reprisal raids from the Portuguese. Time was on the side of the Dutch; they could afford to move slowly against Portuguese Malacca, and meanwhile to concentrate their main efforts on the trade at Bantam and the penetration of the Moluccas. Slowness was all the more advisable after 1604, when an English peace treaty with Spain and Portugal put an end to any hope of Anglo-Dutch co-operation against Malacca, and revealed the essential reality of the commercial rivalry between the two Companies in the East.

Both Companies had gained entry to pepper markets in Sumatra and Java outside Portuguese control; they now raced to the clove islands of the Moluccas, where Portugal was still in possession. Henry Middleton, in command of the English Company's second expedition, reached Amboyna on 10 February 1605, and, on the strength of the peace treaty of the previous year, obtained the Portuguese governor's permission to trade there. But the Dutch, who had been forced out of their earlier foothold in Amboyna, arrived with five ships on the following day, and after a brief struggle they forced the Portuguese fort to surrender. Amboyna thus became the first Dutch possession in island South-east Asia, its chiefs acknowledging Dutch sovereignty by treaty of August 1605.

Portugal's sea-power seemed too weak to support her remote outposts, and the events at Amboyna were repeated shortly afterwards at Tidore, where Middleton again had to stand by while the Dutch captured the Portuguese fort. In Ternate the Dutch encountered no opposition and secured an agreement from the Sultan for the exclusive supply of cloves. These Dutch successes in the Moluccas were only temporarily checked by the despatch of a Spanish fleet from Manila to Ternate and Tidore in January 1606, and in the following year the Dutch consolidated their hold on Ternate by a treaty in which the Sultan acknowledged the sovereignty of Holland in return for protection, symbolized by the Fort of Orange built in the same year.

Dutch pressure on the strongholds of Portuguese trade was considerably increased in these years. Both Lisbon and Goa were blockaded in 1606. In the Straits, although the Portuguese were able to launch an attack against Achin, their old enemy, in the same year, they themselves were attacked by the Dutch and the Johore Malays together at Malacca. There was much hard bargaining between Dutch and Malays over their respective claims to the Malacca territory, which, as the Dutch historian Valentyn wrote, was 'very much like selling the skin of the bear before it has been caught' ; and in fact the fortress garrison, which now included no more than eighty Portuguese, held out against two successive landing forces until relief came from Goa ; and it withstood another Dutch attack in November 1608.

But although Malacca itself could still hold off Dutch assaults, the Portuguese were suffering severe shipping losses in the Straits. In Western waters too the Dutch were taking strong offensive action, and their victory over superior Spanish naval forces in Gibraltar Bay in 1607 impelled Spain to open the negotiations that led to a twelve-years truce in 1609. With an eye to the outcome of these negotiations the Dutch took steps to improve their position in the East, especially in the Moluccas, the key to the whole Eastern trade. A strong fleet sent to the Banda Islands early in 1609 forced Bandanese agreement to the construction of a fort and a Dutch monopoly of spice supplies. Here again the English were present as spectators of the progress of a rival Company that would immediately exclude them from any share in the trade. For while the Dutch were prepared to tolerate the English Company's comparatively weak competition at Bantam and in Sumatran ports, they were determined to establish an exclusive trade in the Moluccas. This determination was strengthened when the negotiations with Spain, in which the Dutch had hoped for English support, failed to achieve agreement on a basis for permanent peace in the face of Spanish insistence on exclusive dominion in the East and West Indies. Thus from 1609 onwards the Dutch, denied by the Spanish-Portuguese government an acknowledgment of even partial rights in island South-east Asia, and no longer aligned diplomatically with the English, forged ahead on their own to build up, during the ensuing twelve years of truce with Spain, a *de facto* exclusive dominion in the Moluccas. When their first Governor-General of the Indies, Pieter Both, arrived at Bantam in January 1611 he carried instructions that 'the commerce of the Moluccas, Amboyna and Banda should belong to the Company, and that no other nation in the world should have the least part'.

The English Company continued to seek co-operation with the Dutch, hoping to establish some *modus vivendi* between the two concerns in island South-east Asia. The Dutch government was approached, and talks began in London in 1613. The English had everything to gain from co-operation. They could not hope to extend their trade in the face of direct opposition from the Dutch, whose Company was virtually backed by the whole financial resources of the State, and whose ships were far superior in armament and in fighting power. On the other hand the English Company had little to bargain with ; it had, in fact, nothing substantial to offer the Dutch in return for a formal recognition of the right to participate in the trade with South-east Asia. Its hands were tied by James I, who, while urging a settlement, refused to agree to any proposal for co-operative action against the Portuguese, without which the Dutch would regard no settlement as acceptable. And even without this restriction on the English Company's action, had it been diplomatically possible to agree formally to co-operate with the Dutch in direct measures against the Portuguese, the English lacked the resources and equipment to make any such co-operation effective on their part. In any case, the logic of the situation in the East Indies was not likely to be affected by diplomatic adjustments in Europe. With or without English co-operation, the Dutch had the strength and the organization with which to fight their own battles in the East. They were prepared to talk in London or The Hague, but in the East they were committed to action. They were not unwilling to discuss with the English the price of admission to a junior partnership in the East Indies trade, but they would do so fully conscious of the fact that a large amount of the business was already in their own hands.

While negotiations continued in Europe, both Companies pressed on with independent action in the East. The Dutch took energetic steps to provide what legal sanction they could for their position in South-east Asia by building up a network of treaties with the local rulers. The English, operating on a much smaller scale, and with only one properly constituted factory—that at Bantam—in the whole area, appeared nevertheless to have gained fresh vigour from a reorganization of the Company, in 1612, which ended the system of separate voyages and began the first joint-stock operations. In 1613, although the Dutch were unchallenged in the Moluccas, there were English agents as well as Dutch at Macassar in Celebes, at Sukadana and Banjermasin in Borneo, and, in Siamese territory, at Patani and at Ayuthia itself. In the Java ports of Jacarta and Grisek the Dutch had a free hand, but they were now confronted with renewed English competition at Achin in Sumatra.

The reopening of English trade at Achin was prompted by a revival of Achinese power after a period of quiescence lasting something over a quarter of a century. Since Lancaster's visit to Achin in 1602 the English had found it easier and cheaper to procure supplies of pepper at Tiku and Periaman, ports on the west coast of Sumatra, rather than at Achin itself. Now, however, Achin had brought these ports under her control, and she was extending her influence in other directions with such effect that it was necessary to negotiate with her for trading rights in Sumatra generally. After months of discussion, Thomas Best in 1613 succeeded in arranging new terms for English trade with Achin, to include the ports subordinate to her. In dealing with the English, the Sultan of Achin referred to himself as King of all Sumatra, and although this represented ambition rather than achievement, it was clearly important to cultivate good relations with him. The Court of the Company in London even considered seriously the Sultan's request for an English wife, and 'a gentleman proposed his daughter, of most excellent parts for music, her needle and good discourse, and also very beautiful and personable'. Certain religious objections to the proposed match were answered to the satisfaction of the Court, and 'the lawfulness of the enterprise proved by Scripture'. It only remained for the girl's father to satisfy the meeting that there were no adequate grounds for the 'supposition that the rest of the women appertaining to the King may poison her if she become an extraordinary favourite'; after which, it was recorded, 'if the King [of England] consent, it was thought it would prove a very honourable action'. But nothing more is heard about the affair; perhaps James I refused his consent.

Once again Achin was coming to the forefront of the struggle for power in the Straits. Her old enmity against the Johore Malays, who had made a truce with Portuguese Malacca, flared up anew. She invaded Johore itself in 1613 and carried off its Sultan; and when his successor made terms with the Portuguese in 1615 she invaded the country again and drove him out. In 1615 and 1616 Achinese fleets tested the defences of Malacca. The Dutch, too, struck at Malacca in 1615, but although they inflicted heavy damage on the defence squadron they were not yet able to carry out the amphibious operations that would be necessary in order to take the fortress itself.

The English Company had scored a great success in its agreement with Achin for trade in Sumatran pepper. But even highest quality pepper could not compare in market value with nutmegs or cloves, and, for that reason, the Company now decided to embark on a new attempt to break in on the spice trade at Amboyna and the Bandas, a decision which was reinforced when the Anglo-Dutch talks broke down in 1615. Such a decision, constituting as it did a direct challenge to the real basis of the Dutch commercial position in island South-east Asia, was bound to meet with the sternest opposition; it led, in fact, to the final trial of strength that was to determine which of the two Companies would dominate the South-east Asian trade. The first English attempts to reopen trade with the Spice Islands in 1615 were thwarted by the Dutch, but in 1616 the English Company scored an outstanding success in obtaining the cession of two islands in the Banda group—Wai and Run—from the local rulers.

Not only in the Spice Islands but in Sumatra and Java as well, the English gave evidence of a new forward policy. They opened new agencies in the Sumatran river-ports of Jambi and Indragiri in 1616, and in the following year a factory at Jacarta. And in 1618 they sent Thomas Dale, who had gained a reputation for firmness and efficiency by his administration of the colony of Virginia, with a fleet of six ships to add force to their policy in the whole area. But in the same year the Dutch appointed a new Governor-General

who was to prove more than a match for Dale in determination and
vision—Jan Pieterzsoon Coen, the real founder of Dutch power in
the East Indies.

It was in the Java ports of Bantam and Jacarta, where both
Companies had their main factories, that the hostilities foreshadowed by these events broke out. Towards the end of 1618
Dale seized a Dutch vessel in the harbour of Bantam as a hostage ;
and when shortly afterwards the ship and its valuable cargo were
destroyed by fire, Coen retaliated by ordering the destruction of
the English factory at Jacarta. A clash between the rival fleets
followed, but as the Dutch were outnumbered Coen decided to
call in additional naval support from Amboyna before attempting
further action. Dale seized the opportunity to press home his
advantage, and, with the help of local troops, besieged the Dutch
fortified factory at Jacarta early in 1619. But then disputes arose with
the Javanese over the surrender terms to be imposed on the
garrison, and when Coen returned from Amboyna he quickly
restored the Dutch position in Jacarta. Dale now decided to remove the English agents and their goods from Bantam to the
Coromandel coast of India, and to attempt to organize a new
expedition from there. But his fleet of six ships, dispersed to take
on cargoes at various South-east Asian ports, had been completely
destroyed by the Dutch before the end of 1619.

The English forward policy had ended in disaster, and the
Company's position was now weaker than ever. But the final act
in this drama of Anglo-Dutch conflict in the East Indies was postponed by the intervention of diplomacy in Europe. Renewed
negotiations—lasting over seven months, and on several occasions
broken off on the arrival of news of hostilities in the East—culminated in a Treaty of Defence in July 1619. James I had prevailed
on the English Company to accept terms—terms which, in fact, it
was both unable and unwilling to carry out. Each Company was
to provide ten warships for joint action against Portuguese and
Spaniards in Eastern waters. There was to be an equal division of
the pepper trade in the Java ports ; while in the Moluccas, the
Bandas and Amboyna the Dutch were to have two-thirds and the
English one-third of the spice trade, each Company contributing
a corresponding proportion of the expenses of fortresses and

garrisons. By this arrangement the English were to be admitted
to a recognized partnership in the East Indies trade, but at precisely
the price that they had refused to pay in the negotiations of 1613-15
—the price of committing themselves to definite obligations under
an agreement which really constituted an offensive alliance against
Spain and Portugal overseas.

For the Dutch this was, on paper, a diplomatic victory; for
their truce with Spain would end in 1621, and they had now
enlisted English support in the work of undermining Spanish-
Portuguese power in the East in preparation for the renewal of
war in Europe. But English support was not in fact a realizable
asset. Even if the Company had been able to meet the material
demands of a policy of active co-operation with the Dutch, it
would yet have remained constitutionally averse to the policy
itself, fundamentally unwilling to become involved in the obligations of a frontal attack against Spanish-Portuguese power in
South-east Asia. The aims of the English Company were commercial—perhaps narrowly so ; and it hoped to be able to restrict
itself to purely commercial methods. What the Company wanted
in the East Indies was not open war but open markets.

When the Treaty of Defence was published in the East Indies
early in 1620 Coen had to accept the changed situation and refrain
from direct action against the English, but no treaty could conceal
for long the reality of the fundamental opposition between the two
concerns in island South-east Asia. Coen made the position of the
English in Jacarta (named Batavia by the Dutch in 1619) as un-
comfortable as possible, at the same time preventing them from
moving their Java headquarters away from under his direct supervision to Bantam. Elsewhere the English Company enjoyed only
a brief hour of commercial freedom. At Japara, on the north
coast of Java, they maintained an agency and a ship-repairing base ;
in the Bandas they retained Run Island and acquired control of
Lontor. But the marriage of Anglo-Dutch interests in the East
Indies under the Treaty of Defence had been a forced one ; the
honeymoon was short and unsuccessful, and before long the
partners had fallen out. When the truce between Spain and the
United Provinces ended in 1621 and war between them began

again, it became clear that the treaty had not succeeded in tying the English up with Dutch purposes in the East—that, in fact, while the English would accept the benefits which the treaty conferred, they would not perform the obligations which it imposed. But, in the Dutch view, there was no room for neutral commerce in the East Indies; if the English would not co-operate in a general plan of operations against the Portuguese, they could not expect to receive any consideration.

The treaty remained in legal force for twenty years, but in less than as many months it had broken down in practice, and negotiations had to be resumed in an effort to settle constant differences and disputes. The English encountered increasing obstruction in Batavia, and by 1623 they had been almost driven out of the Bandas, though retaining nominal possession of Run Island. Competition for pepper supplies in the Java ports had become fiercer than ever as a result of Achin's policy of restricting European trading in Sumatra, forcing the Dutch to abandon the Achin trade in 1622. And now an event occurred that was to put an end to any hope of Anglo-Dutch co-operation in South-east Asia.

The English President and Council at Batavia, lacking sufficient funds to meet the expenses of forts and garrisons due from them under the Treaty of Defence, had already resolved, early in 1623, to wind up the Company's business in the Moluccas, the Bandas and Amboyna, and to order the closure of their factories in those parts. Orders to this effect were sent to Amboyna, but before they arrived the 'massacre' had taken place. In February 1623 ten Englishmen, nine Japanese and one Portuguese were executed by the Dutch in Amboyna on a charge of conspiracy. News of this event reached Batavia in June, and hastened the withdrawal of the English Company to its stations in India. Business had already been closed down in Patani and Ayuthia in 1622, but factories were retained at Japara (until 1648), Achin, Jambi and Macassar, as well as at Batavia and at Bantam, which remained an English foothold in South-east Asia until 1682. Continued disputes with the Dutch after Amboyna led to the closing down of the English factory at Batavia in 1628, the factories and goods being transferred to Bantam.

The Dutch had now virtually eliminated English commercial competition in South-east Asia. They had expelled the English from the Spice Islands altogether, and elsewhere in the area they had ensured that a limited English trade could be carried on only by the permission and under the supervision of their headquarters at Batavia. The English were driven back on their commercial interests in the ports of India, where they hoped to develop a peaceful trade in consonance with their declared policy that 'a war and traffic are incompatible'. Both Companies had already realized the essential part played by Indian cloth in the exchange economy of South-east Asia ; they had set up buying agencies at points on the Indian coast where textiles could be purchased for silver and thence distributed to their factories further east for barter exchange in the pepper and spice markets. It was on the Coromandel coast of India that calico production was most closely related to the requirements of South-east Asian markets ; in this area the Portuguese had founded agencies at Negapatam and San Thomé (Madras), and during the first ten years of the seventeenth century the Dutch had established factories at Masulipatam, Petapoli, Tegnapatam and Pulicat. From 1611 the English Company was trading at Masulipatam, and in 1613 it opened a factory there. But for both Dutch and English these establishments were, in origin, essentially subsidiary to the trade with the East Indies. It was only after failure in their first objective—the spice markets of island South-east Asia—that the English turned aside to concentrate on the apparently less attractive proposition of trade between India and other parts of the world.

In these early Company days life was far from easy for the European servant in the East. The rigours of the voyage out had not considerably diminished since the previous century, when the Portuguese reckoned the death-rate as nearly six out of every seven who left Europe. Lime juice or 'lemon water' was issued during the voyage to counteract the scurvy ; in 1619 the English Company decided, as an experiment, to follow the Dutch example of substituting white wine for this purpose, 'to refresh the men and scour their maws'. But those who survived the voyage and reached the East Indies were left with little resistance to disease. In two

English ships trading in Sumatran ports in 1634, forty-four members of the crews died.

If a Company servant's health survived the dangers and discomforts of the voyage, it would be even more severely tested by the living conditions in the factory area to which he might be posted. Bantam was regarded as a particularly unhealthy post; the European factories there were situated in the Chinese suburb, described as 'a stinking stew'. Jacarta seemed, by comparison, salubrious. The most frequently attributed cause of death was 'the flux'. This disease, apparently, might be contracted through various, and even contradictory, causes. Instances are recorded of death from the flux through 'the inordinate drinking of a wine called toddy'; but it was the opinion of Captain Cope in 1754 that 'those gentlemen who drink strong liquors to excess usually avoid the flux—but are carried off by fevers'; it was clearly a difficult choice for a Company servant. Recommended remedies for the flux were also various; lemon water and white wine were suggested in 1607, and later 'infallible remedies' proposed were 'the fruit guava and the pomegranate', boiled mangosteens, and even the drastic expedient of 'bathing in the cold water'.

Both Companies kept a careful watch over the conduct of their servants in the East Indies and made strenuous efforts to enforce discipline and sober behaviour. The English Company maintained a lofty moral tone in its dispatches; it was even ready to censure the behaviour of the preachers whom it had chosen, with great care, for ministry in the East. A preacher who applied for appointment was usually required to preach a sermon before the Court of Directors in London, and a poor sermon would disqualify the candidate. But a good sermon was not everything; the candidate was liable to further examination. When a Mr. Fuller applied for appointment as a preacher in 1629 the Court demanded why, 'he being a married man and having received £700 or £800 with his wife, he would undertake such a voyage and absent himself so long from her'. The preacher frankly confessed that 'that was the chief cause of desiring this employment, for that she is a woman whose life and conversation is incompatible and not to be endured'. The Court desired Mr. Fuller 'to have patience till Friday'.

There was already the tendency of the Englishman at home to blame 'the man on the spot' for the comparative ineffectiveness of English efforts in the East. We 'besot ourselves with pint and pot', writes Mun in 1621, while the Dutch have 'taken up our wonted valour'. But the men on the spot looked at the matter differently. 'The Dutch horse,' wrote the factors from Bantam in 1618, 'will not travail without provender at his nose, nor are we English able to endure without beef, bread and good drink, of all which we are too much destitute at present.'

Chapter Ten

EUROPEAN COMPANY TRADE IN THE SEVENTEENTH CENTURY

After Amboyna the English Company resigned itself to the necessity of leaving the South-east Asian trade almost entirely to the Dutch and confining its interests to the Indian trade. For its new purposes it was even willing for a time to support Dutch action against the Portuguese in Indian waters. There were in- stances of Anglo-Dutch joint action in 1624 and 1625 when attacks were made on the Portuguese squadron stationed at the entrance to the Persian Gulf, and in 1626 when combined naval forces attacked the Portuguese settlement on the island of Bombay. But although England and Spain were at war from 1625 to 1630, the English Company actually curtailed its operations against the Portuguese in the East during that period; and the Treaty of Madrid in 1630 announced the cessation of commercial hostilities between England and Portugal. When Portugal broke away from Spain in 1640 and declared her independence, her relations with England were further improved; and in 1654 she formally recog- nized the English right to trade in Asia.

In South-east Asia the Dutch were left to build up a command- ing commercial position at Batavia and to prepare for the final expulsion of Portuguese power from the Straits of Malacca. Taught by the failure of earlier direct assaults on Malacca itself, they worked slowly and methodically, gradually wearing down what remained of Malacca's hold on the trade through the Straits, drawing the strings of the whole network of South-east Asian maritime trade into their hands at Batavia, and patiently accumu- lating both sea and land forces in sufficient strength to ensure the downfall of the Malacca fortress.

Cut off from direct access to the main produce markets of island South-east Asia, Malacca had now almost completely lost her entrepôt trade. Only with Macassar, where limited supplies of spices could be obtained, did she manage to maintain direct contact. And the products of the islands were no longer being brought to Malacca by local trading vessels in exchange for cloth and other commodities. The commerce of Malacca, Resende notes (*c.* 1638), 'is almost entirely extinct, for never or only rarely do any natives come to Malacca to seek anything, having all they require from the Dutch'. Portuguese ships still carried on a direct trade with Macao, Manila and ports of the Indo-Chinese coast, but they were subject to increasing attacks from the Dutch, and from the *orang selat* who assisted them, in the Singapore Strait; and besides, this trade was being starved by Malacca's growing inability to obtain and supply island produce. Apart from imports from India, themselves greatly restricted, Malacca could supply China with only a little pepper and an even smaller quantity of cloves.

In the Malay Peninsula itself there was little of commercial value to be obtained. The tin supplies of Perak, largely under Portuguese control in earlier years, had been greatly reduced since the Achinese began to harry that state in 1620; the Portuguese fort had been virtually abandoned; the ruler of Perak was refusing to pay the tin tribute to Malacca unless he received protection; and the Dutch were gaining a hold on the trade. Only small and irregular supplies of tin could be obtained through the five or six thousand Menangkabau people living in Naning, in the hinterland of Malacca. These people, whose ancestors had crossed over from Sumatra during the fifteenth century, and who now lived under the jurisdiction of a Temenggong appointed by Malacca, also helped to supplement the town's failing food supplies.

Malacca was being starved not only of the staple commodities of her former entrepôt trade but of essential food supplies. The town had always been largely dependent upon imported rice and vegetables. The Portuguese complained that this dependence was unnecessary—that the country behind Malacca was well watered and fertile, and capable of supplying her basic food requirements, but that the Malay farmer did not make the best use of it. The Malay, in other words, grew only enough food for the needs of his family; he farmed for subsistence and not for commerce. Consequently, rice had to be imported for the town population; and the frequent blockades and interruptions of food shipments from Java and elsewhere caused severe shortages and high prices. For the soldiers of the Malacca garrison, as Resende wrote, 'the King's pay is very small, and the country very dear'.

And yet, in spite of changing circumstances, Portuguese Malacca still clung to the principle that 'no ship coming from the Straits region shall pass without putting in at Malacca and paying duties on all the cargo : 10 per cent on the cargo itself and a further 2 per cent to the town for the fortification and artillery'. On top of this, the Malacca officials, deeply involved in private trading, used their position to insist on the right to purchase part of an incoming cargo at reduced prices. Their exactions perhaps did as much as Dutch competition and blockade to ruin Malacca's commerce.

The Portuguese succeeded in maintaining friendly relations with Johore and the states of the Malay Peninsula generally between 1615 and 1637, but Achin remained an implacable foe of both Portuguese and Malays. In 1620 the Achinese overran Perak, Pahang and Johore, and destroyed the pepper plantations of Kedah that competed with their own. They made a direct assault on Malacca in 1629, but their fleet was badly mauled by combined Portuguese and Malay forces. From 1630 onwards the Dutch blockade of Malacca was maintained with increasing rigour ; but although the Dutch won Johore over to their side in 1637, and during the next few years received active support from Achinese or Johore forces on one occasion or another, these would not combine in a single operation. However, with the appointment of Anthony van Diemen to the Governor-Generalship in 1636 the Dutch were resolved that nothing should stand in the way of their determination to take Malacca. In 1636 they attacked a fleet of twenty Portuguese ships in the harbour of Malacca, and in 1639 Dutch and Achinese forces completely invested the town itself.

In June 1640 the final assault on the fortress began. The Achinese, who had carried out so many attacks on Malacca, refused to join in this last attack because the Dutch had obtained the co-operation of the Johore Malays. Landings were made in August and the defending forces driven into the fortress, which was then bombarded from land and sea. The powerful artillery of the fortress—forty-one pieces in all according to de Resende—

replied vigorously, and the Portuguese showed no inclination to surrender. At the end of September some nine hundred Dutch reinforcements arrived and, propaganda leaflets were smuggled into the fortress urging the defenders to cease their futile resistance since the Portuguese empire in the East was doomed. The defenders were now facing starvation ; but the attackers were suffering from fever, dysentery and plague. The new year opened with the cannon still roaring on both sides. But although the fortress still stood, no relief had come from Goa. On 11 January 1641 the Dutch resolved to storm the walls, and three days later, after a desperate resistance, Malacca capitulated. The Dutch treated the Portuguese honourably, allowing them complete freedom of repatriation.

With the capture of Malacca the Dutch Company obtained command of the Straits of Malacca as well as the Sunda Strait, but it was in Batavia that its headquarters remained and its control of the main lines of South-east Asian trade centred. Batavia began to assume the character of a European-administered colonial seaport town, with a heterogeneous and expanding population of Asians, during the Governor-Generalship of van Diemen (1636–45). He encouraged Chinese settlement by supporting the sugar industry, which was in Chinese hands.

From Batavia Dutch commercial interests looked outward across the sea to Malacca and to the Moluccas. Within Java itself the political balance of the various states remained for the most part unaffected by Dutch, as earlier by Portuguese, activities. When the last Hindu dynasty of Majapahit—which had established its rule over that shrunken kingdom in East Java in 1486—was overthrown in a series of wars between 1513 and 1528, conservative interests fled eastward and became concentrated in the island of Bali, which became—and has remained—a living museum of Hindu-Javanese tradition and culture. The interests of the separate Moslem commercial states of Java's north coast continued to be bound up with the inter-port trade of island South-east Asia and the Malay Peninsula ; although Demak and Japara lent support on occasion to Malay or Achinese attacks on Portuguese Malacca, they normally carried on an exchange trade with that port, as well as with ports in Celebes and the Moluccas, during the sixteenth century. At the same time, however, centripetal tendencies were beginning to reassert themselves in Java's political structure. By the end of the sixteenth century the central Javanese state of Mataram was successfully building up an inland empire, based upon agricultural production, at the expense of the commercial sultanates of the north and north-east coasts, which it gradually absorbed. Thus from the early years of the seventeenth century the main forces of Javanese political, economic and cultural life were becoming centralized in Mataram. And this process was accompanied by the gradual decay of Javanese-owned shipping and overseas trading concerns; for Mataram's rulers, seeking the static stability of seclusion, had no ambitions for foreign trade or overseas influence; they were, in fact, not unwilling to concede to European merchants the management of the commercial affairs of their seaports.

Mataram's overlordship extended over Java westward as far as Cheribon, where it had halted after an unsuccessful attempt to establish control over Batavia in 1628–9. On the other side of Batavia lay the rich pepper country of Bantam, in whose seaport capital the English Company still maintained a resident agency. Here and in other South-east Asian ports where the European Companies had gained concessions but not exclusive rights, they had to compete with Asian merchants—Indians, Arabs, Persians, Chinese—and were often outdone by them in business ability. Moreover, in the years after 1650 Bantam, in contrast to Mataram, began to take the initiative in developing its overseas trade, maintaining a merchant fleet of its own and cultivating direct commercial relations with other centres in Asia. Bantam, in fact, began to appear as a serious rival to the Dutch Company in Batavia; it seemed to be aspiring to the position of a new Malacca, a modernized Moslem commercial power, in the Malayan archipelago. Guided by the progressive policy of its Sultan, Abdul Fatah Agung (1651–83), Bantam sought diplomatic relations with Turkey and England, employed European sea-captains, technicians and advisers, and purchased quantities of firearms. In 1681 envoys were sent to England—Evelyn mentions them in his *Diary*—and returned with five hundred barrels of gunpowder. However, Bantam's era of independent progress was soon ended; its political stability depended too much upon the personal influence of its ruler. In 1682 the Sultan quarrelled with his son, whom he had earlier brought into close association with himself in the government of the country, and when open conflict broke out between them the son took the fatal step of appealing to the Dutch in Batavia for assistance. The Dutch seized the opportunity of intervention; they drove out the old Sultan and installed his son on terms which gave then a virtual monopoly of the pepper trade. The English Company's agents were then ordered to leave. They obtained quarters in Batavia; but in the following year, 1683, having broken the Dutch prohibition against trading in cloves, they were finally expelled from Java. Individual English merchants continued to reside in Batavia from time to time, and the Company's ships occasionally called there for trade in non-prohibited commodities.

Meanwhile the Dutch Company had been presented with another, and much larger, opportunity of gaining commercial advantage by intervention in civil war. Dutch forces were called in when a prince of the island of Madura rebelled against the Susuhunan or emperor of Mataram in 1674; they occupied part of Madura and the port of Surabaya. But the war extended to East and central Java, and dragged on for five years; and the cost of Dutch assistance rose steadily year by year. In the end Dutch forces had to drive into the interior of the island and fight their way to Kadiri, in East Java, in order to deal with the rebel prince and his supporters; after which the authority of the Mataram ruler was restored, with a Dutch garrison for his protection, in the new capital of Kartasura. In return for its help, the Dutch Company by 1679 had obtained the extension of the territory under its own jurisdiction from Batavia eastward to the river Chimanuk, and southward across the hill country of Priangan to the coast, thus driving a wedge between the territories of Bantam and Mataram. In Mataram itself the Company obtained the cession of Kartasura's port of Semarang, and a general monopoly of duty-free trading rights in other ports. These gains were confirmed and consolidated after the death, in 1703, of the Susuhunan who had conceded them, when the Dutch occupied Kartasura before approving the installation of the new ruler. By a fresh agreement in 1705 the

Company's territory was extended eastward to include Cheribon, and its commercial domination of Mataram's seaports was completed.

Control of the Java ports accorded with a major aim of Dutch commercial policy in South-east Asia. The Company's purpose was not simply to capture the carrying trade between Asia and Europe, but also to control, and where possible to monopolize, the even more profitable inter-port trade in Asia. The latter aim had been partially achieved by the Portuguese, but the superior resources, organization and technique of the Dutch enabled them to carry it through to much greater effect. And it was over the inter-port trade system of South-east Asia that the Dutch position gave them their strongest hold. With Malacca and Batavia as their control-points, with their hold on the exchange ports of Java, and with their command over sources of supply in India and in the Moluccas for cloth and spices respectively, they were in a position both to direct and to feed the main channels of South-east Asian trade.

Exclusive control of the whole trade, or even of that of island South-east Asia alone, was, of course, an ideal and not a practical possibility. It was only within the limits of its actual jurisdiction that the Company could hope fully to restrict the purchase, resale or shipment of key products—such as spices, pepper, gold, tin, opium and precious woods—to its own agents. In the Moluccas it maintained an effective monopoly of the highly profitable spice trade—the real basis of its commercial strength; but only by perpetual vigilance against interlopers, and by ruthless restriction of movement and of production within the island area. Elsewhere, however, the Dutch Company's commercial monopoly was never complete. Although it possessed by far the largest share of the world trade in pepper, it could never fully exclude rival Asian or European trade in that commodity, the production of which was carried on in widely separated areas throughout South-east Asia, and could not be restricted, as could spice production, to within narrow geographical limits. The marketing of pepper in Java was almost completely controlled by the Dutch, but quantities of pepper were collected in other areas and distributed to both Asian and European ports by English, French and Danish ships, and to

Chinese ports by Chinese ships. After Dutch control of the Java ports had been established, the Company shipped about 3,500 tons of pepper annually to Europe and perhaps an equal amount to China and other parts of Asia. According to a contemporary estimate of the total import of pepper into Europe in the years between 1682 and 1688, English ships imported an annual average of 900 tons, French and Danes 500 tons, and Dutch 3,600 tons.

In the Moluccas, after the expulsion of the Portuguese, and the elimination of English competition in 1623, the Dutch proceeded to transform trading concessions into controlling rights over production as well as marketing and distribution. This ultimately involved full political control over the rulers of the Moluccas. In these islands, whose natural products were the most commercially valuable—and whose people were perhaps the least politically developed—in the whole of South-east Asia, Dutch trading interests quickly led to political domination. The subjection of the Banda Islands, already completed by 1623, gave the Dutch Company a monopoly of the world supply of nutmeg and mace. The island of Amboyna, still nominally under the suzerainty of the Sultan of Ternate, was chosen to take the position—analogous to that of the Bandas—of the sole source of the world supply of cloves. This policy demanded the extension and maintenance of Dutch control over the Moluccas proper in order to prohibit the production of cloves in those islands, where the clove was, in fact, indigenous. And the maintenance of Dutch control, in its turn, involved the Company in a series of wars and repressive actions, punctuated by more or less unstable agreements with the rulers, until, towards the end of the seventeenth century, the Moluccas were finally subdued.

During this period the Company carried out the destruction of clove plantations wherever found in unauthorized areas outside Amboyna, thereby achieving the dual purpose of restricting and monopolizing output. This stern policy, which greatly shocked the liberal principles of a later age, can only be properly judged in the light of the accepted commercial principles of the time— essentially those principles of mercantilism that were applied by England, France and Holland alike to their overseas territories in the seventeenth and eighteenth centuries. Moreover, it would be wrong to assume that the destruction of clove plantations deprived the Molucca islanders of the essential basis of their livelihood ; on the contrary, it relieved them of the burden of poorly-rewarded labour on the plantations, which formed probably a major obstacle to their material and social well-being. For the island clove industries were organized and operated for the sole benefit of the rulers and their households, and although a small proportion of the wealth which the industry brought to the islands may have seeped through to the mass of the inhabitants, yet the system bound them to perform what was virtually servile labour on commercial crops at the expense of subsistence farming, fishing, and the normal activities of the village community. Whilst the welfare of the native inhabitants was no direct concern of the Company, it may well have indirectly furthered their real interests by destroying the vested interests of the rulers in clove production.

The Company had no desire to interfere in the internal administration of the islands otherwise than for primarily commercial purposes. War was for it an occasionally necessary commercial technique. Though economic control shaded off imperceptibly into political control, the Company always sought commercial advantage, not political responsibility ; and in the seventeenth and eighteenth centuries it was still possible for a European Company in Asia to secure the one and avoid the other. In the Moluccas the Company ruled, if it could be said to have ruled at all, by indirect methods ; except in Ternate, which was reduced to a status of complete dependency in 1683, the Sultans were left as nominally sovereign rulers in relation to their people, though bound to the Company in economic matters by treaty engagements.

But economic matters provided a wide enough field for direction and control. The restriction of clove production ; the prohibition of trade or diplomatic relations with other parts of Asia—so that the whole Moluccas area should be a closed preserve for Dutch exploitation ; the exclusive importation of cloth and other staple consumer goods ; the general direction and organization of labour for the production of commercial crops in Amboyna and the Bandas : these powers were all obtained by a mixture of diplomacy and duress. The organization of labour for Dutch purposes led to the requisitioning of slaves, especially at Macassar and on its dependent island of Sumbawa, which furnished servile labour in considerable quantity during the seventeenth and eighteenth centuries.[1] In the seventeenth century such supplies were augmented by the import of slaves from Africa and by slave-raiding on the coasts of Asia generally.

By such measures the Company established its position as the sole supplier of the world's requirements of cloves and nutmeg. During the seventeenth and eighteenth centuries it shipped to Europe between 1,400 and 1,800 tons of cloves a year. With a purchase price of 3d. per lb. in the Moluccas, and a cost price of perhaps 6d. per lb. at Amsterdam, cloves sold at the more or less constant rate of 6s. 3d. per lb. Besides this, the Company distributed large quantities of cloves and nutmeg throughout Asia.

After the capture of Malacca in 1641 the Dutch restored and extended its fortifications, completing 'a respectable fortress of great strength with solid walls and fortified with bastions, well provided with guns. . . .' (Valentyn). Indeed Malacca under Dutch rule was first and foremost a strategic fortress dominating the Straits ; only secondarily was it a trading post. As an entrepôt port it was definitely overshadowed by Batavia. In his report of 1678 the Governor observed that although many ships, both Company-owned and others, called at Malacca, few of them unloaded more than a small proportion of their cargoes (usually food and clothing), but carried the bulk of their goods to other ports. The only large shipments unloaded at Malacca were specially requisitioned supplies ordered by the Company from Batavia or other ports in Asia. Many such shipments consisted of food supplies ; for Malacca, as always, was unable to support itself in food, and had to depend upon imported supplies of rice and vegetables from Java, Siam and Bengal. The Dutch complained, as the Portuguese had done, that the Malays in the Malacca district would grow little more rice than was enough for their own needs. In 1668 the Malacca rice-fields produced 76 loads of 3,000 lb. each,

[1] By treaty of November 1667 the Company secured exclusive duty-free trading rights at Macassar, and regular tribute of slaves. Similar terms were later extended to Sumbawa (treaties of 1669, 1673–75, 1701, 1765).

but the Malacca government estimated its rice requirements for all purposes at 200 loads per annum.

Apart from food supplies, Malacca's main imports were textiles from India. The major export commodity was tin, which was found in various parts of the peninsula : in Perak (which was subject to Achin), in Kedah, Ujong Salang and Singora (subject to Siam), and in Sungei Ujong and Klang (in Johore territory). The Dutch Company maintained, as far as it could, a strict monopoly in the export of tin and the import of Indian cloth. Besides these controls, all dealings in pepper, cloves, opium, nutmeg, mace and resin were restricted to the Company and its agents. Moreover the Company sold stocks of pepper and cloves for export on very definite conditions : that these commodities might be exported only to Macao, the China coast or Manila. This was to prevent inroads into the Company's monopoly of the pepper and clove trade in the East Indies, or into the export trade to Europe. The business in nutmeg, mace, opium and resin was small; Batavia was the main entrepôt for such goods. Resin, for example—a plentiful product of the Malayan jungle, but in short supply owing to banditry and unrest inland from Malacca (attributed by the Dutch mainly to the Menangkabaus of Naning)—had to be imported from Batavia after being collected from Palembang in Sumatra. Trade restrictions were reinforced by restrictions on shipping within the Straits. Only the Company's ships were permitted to call at Indragiri, in Sumatra, because the Dutch monopolized the gold and pepper market there according to the terms of a treaty of 1664. Voyages from Malacca to Palembang were similarly prohibited.

In practice the Dutch found it impossible to maintain a monopoly of cloth imports or of tin exports except at Malacca itself. 'The Moors [i.e. Indian Moslems] snap up all the tin in Perak under our very noses, and stuff the country full with their piece goods,' they complained in 1647. An attempt to solve the problem, on the lines of earlier Portuguese methods, was the enforcement of a permit system on all ships passing through the Straits. Indian Moslem traders were at first refused admission to Malayan ports and also prevented from calling at Achin, which could offer tin supplies through its control of Perak. But the Dutch soon found it

impossible to keep Indian cloth traders out. Governor Bort of
Malacca, writing in 1678, admitted that the Dutch were unable to
compete with the Indians in an open port ; and since their resources
were unequal to the task of maintaining a permanent blockade of
independent ports on the Malay Peninsula such as Kedah, Ujong
Salang and Tenasserim, as well as Achin, they had to content themselves with a policy of attracting Indian cloth importers as far as
possible to Malacca itself. The remaining Malayan ports, as well
as Achin, remained more or less open to Indian and also to European traders—English, Portuguese, French and Danes. The
Dutch had attempted a blockade of Achin from 1656 to 1659 in
order to keep the Indians out of the cloth trade there, but without
success. They found that one result of keeping the Indians out
was to let the English in ; and by 1660 the Dutch had come round
to the view that their best policy was to issue permits for Indian
traders to Achin if only in the hope of excluding English and other
European traders, who were no more successful than the Dutch in
competing with Indians on equal terms. But in 1688 Dampier
reported that the roads at Achin were 'seldom without ten or
fifteen sail of ships of several nations', and that in the town there
were 'a great many foreign merchants, English, Dutch, Danes,
Portuguese, Chinese, Gujeratis'. Near the gate of the Sultan's
palace there stood two English brass cannon, the gift of James I.

Thus the initial policy of direct control of all the main ports in or
near the Straits had to be abandoned for one of indirect control by
means of the regular patrol of the Straits by Dutch sloops, which
would compel all ships to call at Malacca, pay dues there, and apply
for permits to proceed to their destination. The Indian hold on the
import of cloth had remained an unchanging feature of the trade
of the Straits region, and both Portuguese and Dutch were forced
to adopt similar methods in their attempts to break it.

To control the tin trade of the Straits area was an equally difficult
task. Kedah agreed in 1642 to sell half its tin produce to the Dutch
Company at a fixed price, and not to transact business with any
merchant who could not produce the Company's permit. Perak
refused a similar agreement on the grounds of its dependence upon
Achin. However, with the death of their Sultan, Iskandar Thani,
in 1641 the Achinese had come under the rule of the first of a

I

succession of Sultanas ; and the change disposed them to favour diplomacy rather than war. In 1650 the Dutch succeeded in persuading Achin to agree to an equal division of the Perak tin produce. A Dutch factory was then established on the Perak river, but its occupants were murdered in the following year. The factory was reopened in 1655, and the Dutch carried on a desultory warfare at sea against the Achinese, whom they held to be responsible for the conduct of Perak. But the station on the Perak river was on a 'bad, marshy site' ; it was abandoned in 1661 and a new factory established on Pangkor Island, which was described by Dampier in 1689. In 1690, however, this post was attacked by Malays, and the fort that had been built there was abandoned. Elsewhere the control of tin supplies seemed equally elusive. When news reached Malacca of the discovery of tin mines up the river Siak, on the east coast of Sumatra, the Dutch quickly concluded an agreement for the sole purchase of supplies there (1676), but they soon found that a Johore port official (Shahbandar) was collecting most of the tin and shipping it to Bintang Island, in the Johore dominions. Although the islands of Banka and Billiton were ceded by the Sultan of Palembang in 1668, the tin produce of Banka Island was as yet unknown to the Dutch ; it was being sold secretly to Chinese traders.

Unless by force, no tin would come to Malacca if it could find an alternative market. In 1663 Perak was sending its tin quota to Achin, but 'declining to give the Company its competent half-share'. Governor Bort noted in 1678 that both Perak and Kedah were under contract to deliver half their tin to the Company, but the agreements had seldom been carried out. What supplies did reach Malacca could be legally sold only to the Company at its own price. At the end of each year the accumulated stocks of tin were sent from Malacca to Dutch agencies in India for the purchase of cloth ; any surplus over and above these requirements would be sent to Batavia.

Although much of the trade of the Straits area eluded Malacca's control, the Dutch position was at any rate more secure politically than that of the Portuguese had been. Achin was no longer a danger to Malacca after about the middle of the seventeenth century. Johore, however, was still a considerable power. She claimed a general suzerainty over the Malay Peninsula (excluding Malacca and the inland district of Naning under its jurisdiction), and also over the Riau Archipelago and the minor states of Bengkalis, Siak and Kampar on the east coast of Sumatra. At Bengkalis, opposite Malacca, a busy exchange trade was carried on between Malays, Javanese and Indian Moslems in spite of Dutch attempts to prevent ships from calling there. The capital of Johore itself, on the Johore river, was also a mart for tin, pepper and cloth, in which traders from all parts met and exchanged their goods. After 1669 Johore absorbed the Sumatran state of Indragiri—on the southern side of Kampar—where the Dutch had hoped to exploit a monopoly of the gold and pepper trade conceded to them only a few years before. The Dutch had no option but to tolerate such commercial competition, and they were careful to maintain peaceful, if not exactly friendly, relations with Johore.

After 1670, however, the Dutch were relieved from the pressure of competition from Johore by the new rivalries that were developing in the Malay world. Disputes over a broken marriage contract led to war between Johore and Jambi, on the Sumatran coast. In 1673 Jambi attacked Bengkalis, a dependency of Johore, and then invaded Johore itself, destroying the capital at Batu Sawar, and driving the Sultan into exile in Pahang. Later the capital of the Johore dominions was transferred to Riau, in the island of Bintang, but this move only exposed the sultanate to the attacks of new enemies. Siak threw off its allegiance and chose a Menangkabau ruler, who invaded Johore early in the eighteenth century and made himself Sultan. The deposed Sultan intrigued with Bugis adventurers from Macassar in the hope of winning back his throne, but the attempt was a failure and he had to flee to Pahang (1718). Later, however, the Menangkabau Sultan was himself driven out of Riau by the Bugis, who set up a puppet Malay Sultan of Johore and Pahang in 1722. From that date a Bugis ruled as under-king (Yamtuan Muda); and a number of Bugis buccaneers who had settled around the river-mouths of the west coast of the Malay Peninsula, between Malacca and Perak, transferred their headquarters to Riau.

The first thirty years of the seventeenth century saw a revival of Burman power under the Toungu dynasty, and the reconquest of much of the southern territory that had been recently lost to the Siamese (see p. 78). Pegu's port of Syriam was taken in 1613, and the Portuguese adventurer de Brito who had installed himself there was caught and executed. Martaban was recovered from the Siamese, but Tenasserim withstood a Burman siege of 1614. Chiengmai, east of Toungu in Siamese territory, was recaptured in 1615.

Then in 1628 the Toungu ruler moved his residence southward to Pegu, and for a time it seemed as if Burma's political life, centred in the coastal region and based on a real union of Burmans and Mons, would henceforth be exposed to the modernizing influences of the outside world. But the Burman court seems to have found the Mon country uncongenial, and there were perhaps other considerations that pointed to the unsuitability of the southern region as a political centre. The Mon people had no liking for Burman rule ; Pegu itself was particularly exposed to attack from Siam ; and the delta region of the Irrawaddy, far from being the thickly populated rice-growing area it was to become in later times, was poor and unproductive. In 1635 the court retired inland to Ava, near the present Mandalay, which was four hundred miles distant—a river journey of up to two months—from the sea. Henceforth, until late in the nineteenth century, the political centre of gravity remained in Upper Burma ; and although the Toungu kings invited European trade with their ports on several occasions in the seventeenth century, they gave little real encouragement to trade ; and Burma as a whole lived a withdrawn, self-sufficient existence of its own, uninfluenced in any vital respect by the changing conditions of the outside world. Shielded from the impact of new ideas, the culture of Burma developed along narrow and rigidly traditional lines ; and although this made for a certain unity and strength of culture, it was a unity based upon a self-imposed isolation, a static unity which, as Burma—like China—was to find in the nineteenth century, was bound to collapse in the long run when new ideas could no longer be kept out, but would come flooding over the dams and dikes of her medieval isolation.

The decision of the Burman court to withdraw to Upper Burma was in a sense justified by events in the second half of the seventeenth century, when Burma was affected by disturbances which followed from the overthrow of the Ming dynasty in China. When the last of the Ming princes, expelled from Yunnan in 1658, fled to Burma, he was pursued by Manchu forces which raided northern Burma and at one time besieged Ava itself. A few years later, in 1662, the Siamese made good use of the opportunity to recapture Chiengmai and overrun Pegu. But the Toungu government, securely entrenched in its homeland in Upper Burma, was capable of surviving such inroads into its territory; both Chinese and Siamese eventually withdrew their forces, and Burman rule over Pegu and Chiengmai was restored.

European trade with the seaports of Burma and Siam in the seventeenth century was fitful and erratic, and subject always to sudden changes of policy on the part of both the Eastern rulers and the Western Companies. These countries, as we noted earlier, lay off the main line of European commercial activity in Asia ; the long spear of the Malay Peninsula was interposed between them and the Straits of Malacca ; and as a result they were only slightly affected by the operation of Western commerce and diplomacy before the nineteenth century.

As early as 1620 a direct invitation to 'free trade' was issued by the Toungu ruler to the English Company, but the President and Council at Batavia were fully occupied by their difficulties in the East Indies at that time. Dutch agents began trading at Syriam in 1634. The withdrawal of the Burman court to Ava in the following year, however, did not enhance the prospects of a regular trade with official backing, and in fact the Burma trade was never a paying proposition. For most of the century the Dutch maintained a footing at Syriam and Ava, if only for the purpose of keeping the English out—an English factory established in 1647 lasted less than ten years—but the Dutch themselves abandoned their interest in Burma after 1679. This left the field, unpromising as it was, open to the English Company, and serious consideration was given to the re-establishment of a factory at Syriam in 1680 ; but the Ava government would not agree to supply saltpetre for the Company's ammunition requirements in India, and the project was abandoned.

European commercial activity was hardly more successful in Siam, but competition was keener there owing to the strong intervention of French, as well as Dutch and English, interests. French vessels had appeared in Eastern waters from 1620 onwards, but organized trade began with the formation of the French East India Company in 1664. Indian factories were founded at Surat and Masulipatam in 1668–9; the site of Pondicherry was acquired in 1673. The first French approaches to Siam, however, were made between 1660 and 1680 by missionaries, some of whom gained great favour by combining their religious teaching with instruction in military engineering and fortress-building. A French medical missionary was appointed governor of Puket Island.

Commercially, the Dutch were still in the strongest position at Ayuthia. As a result of a show of force in 1664, when they blockaded the Menam river, they had obtained definite trading concessions. English trade at Ayuthia was comparatively trivial; the Company's factory had been revived there by 1661, but there was much personal adventuring, and the line between official Company trade and that of the unlicensed 'interloper' was anything but clear. The most successful adventurer among many was a Greek named Constantine Phaulkon; he first came to Ayuthia in the English Company's service in 1675, and then, after several years' trading, entered the service of the Siamese government, in which he attained a position of great influence as Superintendent of Foreign Trade.

The French missionaries in Siam were soon followed up by agents of the French East India Company, who opened a factory at Ayuthia in 1680. Diplomatic relations between France and Siam, helped forward by Phaulkon's patronage, were cultivated with great enthusiasm. A Siamese embassy left for France at the end of 1680 with young elephants and rhinoceroses for Louis XIV, and a letter written on a sheet of gold. Their ship was wrecked off the coast of Madagascar, and all passengers, human and animal, were lost; but a second embassy reached France safely in 1684. In the following year two French warships brought an embassy to Siam, and a commercial treaty was signed. The French Company was admitted to full trade with Siamese royal agents (to whom Siam's foreign trade was normally confined); it obtained a monopoly of the tin exports of Puket Island or Ujong Salang, and the cession of Singora. It was also granted extraterritorial jurisdiction over its servants in Ayuthia, a privilege which the Dutch had already secured there as well as in certain Sumatran ports.

These successes of the French Company in Siam spurred the English Council at Madras to action. The English Company was trying out a forward policy in India at this time, and it was in the mood for forceful methods. In 1686 it planned an attempt to seize Chittagong and became embroiled in hostilities against the Moghul government. The Madras Council also proposed to capture the island of Negrais, in the mouth of the Bassein river in Burma, and to use it as a base for an attack on the port of Mergui, in Siamese territory. The first part of this project was abandoned, but the Company despatched two frigates direct to Mergui in 1687. A considerable number of English interlopers were stationed at that port, some of them—including the prominent Richard Burnaby and Samuel White—working in Siamese service. The arrival of the English ships, calculated to cause the immediate surrender of Mergui to the Company, merely resulted in incriminating the Englishmen ashore ; Burnaby and about fifty others were slain by the Siamese, and Siam formally declared war on the English Company.

Meanwhile French influence in Siam had attained almost its highest point. Siamese envoys to France in 1685 had gone so far as to invite French troops to garrison their forts, and six hundred French soldiers and three hundred technicians arrived at Ayuthia in September 1687. The troops were dispersed to various key points such as Mergui and Bangkok, and the trading privileges of the Company were renewed and extended. But the installation of military forces marked the final hour of French ascendancy in Siam. A sudden reaction against French influence set in among Siamese court circles in 1688 ; Phaulkon, who all along had favoured the French above the other European Companies, was executed ; missionaries were imprisoned and Christian converts were slain. The French troops at Bangkok were permitted to withdraw to India, but many of those stationed in more outlying posts were killed or imprisoned.

The Dutch now replaced the French as the most favoured nation in Siam's foreign trade ; by a new agreement of November

1688 they obtained a monopoly of the export trade in hides and tin. The English also gradually recovered their position as Siam's war against the Company petered out. It was rather on the more accessible ports of Burma, however, that English traders from India naturally converged. The Ava government continued to press for the reopening of an English factory at Syriam, but the Company refused to commit itself to anything so positive. Instead, the authorities at Madras were content to issue permits for individual trading ventures to Syriam; and although one of the individuals engaged in this trade carried the splendid title of 'Chief of the Affairs of the English Nation', he was in fact a private merchant resident at Madras who visited Syriam every year.

In the East Indies the English were excluded from any serious competition in the clove and nutmeg trade since the Amboyna affair, but the Company held on to its factory at Bantam until 1682. It possessed a paper claim to the island of Run in the Banda group, but this was surrendered to the Dutch under the Treaty of Breda in 1667. The Bantam factory was closed down owing to Dutch pressure in 1682 and it was never restored. But new factories were soon afterwards opened on the south-west coast of Sumatra, at Indrapura (1684) and Bencoolen (1685). The former lasted only a short time, but the Bencoolen factory survived as the only considerable depot of the English Company in South-east Asia until the foundation of Penang in 1786.

In the Malayan region during the second half of the seventeenth century individual English traders continued to put in an occasional appearance at various ports and to pick up what business they could, their success depending to a large extent upon the direction of Dutch policy at the time. In 1656, for example, the English President at Surat sold a cargo of cloth to Kedah—where he had his Indian agents—in exchange for tin and pepper; his ship, however, was stopped by the Dutch as it came out of the Kedah river and the tin was confiscated. But in 1661 English traders were still arriving at Kedah, with cloth, iron and steel; one of these private merchant-adventurers was having ships built for himself at Kedah and was acting as a business agent of the Sultan, shipping tin, gold and elephants to the Coromandel coast of India and bringing back Indian cloth. For a time a small factory was operated in Kedah (1669–75). Malacca itself was visited by English traders, and Governor Bort noted in 1678 that the English were beginning to take a hand in the import of rice to Malacca from Siam. The Dutch conceded that the English were esteemed in these parts 'for their natural character and their large purchases'.

Individual traders and agents of the Company also visited Johore. Johore had co-operated with the Dutch since their arrival in Malayan waters, and in the first agreement of 1606 the Dutch had obtained the concession of duty-free trade to the exclusion of all other Europeans. However, when an agent of the English Company applied to Johore for the right of duty-free trade in 1647 the concession was granted, though only as a temporary arrangement with the agent himself; the Company would be required to pay a 5 per cent duty on imports, an export duty on tin and pepper, and the usual port dues. An English request for permission to maintain a permanent warehouse in Johore was refused in 1661.

The English, then, were far from being unaware of the possibilities of trade in the South-east Asian region, from which they were never fully excluded between the Amboyna massacre and the foundation of Penang by Francis Light. After the final loss of Bantam in 1682 they concentrated more than ever on the Indian trade, but they never fully lost sight of their earlier ambition for trade with the farther East. Indeed the successful foundation of Penang and Singapore came at the end of a long series of attempts on the part of the English to establish other permanent footholds in South-east Asia besides that at Bencoolen. However, these attempts, it must be admitted, were sporadic and unsustained; they represented no fixed direction of policy on the part of the East India Company.

Chapter Eleven

COMMERCE AND CONFLICT IN THE EIGHTEENTH CENTURY

SOUTH-EAST ASIA at the beginning of the eighteenth century had been exposed to the operations of European commerce for almost two hundred years. Yet the effects of direct contact with the agents of Western commercial enterprise had hardly made themselves felt, and the influence of the West in general had made practically no impression. European commercial activity had so far only scratched the surface of life for the inhabitants of South-east Asia. The ancient life of the peasant villages remained practically unchanged, for the aims and methods of production had not been materially altered. There had been increased control of the distribution of South-east Asian products in certain areas, especially in the Moluccas, and there had been some regulation and direction of production in parts of Java, where commercial aims had been advanced by war and by the consequent establishment of claims to a general politico-commercial supervision. These measures, however, had not carried European commercial exploitation in South-east Asia much beyond the stage reached by Indian or Arab traders in earlier centuries. They imposed controls and restrictions, more or less enforceable, on the commercial relations between the main centres of South-east Asian production and the outside world, but they did not bring about any basic modification of the internal structure of South-east Asia's economy.

The aims of European activity were still predominantly commercial ; its methods were those of the chartered trading company which, although closely linked through its directorate with the State, was not a consciously political agent but an avowedly commercial one. It may perhaps be true that European aims in South-east Asia have always been and have remained predominantly commercial down to the present day ; and it is possible for the historian to see that commercial and political aims have from the earliest days been very closely interrelated, in effect if not in intention. But it was not until the nineteenth century that European aims became *consciously* both political and commercial. It was not until then that those areas of South-east Asia which for the most part had already been subjected for a considerable time to European commercial penetration became colonies in the modern sense of the term. Before then, although there was political action there was no political policy ; there was only commercial policy.

In practice, however, the commercial policy of the Dutch in the seventeenth and eighteenth centuries carried within itself inevitable political implications and consequences. And although these were, on the whole, hardly realized, or at any rate rarely admitted, by the Company as such—that is, by the governing body in Amsterdam —they had to be faced and dealt with by the authorities in South-east Asia. The directors in Amsterdam were concerned with commercial results rather than with any political measures through which results might be obtained ; it was left to the Governors in Batavia to work out, largely on their own initiative, the practical application of commercial policy to local political conditions. At first the commercial aim of the Dutch was simply to interpose themselves as monopolist middlemen and carriers between the main sources of supply of the most valuable products of South-east Asia and the world markets in which those products were demanded. In particular, they aimed at monopolizing the export of pepper, spices and sugar, and the import of cloth and opium. But a policy of commercial monopoly is one which by its very nature carries with it political implications. These may not necessarily be of a far-reaching nature, but they must include at any rate a willingness to use force in order to further commercial ends which are essentially restrictive and prohibitive. Seventeenth-century commercial policy, which required that the Dutch should simply stand guard over the main outlets and inlets of trade, was generally satisfied by such limited intervention of a political kind as would afford some security for control in the main seaports. Commercial activity and the aims of such political measures as were taken in support of it, were restricted to the coastal fringes. This is true, in a general sense, of Dutch activity in Java and other parts of South-east Asia. The Moluccas, however, must be excluded from this generalization because, by reason of their miniature size and their internal weakness, they invited political intervention of a much more far-reaching nature than elsewhere, resulting in measures of internal direction which foreshadowed the future development of Dutch action in Java itself.

In passing from the seventeenth to the eighteenth century we notice the development of new trends. For one reason or another the Dutch are no longer content to remain on the doorstep of Java; they wish to open the door and go inside. The decline of the Company's trade with India, the weakening of its hold on the carrying trade between various parts of Asia, and the practical difficulties of enforcing monopolist control in the Java ports, all combined to force the Dutch to seek compensation for losses sustained during the last twenty years of the seventeenth century in a further development of their commercial aims in Java, in the transformation of their policy from that of mercantile intermediacy to one of agricultural exploitation. This was not, of course, a change of policy which the Company consciously adopted at any definite date; rather it was the gradual outcome of empirical measures undertaken by the authorities in Batavia in order to meet changing circumstances. It was a policy forced on the Company at the end of the seventeenth century mainly by the diminution in the profits which it drew from the carrying trade in Asia and between Asia and Europe. As a policy it never, in fact, succeeded in reviving the prosperity that the Company had enjoyed during the seventeenth century. The period from 1639 to 1693, when the Company was still a trading concern without territorial ambitions, remained the most profitable period of its history.

The assumption of a general supervision of Javanese agricultural production, which the change of policy foreshadowed, would inevitably entail a political supervision much more far-reaching than any hitherto attempted in Java. Yet it remains true of eighteenth-century as of seventeenth-century Dutch action in Java, that political intervention was motivated and conditioned by predominantly commercial purposes. The trading company was merely making use of the existing political machinery for its own ends. The merchants came from the doorstep into the house itself, but they came as merchants rather than as masters ; provided they could get at the larder, they had no intention of occupying the house or of interfering with the domestic arrangements.

Already before the end of the seventeenth century Batavia had begun the process of expanding its monopoly rights in the Java ports into claims for the automatic delivery to the Company's warehouses of fixed amounts of produce at fixed prices. Bantam was under obligation to deliver quantities of pepper ; the princes of Mataram and the subordinate rulers, or regents, of the north coast and of Madura were bound to deliver a fixed annual amount of rice. This system was extended in the eighteenth century concurrently with the development of new commercial crops such as coffee and indigo. The coffee plant was introduced from the Malabar coast of India ; indigo workers were brought in from the Coromandel coast. Coffee plantations were started in the Batavia district, in Priangan and in Cheribon in 1707, and before long coffee was widely extended as a staple crop, the commercial value of which greatly increased as the eighteenth century wore on. The commercial crops which had been already established were also considerably extended ; 2,200,000 lb. of pepper were exported in 1710, and in the same year there were 130 sugar factories in the Batavia district alone, mostly in Chinese hands.

The exploitation of these crops was effected by political means similar to those which had already been applied in the Moluccas. Regents were required to deliver fixed amounts of coffee, pepper or cotton to the Company at imposed prices, and, in cases where political control had been firmly established, they had also to surrender freely a quota of the produce of their districts in the form of tribute. The forced deliveries (*leveringen*) of commercial crops involved the Company in a general supervision of agricultural production and conditions of employment, which was to lead on to the direct and detailed control of the nineteenth century. They imposed a heavy burden on the peasant population, for the forced cultivation of cash crops upset the rhythm of the village economy ; the peasants were sometimes compelled to grow crops on soil that was quite unsuitable ; and the demands of the Company, conveyed through the regents, were erratic and unpredictable from year to year, at one time urging increased production and at another

ordering the destruction of crops, as was done in the Moluccas.
The tributes in kind, or 'contingents', which consisted of food
crops such as rice, were comparatively less onerous though
necessarily irksome.

The regents under this system acquired a dual status; they
remained the acknowledged rulers of their districts, with control
of law and administration; they became also the commercial
agents or tools of the Dutch Company. They were not necessarily
unwilling tools; to a large extent the system of forced deliveries
forged a link of mutual economic interest between the Company
and the regents so that they combined in a partnership for the
exploitation of the Javanese peasantry. It was a system of agricultural production by remote control, in which the regents were
like the stewards of an absentee landlord, appearing to their tenants
as the agents of an alien and unfathomable purpose. Such a system
by its comparative uniformity might induce internal order and
security in the country districts, but it would be attended by much
hardship for the peasant cultivator. On the other hand, merely
commercial considerations required that the Dutch should supervise to a greater or less extent the organization of labour for their
own purposes, which involved also the protection of labour against
excessive and therefore uneconomic exploitation on the part of
rulers and chiefs. And the protection of labour, undertaken initially
for motives of prudential insurance, received further justification
and support in the later eighteenth century from humanitarian
sentiment.

An increasing area of Java thus became subservient to Dutch
commercial purposes. But although this had disturbing effects on
village economy and on the balance of cultivation, those effects
were not profound; they left untouched the essential framework
of social organization, law and custom. The customary law, or
adat, of the countryside was unaffected, for the good reason that
the Dutch had no need to interfere with it; they wished to acquire
rights, not responsibilities.

If the operations of European commerce had produced little
radical change in South-east Asia, even in those areas where they
were most fully concentrated, the influence of European culture

and custom had been even less noticeable. Europeans and Asians met only in the business contacts of the market-place or in the relationship of master and servant; in such circumstances there could be little appreciation of, or even interest in, cultural backgrounds. Few Dutchmen in the seventeenth century attempted to learn Malay or any other Eastern language. The *lingua franca* used between Europeans and Asians, and among Europeans of different nationalities, was a debased kind of Portuguese. There were other survivals from the period of Portuguese ascendancy; indeed such European influence as had penetrated South-east Asia (apart from the influence of European trade) was Portuguese and Catholic Christian. It survived especially at Malacca and in the Moluccas, the former centres of Portuguese power, although the numbers of Portuguese Eurasians at Malacca had been considerably diminished by emigration after 1645, when the Dutch administration prohibited Catholic worship. In the Moluccas there were districts and villages that adhered to Christianity, and also, although under Dutch influence acknowledging themselves to be Protestant rather than Catholic, to ritual and customs derived from the Portuguese. These *orang sirani* of the Moluccas showed the impress of Portuguese influence down to comparatively recent times. Alfred Russel Wallace, who visited Amboyna between 1857 and 1860, observed that 'the Portuguese element decidedly predominates in the old Christian population, as indicated by features, habits, and the retention of many Portuguese words in the Malay. . . . Though now Protestants, they preserve at feasts and weddings the processions and music of the Catholic Church, curiously mixed up with the songs and dances of the aborigines of the country. Their language has still much more Portuguese than Dutch in it, although they have been in close communication with the latter nation for more than two hundred and fifty years; even many names of birds, trees and other natural objects, as well as many domestic terms, being plainly Portuguese'. Describing a *kampong sirani*, or Christian village, on the island of Bachian, Wallace wrote : 'It is astonishing how little these people have altered in three hundred years. . . . They are still in manners and appearance almost pure Portuguese.' The people of Amboyna, the centre of the vastly profitable clove production, received particular attention from their

European masters, and certainly the Dutch did not neglect to build on the foundations of Christianity which the Portuguese had laid in that island. Alexander Hamilton, the Scottish merchant-adventurer who was trading in South-east Asian waters in the first years of the eighteenth century, observed that 'Amboyna has turned prodigiously religious, having no less than fifty Dutch Protestant churches'; and he added that some Ambonese youths had already been sent to be trained for holy orders in the universities of Holland.

But it was the Philippines that formed the major exception to the general rule that European influence in South-east Asia had not yet begun to make itself felt to any marked extent. These islands had barely been touched by Indian cultural influence in earlier times, and the influence of Islam, which had been operating for little more than a century before the arrival of the Spaniards, was mainly limited to the southern parts, especially Mindinao. The majority of the population in the sixteenth century was still living at the primitive 'Indonesian' stage of culture. The Philippines therefore constituted the one considerable region in South-east Asia where Europeans were not faced with a civilized culture, comparable in a general way with their own, already established and assimilated. And the Spaniards who mastered the islands were able to make good use of these favourable conditions because their interest in the territory was much less a commercial interest than a missionary one. With the Portuguese, crusading and commercial motives had been combined up to a point, and the influence of their religion and customs had survived, as we have seen, in small pockets here and there. The Dutch had shown, so far, an almost entirely commercial interest in the areas which came under their control. By contrast, the Spaniards were conquerors and colonizers on a broad scale and in the spirit of their achievement in Spanish America. After 1571 their dominion fanned out from Manila over most of Luzon and the larger islands southward towards Mindinao, and with it they carried their methods of administrative organization, their feudal structure of landownership, and their missionary activities.

Spanish administration in the Philippines was built on a broad territorial basis after the pattern of that of Spanish America. It

was headed by the Governor, virtually an absolute ruler, though
to some extent restricted in his powers by the *audiencia* or supreme
court, and by the practice of holding a *residencia*, or official enquiry
into the Governor's administration on the expiry of his term of
office. Under the Governor was a provincial organization, in
which the *alcaldes mayores* were responsible for both executive and
judicial functions in each province. Under these officials were
elected native *gobernadorcillos*, who were in charge of the *pueblos*
into which the province was subdivided. Economically, the basis
of Spanish rule was the landed estate held in feudal tenure by a
privileged class of *caciques* or chiefs, on whose lands the peasant
villagers laboured and lived as their class had done for centuries,
with the added benefit under Spanish rule of the consolations and
entertainments of a new religion. For the governmental structure
was paralleled by an ecclesiastical one which brought the parish
priest into the villages, and so helped more than anything else to
make the simpler aspects of Western religion and culture a real part
of Filipino life. Besides this, the Church provided a valuable
system of education throughout the provinces, and for higher
education Manila had its College of St. Thomas, founded in 1611,
which became the first university in South-east Asia as early as
1645.

But although Spanish rule transformed the primitive society of
the Philippines to a considerable degree, it did not invigorate it ;
rather it set it in a medieval mould, froze it into a rigid immobility.
Certainly this permitted the gradual assimilation of Spanish cultural influence, so that by the nineteenth century the Filipinos had
become Christianized and Europeanized to an extent that markedly
distinguished them from the other peoples of South-east Asia.
And yet the cultural process that took place under the sheltered
conditions of Spanish rule was one of superimposition rather than
integration. There was little preservation, much less development,
of the native Filipino culture, feeble as it was ; so that Spanish
influence, though widespread, could never coalesce with an
indigenous body of cultural tradition to form an integrated
civilization. At the same time there was little attempt to relate
Spanish rule to the changing conditions of the outside world, or to
bring the Filipino people into touch with world—as distinct from

K

Spanish—influences. Under Spanish rule the Philippines remained as it were in a state of suspended animation.

Commercial crops such as tobacco and hemp were cultivated in the Philippines, but there was no large attempt at exploitation of these resources for the purpose of world trade or even for that of trade restricted to the mother country ; there was little economic development of any kind. Inevitably Manila became an entrepôt port for Far Eastern trade, but this was largely a matter of Chinese enterprise. The Spanish administration itself undertook no schemes of commercial development; on the contrary, trade between the Philippines and Spain was restricted to a single annual voyage of 'the Manila galleon'. Commercial opportunities and incentives—and commercial exploitation—were almost entirely absent. The small Filipino middle class which emerged from the higher levels of the educational system became petty officials, priests or schoolmasters.

The commercial position of Manila was mainly that of a passive intermediary between China and Spanish America. By about the beginning of the seventeenth century the cultivation of tobacco, maize or Indian corn, the sweet potato and the peanut had been introduced into China from America by way of the Philippines. Chinese junks carried porcelain, silk and other goods to Manila for transhipment across the Pacific to Mexico, earning in exchange large quantities of silver Mexican dollars, which became standard currency in the south China ports. The profits of this middle-man's trade and the settled conditions maintained by Spanish rule were not long in attracting Chinese immigrants to Manila. But the presence of a rapidly increasing Chinese community, profitable but prolific, posed a security problem for the small Spanish population. In 1603 a sudden panic, occasioned by rumours of a Chinese plot, resulted in the massacre of a large number of the Chinese inhabitants.

At the beginning of the eighteenth century there were Chinese living in fairly considerable numbers in various parts of South-east Asia, especially where European authority seemed to afford a measure of security. They were to be found, however, not only as traders and artisans in the chief commercial centres, but also as planters and farmers in outlying parts. Alexander Hamilton in the early years of the century estimated that there were 'about a thousand Chinese families' settled in the dominions of Johore, and he observed that half the population of Trengganu, on the north-east coast of the Malay Peninsula, was Chinese, many of them being apparently engaged in pepper planting. Generally, however, the Chinese tended to form a middle class in South-east Asia, interposing themselves between the European merchant and administrator and the native peasant.

It was to Java that most Chinese settlers were attracted. They were almost entirely Hokkiens from the south China province of Fukien. The civil war which followed on the conquest of south China by the Manchus[1], in which the province of Fukien was deeply involved, had provided a strong impetus to Hokkien emigration to South-east Asia in the later years of the seventeenth century. In about the year 1720 there were probably a hundred thousand Chinese in the whole of Java, and of these some eighty thousand were concentrated in and around Batavia. They were an industrious people, ready to turn their hands to any work that promised even a small reward, and as a class they came to wield considerable economic power. Some were employed in coastal trade or in fishing, others were merchants, shopkeepers or artisans, and many were engaged, either as *entrepreneurs* or as labourers, in the sugar industry which followed the extension of Dutch control from Batavia along the north coastal plain. As capitalists they were able to purchase both legal and illegal concessions, to farm the customs, rent markets, and operate as bankers and money-lenders. They extended their activities into territory beyond the direct control of the Dutch, and purchased and rented land from the rulers. Not infrequently they were able to bribe rulers as well as Dutch officials to connive in contraband trade. At the same time, while the economic influence of the Chinese penetrated into other groups around them, they themselves, no less than the Europeans, remained a community separate and distinct. They held to their own social traditions and customs ; and their right to

[1] The rebellion (1673–81) of the San Fan or Three Feudatories, i.e. the leading generals of Fukien and Kwangtung, with Wu San-kuei, the Chinese general who had conquered Yunnan for the Manchus and then established a virtually independent regime there.

do so was acknowledged by the Dutch in the appointment of a Chinese 'captain' with independent jurisdiction in such matters. Although they took their wives from the local population (since Chinese women did not emigrate), this did not bring them any closer as a group to the people of the country, and they were always careful to train their children up as Chinese.

As time went on the flow of Chinese immigrants to Java became so great that many of them failed to find work to do. Unemployed, or casually employed, bands of Chinese began to gather on the outskirts of Batavia and other coastal towns, constituting a menace to order and security; others roamed about the interior as itinerant hawkers or as mere vagabonds. The Dutch government in Batavia became alarmed, and various restrictive measures were taken in an attempt to deal with the situation. Registration was enforced, roving Chinese were threatened with deportation, and petty shopkeeping in the interior was forbidden without licence. These measures, however, were largely ineffective, and the sale of permits became a profitable sideline for the Company's officials. It was a dangerous situation.

Early in October 1740 rumours about harsh treatment of deported Chinese began to spread in Batavia and other towns; it was believed that some deportees had been thrown overboard from Dutch ships. The Chinese in the countryside became aggressive, thus compromising the urban communities, which were vaguely suspected of complicity in a widespread plot to seize the coastal towns; and when some of the town-dwellers fled for comparative safety into the countryside, those who remained became only more suspect. As a security measure the Dutch administration resolved to clear Batavia completely of Chinese. This started a general panic, which the Dutch were unable or un-willing to control. In an outburst of blind fear and hatred the other inhabitants of Batavia turned on the Chinese; after twelve days of terror some ten thousand had been massacred and the Chinese quarter looted and destroyed. This violent explosion in Batavia set almost the whole of Java aflame. Bands of Chinese made their way inland to Kartasura, where, after several months, opinion in the court of Mataram decided in favour of a general war against the Dutch.

Since 1705, when the Dutch hold on the seaports of Mataram had been consolidated, there had been recurrent unrest in central and eastern Java. The basic cause of this unrest lay in the equivocal position which Mataram now held. Politically she continued to be the symbol of Javanese imperial tradition, but economically she had been partly brought within the Dutch system of control. This dual relationship to Java and to the Dutch set up a kind of psychological conflict, a conflict of aims and interests, within the dominions of Mataram. To some princes and regents a peaceful partnership with the Dutch in the commercial exploitation of the country must have seemed a safe and profitable commitment, but to others the royal court of Mataram appeared to be by degrees bartering

JAVA IN THE 18TH CENTURY

away its political leadership for a minor share in a foreign-controlled business. Between these broadly opposed points of view there must have been many different shades of opinion, and attitudes would often be influenced by personal ambitions and rivalries. Mataram in the eighteenth century stood between two worlds, the medieval world of self-contained and slowly changing traditions and beliefs, and the modern world of intensified and shifting social and political conflict that was soon to be born.

The increasing weakness of Mataram's political position since 1705 had already been clearly revealed. A revolt in East Java could only be stamped out with the help of Dutch forces and after the banishment of several of the leaders in 1723. Ten years later Mataram accepted a new treaty with the Dutch Company. Not

only were her contributions of pepper, indigo and rice to be
increased and her coffee cultivation subjected to additional controls,
but she was also now required to pay the expenses of the Dutch
fortress and garrison at Kartasura and to supply provisions to the
garrisons at Semarang and Japara. The grip of the Dutch Company was steadily tightening, so that in 1740, when the Chinese in
Java had become antagonized by Dutch policy and enraged by the
massacre of Batavia, it seemed to many of those whose opinions
were heard at the court of Mataram that a favourable opportunity
had arisen in which to shake off Dutch control.

The issue was forced in July 1741 by the seizure of the fortress
at Kartasura and the murder of the Dutch officers of the garrison
by a combined force of Chinese and Javanese. This brought the
majority of the subordinate rulers over to the war party, and a
general attack on Dutch power began. But there were still divided
opinions on the war policy in the Mataram court, and when the
Susuhunan appeared to be considering peace terms with the
Company, the Chinese and their Javanese supporters marched on
Kartasura, sacked the town, and installed a new ruler. The latter's
position, however, soon became impossible ; it had no real basis
other than the *ad hoc* support of confederates who were far from
being united among themselves. Meanwhile the Dutch garrison at
Semarang had held out successfully against a siege, and by 1743
the Company was in a position to reinstate the displaced Susuhunan. The signing of a new treaty was the inevitable accom-
paniment of this event. The Company was now confirmed in its
possession of the port of Semarang, and it obtained besides the
districts of Japara, Rembang and Surabaya, the island of Madura,
and the whole of the eastern end of Java from Pasuruan and Malang
to the Bali Strait, as well as a narrow ribbon of territory along the
entire coast of the dominions of Mataram. Mataram had thus not
only lost possession of its seaports ; it was completely cut off from
independent contact with the outside world, and both politically
and economically it had become a dependency of the Dutch
Company. In future the Company would have to be consulted
before the appointment of Mataram's prime minister or Pateh, as
well as on the succession of the chief regents. No communication
between regents was to be permitted except through officials of the

Company. Before long the regents were deprived of most of their judicial powers ; all law cases other than those of minor importance were to be heard by the court of justice (*raad van justitie*) at Semarang or Surabaya.

For the inhabitants of the coastal districts which now came under the Company's rule the change of government brought no relief from traditional burdens. The Company simply took over the claims which Mataram had exercised before, and then farmed many of these out to Chinese ; so that demands on the peasant for rent in the form of rice or labour, for free or cheap deliveries of crops, for toll payments on road and river traffic, and various other impositions, were enforced with new thoroughness and harshness. For the princes and aristocracy of the reduced dominions of Mataram, now centred in a new capital at Surakarta, personal rivalries and the struggle for power remained as absorbing as ever, and had been only intensified by Dutch intervention. They were at war among themselves from 1746 onward, and Dutch forces were involved. In 1749 the dying Susuhunan decided to bequeath his dominions to the Dutch, less out of regard for the Company than out of sheer distaste for his successor. The latter, however, naturally objected to the arrangement, and a three-cornered contest began between the Company and two rival claimants to the throne. Finally, war ended in 1755 with the partition of Mataram into two separate states under a Susuhunan at Surakarta and a Sultan at Jokjakarta.

West Java, although not involved in the Mataram wars, did not remain entirely peaceful during this period. For most of the time Bantam, with its dependent district of Lampong at the southern end of Sumatra, contributed regular supplies of pepper, sugar, indigo and cotton, and for that reason its relations with the Company were smooth. But, as in the previous century, differences between members of the ruling family invited further Dutch intervention, and this in turn caused disturbances which led to Bantam's final subjection. When the prospective heir to the throne was removed from the country by the Sultan, the Dutch had to be rewarded for their acceptance of this measure by a half-share in the gold mines of Lampong and a strip of territory along Bantam's western border. Then in 1748 it was the turn of the Sultan himself to be removed, for he had become mentally deranged ; the Company thereupon formally annexed the whole of Bantam, leaving its administration in the hands of the Sultana. The latter, however, ruled in such an arbitrary manner that by 1750 the whole country was in rebellion against her and her Dutch protectors, and Batavia itself was closely besieged until reinforcements arrived from Holland. But gradually the rebellion was stamped out, and in 1752, on the installation of a new Sultan, the Dutch Company assumed complete sovereignty over Bantam.

East Java, which had been ceded to the Company by Mataram in 1755, now remained the only important coastal area still to be brought under Dutch control. It had really formed no more than a nominal part of the Mataram dominions ; Buginese, Macassars and Balinese had been able to control various parts of the coast in turn, and now English ships were slipping through the Bali Strait and disposing of considerable quantities of opium through Chinese settlers. It required five years of hard fighting (1767–72) to establish Dutch control.

Although the ultimate purpose of all this extension of Dutch control in Java was primarily commercial, and although it brought with it a considerable extension of the field of the Company's commercial operations, yet in the middle of the eighteenth century Dutch trade was still closely concerned with the Spice Islands. Referring to Amboyna, Captain Cope wrote in 1754 : 'Here . . . the Dutch have a garrison of 700 or 800 men to defend the approaches to this island, which is esteemed the most profitable government the Hollanders have in India, next to that of Batavia.'

As a city, Batavia in the eighteenth century was, by all accounts, impressive but unhealthy. John Byron was there in 1765, and he described it as 'a city populous, cosmopolitan and polyglot, teeming with fruit and vermin'. Dutch descriptions were more enthusiastic. Writing home in 1778, a young Hollander roundly declared: 'Batavia is the best-built city in the world.' He proceeded to fill in the picture : 'The wide streets and the quays are planted with canary trees which are all beautifully in line.' And he was impressed by the citadel, which was 'a masterpiece'. 'Nothing is more charming and pleasant than the surrounding country.' But it was a fatal charm. 'Batavia is unhealthy,' he continued, 'in a way not to be imagined. . . . One is rarely without fever here . . . It is incredible how many people die. . . . Batavia is a regular cemetery of Europeans.' And even the native inhabitants, this writer declared, were unhealthy in Batavia. 'In the other stations of Java and of that so-called Great and Little East, people are well and healthy ; here the natives are no more able than we are to resist the climate.' But for those Hollanders who survived it was a good life. If one were lucky one might attain to one of the 'few good situations existing in which one makes an immense fortune in a few years. . . . Luxury simply cries aloud here. The houses are furnished regardless of cost'. We have, of course, no contemporary record of the living conditions of the native inhabitants.

Malacca in the eighteenth century was overshadowed in importance by Batavia, but it was regarded as a much pleasanter station for a servant of the Dutch Company. It possessed the air of distinction and the *panache* that Batavia lacked. 'The Governor here is a much greater being than the Governor-General of Batavia,' wrote the same young Hollander from Malacca in 1786; 'the Councillors . . . roll about in gilt coaches, wear velvet coats, etc.'

The English Company retained a foothold in South-east Asia during all this time at Bencoolen, the pepper port on the south-west coast of Sumatra. A fort, Fort Marlborough, was built there in 1714, which served also to protect a few subsidiary factories on the Sumatran coast, such as Periaman. Good supplies of pepper came down river to Bencoolen, and about 6,000 tons were shipped annually. The Company owned and exploited pepper farms here in the Dutch manner, using Indian convict labour. But Bencoolen had a poor harbour, with a dangerous bar and with no protection from the south-west monsoon ; it lay too far off the main track of shipping ever to become an entrepôt port of any size. For the Company's servants its main attraction lay in the fact that they were permitted to trade on their own account in any commodity but pepper, and Bencoolen's proximity to Dutch trading centres offered wide opportunities for such legitimate private trade as well as for smuggling of contraband goods such as opium.

For both Dutch and English Companies the Sumatra trade was essentially subsidiary—in the one case to that of Java, in the other to that of India ; but Dutch interests in Sumatra were fairly considerable, and were naturally more closely related to their Java trade than was the Bencoolen factory to the English trade in India. Northward along the coast from Bencoolen the Dutch had a strongly fortified factory in Padang, which was a collecting centre for pepper and gold. But the more important Dutch stations were situated on the east coast of Sumatra, facing the Malacca Straits. At Bengkalis, Siak and Jambi—all of which had shaken off Johore's control in the later part of the seventeenth century—the Dutch possessed factories which bought pepper and gold in exchange for cloth and opium. At Palembang they had been granted a major share in the pepper trade to the exclusion of all other merchants except Chinese. But it was easier to gain monopoly concessions than to enforce them. There was much evasion of agreements and contracts wherever the Company had no direct rule, and where traders of other nationalities were often welcomed—as English traders were—because they offered better trading terms than the Dutch. On several occasions in the eighteenth century from 1722 onward the Dutch obtained assurances for the monopoly of the tin production of Banka Island, which was subject to Palembang, but they were never able to make the monopoly complete, for the Chinese miners would sell the tin to any visiting ships, English and others, that offered a fair price ; and such infringements of Dutch monopoly rights steadily increased as the eighteenth century wore on.

The English Company made several attempts during the eighteenth century to establish permanent settlements in South-east Asia besides that at Bencoolen. A fortified factory was opened at Banjermassin, on the south coast of Borneo, by 1701, and a fair business was done in pepper there despite the fact that, as Hamilton reports, the head of the factory was more of a naturalist than a merchant, and 'would spend whole days in contemplating on the nature, shape and qualities of a butterfly or a shellfish'—an early example of the pleasant English habit of amateurism so frequently met with in the East. But the English at Banjermassin soon made themselves unpopular with the local ruler by their interference with native craft, and in 1707 they were driven out. Occasional trading visits continued until 1756, when the Dutch obtained a monopoly of pepper exports.

Another English attempt to establish a settlement in Borneo came in 1762 as one of the minor consequences of the Seven Years War. A French force had already expelled the English from Bencoolen and other subsidiary factories in Sumatra in 1760. When Spain declared war early in 1762 an English expedition was sent from Bengal against the Philippines, and it captured Manila in October. These gains were restored by both sides under the terms of the Treaty of Paris in 1763, but the English Company had made a separate acquisition which was unaffected by the treaty. This was the island of Balambangan, situated off the northern tip of Borneo, which was ceded to the Company by its overlord, the Sultan of Sulu, in gratitude for his release from captivity in Manila. The actual grant included the northern parts of Borneo which had been taken from the Sultan of Brunei, and the English also occupied the island of Labuan, though only for a short period. The settlement at Balambangan itself did not last long ; a fort was built there about 1771, but four years later it was attacked and destroyed by the local inhabitants, and the Company's servants withdrew. However, the expedition to Manila and the brief experience of trading in the direction of Borneo served to heighten the interest of Bengal political and mercantile circles in South-east Asian trade. It was in 1771, when the advantages of an eastward station on the China trade-route were being considered more seriously than ever before by the English Company, that Francis Light first drew the attention of his firm in Madras to the possibility of a settlement on the Malay Peninsula.

Apart from such attempts on the Company's part to open up regular trade, an increasing number of privately organized voyages to South-east Asia were being undertaken in 'country' ships owned or chartered by English merchants in India, as well as by Indians and Armenians. Both private and Company trade with south China increased steadily during the eighteenth century, but the private merchants sometimes went no further than South-east Asian ports if they could manage to dispose of their cloth and opium there in exchange for spices or pepper. One such was

Alexander Hamilton, who wrote an excellent account of several voyages which he made between India, South-east Asia and China during the years 1693 to 1718. In 1703 he called at Johore, and the Sultan took such a liking to him that he offered him the island of Singapore as a present. Hamilton turned the offer down—over a hundred years before Raffles founded modern Singapore—remarking that 'it could be of no use to a private person, tho' a proper place for a Company to settle a colony on'. From the Dutch point of view merchants like Hamilton were interlopers and smugglers ; but although for this reason they were coldly received and carefully watched, English traders sometimes called at Malacca and Batavia as well as at ports less closely controlled by the Dutch. Occasionally they managed to penetrate the forbidden area of the Moluccas, especially as Dutch control slackened off in the later part of the eighteenth century. In 1774 Captain Forrest made a successful voyage from Balambangan through the Moluccas and across to Bencoolen, obtaining spice plants for cultivation in the English Company's territory. But the best known English private trader to South-east Asia in the eighteenth century is Francis Light, founder of Penang.

In Burma and Siam during the eighteenth century European traders were very much at the mercy of the frequent waves of war and violence that swept over those countries. Conditions in Lower Burma were especially dangerous and unstable. The Mons of Lower Burma remained unreconciled to their subjection to Ava, the home of the Toungu dynasty in Upper Burma ; while at the same time Ava became less and less capable of exerting real authority beyond the limits of its own immediate territory. Ava's weakness could no longer be concealed after 1738, when invading forces from the state of Manipur, to the west of the Chindwin river, succeeded in fighting their way to within striking distance of the capital itself. This was the moment for the Mons to shake off Ava's rule. In 1740 they declared their independence and installed a king of their own at Pegu. Then, driving northward against Ava, they took Prome and Toungu. A Burman counter-attack in 1743 resulted in the temporary capture of the port of Syriam from the Mons, but the town was quickly recovered, and Mon raids continued further and further into Upper Burma until finally, in 1752, Ava itself was taken. This was the end of the Burman Toungu dynasty.

Almost immediately, however, a resistance movement began in Upper Burma under the leadership of one Alaungpaya, who was to be the founder of the last dynasty of Burma. At the end of 1753, when he seemed ready to attack Ava, the Mons suddenly evacuated the city and fled southward. Then the Mon garrison was driven out of Prome, and Alaungpaya defeated an attempt to retake that town in 1755. Pushing on southward, the Burman forces reached the town of Dagon, which was now renamed Rangoon. Syriam was taken and destroyed in 1756; Pegu fell in 1757. Once again the whole of Upper and Lower Burma had been brought under a single rule, and this time it was to remain so. The history of the Mons as a separate people had ended. But the unification of Burma was not to bring an end to war and disturbances. Alaungpaya, Burma's new king, had not ceased to be a warrior. Having first invaded Manipur, occupied Imphal and deported thousands of the inhabitants, he then turned to attack Siam.

Relations between Burma and Siam had been generally peaceful for almost a hundred years. But the town of Chiengmai, which had already changed hands several times, was always a potential cause of strife between the two countries. At the beginning of the eighteenth century Chiengmai had been in Burman hands for some time, but a rebellion broke out in 1717 and an army sent to reassert Burman authority was defeated in 1728. Ava at the time had to accept the situation, but now it again possessed a powerful and aggressive force under Alaungpaya, who had additional reason for invading Siam when the Mon armies which he had driven out of Pegu fled eastward into Siamese territory. The invasion, which began towards the end of 1759, was an example of the strategy of indirect approach. The Burman army first marched southward to Tavoy and Tenasserim, then across country to the Gulf of Siam, and northward to Ayuthia. During the siege of Ayuthia, however, King Alaungpaya received injuries from a burst cannon, and his army withdrew. The king died in the same year, 1760, but the war against Siam was not abandoned. In 1763 Chiengmai was retaken, and then in 1765 a three-pronged attack was planned against Ayuthia, one Burman army closing in from Chiengmai in the north, another crossing the border and advancing from the west, and a third driving northward from Tenasserim. Caught between these armies, the Siamese were defeated; and in 1767 Ayuthia was captured, plundered and almost completely destroyed.

But now Burma herself was being threatened by invasion from another direction. The Chinese province of Yunnan had been recently brought under the Manchu imperial administration, and when troubles occurred on the Burma-Yunnan frontier these were attributed by the Chinese to Burman aggression. China under the Manchu emperor Chi'en Lung (1736–96) was in an imperialist mood. She had extended her control across central Asia into Tibet and had compelled the Gurkhas of Nepal to acknowledge her suzerainty. Now she determined to bring Burma, her immediate neighbour, under control; and an army was sent across the border from Yunnan in 1766. But Chinese generalship was no match for that of the Burmans. The Chinese were driven back several times; and although they advanced again and were at one stage only thirty miles from Ava, they were completely outmanœuvred all along. China had to ask for peace terms, which were agreed in 1770. For Burma the defeat of the Chinese invasion had been a great military achievement.

In Siam, meanwhile, the effects of these events were seen in the relaxation of Burman control and the growth of a resistance movement originating among Siamese refugees in Cambodia. By the end of 1768 Ayuthia had been recaptured. The critical decision was then taken to build a new capital near the sea, at Bangkok—a decision to which Siam would largely owe her ability to adapt herself to the increasing pressure of the Western world, and so to retain her independence, during the years to come. By 1770, when Burma had dealt successfully with the Chinese invasion, the Siamese were in a position to repel every attempt to re-establish Burman domination, and in 1775 they retook Chiengmai. Ten years later Burma failed in a final attempt to conquer Siam.

These extremely unstable political conditions in the Indo-Chinese peninsula were most unfavourable to foreign trade. After the collapse of French influence in Siam in the previous century the Dutch alone continued to maintain a factory at Ayuthia. In Burma's port of Syriam both French and English Companies after 1720 were represented by a semi-official Resident who was responsible for the supervision of shipbuilding and repairs. But although Burma supplied excellent teak wood, the ships built under the poorly organized conditions at Syriam were not always satisfactory. However, such work as the Companies were carrying on at the port was brought to a sudden and violent end in 1743 during the Mon revolt. Syriam was first taken by the Burmans and most of the commercial establishments were destroyed, the English factory alone escaping. Then the town was recaptured by the Mons, and this time the English factory was less fortunate. The Mons, after declaring their independence in 1740, had offered the post of Shahbandar or Port Officer to the English Resident, who, however, declined the offer on the instructions of Madras. This was now regarded by the Mons as a sign of lack of sympathy with their cause, and the factory was burnt to the ground. The Resident and his staff were permitted to withdraw to Madras.

Having failed to find sympathy in the English, the Mons found it in the French. The French East India Company was reconstituted in 1720, and during the next twenty years it steadily developed its trading interests in India. Having occupied Mauritius in 1721, it founded establishments at Mahé on the Malabar coast of India in 1725 and at Karikal on the Coromandel coast in 1739. Both Pondicherry, the Indian headquarters of the French, and Madras, the main English factory, were situated on the Coromandel coast facing out on the Bay of Bengal, which was therefore to be the main theatre of the coming Anglo-French naval contest. At Syriam the French had a shipbuilding yard alongside the English from 1729 onward, but it was destroyed by the Burmans in 1743 and had to be abandoned.

After 1741 French policy was directed by Dupleix, Governor of Pondicherry, who gave a new turn to European activities in India by first adding the aim of political power to that of commercial profit. That the increase of French power in India would be obtained at the expense of the English Company became apparent on the outbreak of the War of the Austrian Succession, in which

French and English took opposite sides in Europe. The Indian sideshow of the main war was fought from 1744 to 1748. The French capture of Madras in 1746, after La Bourdonnais had driven off an English naval squadron, underlined the decisive importance of sea-power in the Bay of Bengal. The war also drew attention to the strategic advantages which would be secured from a base to the east of the Bay. Because the French and English headquarters on the Coromandel coast were exposed to the full force of the north-east monsoon between October and March, the naval forces of both sides had to retire westward during those months—the French to Mauritius and the English to Bombay. A base on the east side of the Bay of Bengal—in Burma, the Malay Peninsula or Sumatra—would afford shelter from the north-east monsoon, and at the same time would enable naval forces to move out quickly into the Bay and take up defence positions as soon as the monsoon changed.

Accordingly, when the Mons appealed to the French for aid in their struggle against the Burmans, Dupleix readily agreed to send an agent to Pegu in order to further French influence there. Soon after his arrival in 1751 the agent, Sieur de Bruno, reported back to Pondicherry that the Irrawaddy delta could easily be conquered by a small force of French troops. Meanwhile information of French plans for intervention in Burma had reached the English Company at Madras, and when it became known that de Bruno had established an influential position at Pegu it was decided to counter the French move by sending an expedition to occupy the island of Negrais, inside the mouth of the Bassein river—a revival of an earlier plan of 1686. An attempt to negotiate with the Mon government for the cession of the island was defeated by de Bruno's influence, and the occupation was carried out by force in 1753.

But less than a year later the situation for both French and English was completely changed when the Burmans under Alaungpaya drove the Mons out of Upper Burma and then began their southward drive against Pegu. The French were committed to the Mon cause, and de Bruno lent his assistance in organizing the defence of Syriam. The English opened negotiations with the other side and seriously considered lending military assistance to Alaungpaya. But events were now moving so quickly that only immediate withdrawal from Burma could save the Companies' servants from disaster. When Syriam was captured by the Burmans in 1756 de Bruno was taken and put to death along with the officers of two French ships that had just arrived. The English hung on at Negrais in the hope that Alaungpaya would consent to their possession of the island. Though not unwilling to do so, he insisted on direct personal negotiation with the King of England, and by the time his letter—written on a sheet of gold studded with precious stones—reached George II in 1758, the Company had decided that Negrais was, after all, not worth its cost, and no reply was ever sent. In 1759 the Burmans captured the English settlement on Negrais and killed all the inhabitants.

The English Company kept clear of Burma for another twenty years. The French, although forced to surrender their military power and political ambitions in India at the end of the Seven Years War in 1763, were still commercial competitors as well as likely enemies in the event of another war. They began again to use Rangoon as a shipbuilding base in 1768, and English suspicions of French intentions in Burma were kept alive until the end of the century. But the position of foreigners in the Burman ports was as insecure as ever. When Mon troops mutinied against the Burmans in 1773 and took Rangoon, the shipyards were destroyed; and when the town was recaptured by the Burmans shortly afterwards, the French residents were put to death.

On the eastern side of the Indo-Chinese peninsula European action from Portuguese times onwards had always been slight and sporadic. The only real attempt to carry on sustained effort there was that of the French missionaries, who had begun their work among the Vietnamese soon after 1620. The southward expansion of the Vietnamese people had continued from about the tenth century. By the end of the seventeenth century Champa had been fully absorbed; politically the Vietnam area of the Indo-Chinese peninsula had become separated into the modern divisions of Tonkin and Annam; and the movement of Vietnamese colonization was continuing southward. Both central and southern Vietnam attracted Chinese immigration from about the same time. French missionaries naturally sought the patronage

L

of political authority, showing themselves no less disposed than the European merchants in South-east Asia to turn local rivalries to their own advantage, and to identify their own advantage with that of their home country. Rivalry between the ruling families of Annam and Tonkin flared up in 1786 into a war for the imperial throne of the combined countries of Vietnam. The Nguyen family of Annam, which was to emerge victorious in 1802, received material support from a French bishop, Pigneau de Béhaine. In return for procuring the assistance of a military expedition from Pondicherry, the bishop obtained for France the port of Tourane and the island of Condore in 1787. But this arrangement was one of the many that were swept aside by the French Revolution of 1789.

Chapter Twelve

THE SHAPING OF A NEW BALANCE OF POWER

THE last quarter of the eighteenth century saw important changes in the balance of commercial and political forces bearing on the South-east Asian region, changes which prepared the way for the new conditions of the nineteenth century. The English Company, still a commercial concern in name but as far as India was concerned a political power in fact, returned in strength to take up new positions on the Straits of Malacca. The Company had attained a new status both in India and in Britain itself. In India it had acquired territorial responsibilities (after 1765 it was the tax- and rent-collector of Bengal), which called for the transformation of a commercial machine into a government service. In Britain the Company was more and more regarded as an instrument of state, requiring a large standing army, the control of a Governor-General and Council (from 1773), the establishment in Calcutta of an independent Supreme Court, and the creation of a Board of Control responsible ultimately to Parliament (1784). As a commercial concern its main interest by the end of the century was in the trade through the Straits of Malacca to China. Indeed it was the China trade that saved the Company from being bankrupted by the expenses of its inefficient and corrupt administration in India. Vast quantities of tea were shipped from Canton, and the Company had a major interest in the export of opium from India to China—for although it did not ship opium itself, it licensed the country vessels which did so, and it possessed a monopoly of all opium grown in Bengal.

The Dutch Company was less fortunate. Even the huge supplies of coffee which it controlled and exported from Java were not enough to save it from bankruptcy. The Dutch Company had been an instrument of state from the beginning, but it remained primarily a commercial instrument which could never successfully

adapt itself to its developing quasi-political functions. It had all
the defects of the British system in India—corruption, bribery, the
sale of offices—without its compensating features or its growing
assets, such as the immense land revenues derived from direct rule
over newly acquired provinces, or the measures of reform which
were gradually introduced into the Indian administration from
1774 onwards. Moreover, in the wider sphere of world competition,
Holland by the middle of the eighteenth century had lost her
position of international leadership in commerce and finance. For
all these reasons, Dutch Company organization was unable to
survive the wars of the last quarter of the century.

The foundation of British power in South-east Asia in modern
times was laid by a private trader, Francis Light. The lever which
he used to gain admission for British influence was found in the
political rivalries of the Malay Peninsula, which had been greatly
intensified in the eighteenth century by the intrusion of Bugis
interests. The Bugis of the Celebes, expert seamen and hardy
fighters, had descended on the coasts of Java, Sumatra and the
Malay Peninsula during the later years of the seventeenth century,
and neither the Dutch nor the local rulers were able to prevent
them from settling on chosen sites near the river-mouths or from
preying on commerce in the narrow waters of the Straits area.
After 1722 they had the weak sultanate of Johore in their power,
and they made their headquarters at Riau, the capital of the Johore
dominions. From there they extended their control northwards
over much of the Malay Peninsula, cutting Dutch Malacca off from
the tin supplies of Selangor, Perak and Kedah, and trading in the
tin with English and other foreign interlopers. The Dutch, therefore, responded readily to the invitation of the Malay Sultan of
Johore in 1745 to assist him in throwing off Bugis control in
return for the cession of Johore's nominal dependency of Siak—
if the Dutch could capture it from its Menangkabau ruler, which in
fact they did in 1755. Siak was lost again soon afterwards, but not
before the Dutch Company had obtained a new agreement from
Johore for the monopoly of her tin and the exclusion of all other
European traders. But these and similar concessions of the time
could mean little as long as the conflict of interests in the whole

area continued to enable the Malay ruler of Johore to play the Dutch off against the Bugis. The issue was clarified, though only for a time, by the re-establishment of Bugis control over Johore in 1760. From then until 1782 the Dutch had to make the best of the situation; they maintained fairly friendly relations with the Bugis, but partly at least for the reason that they could do nothing to prevent them from selling their tin to visiting English traders.

About the year 1770 the Bugis of Selangor were pressing the Sultan of Kedah for payment of tribute in silver. Dissatisfied with his response, they invaded Kedah and plundered its capital. About the same time Francis Light crossed over from Achin to examine trading prospects in Kedah and visited the Sultan, who had moved northward to the adjoining state of Perlis. An appeal for assistance in expelling the Bugis, written by the Sultan in March 1771, reached the East India Company at Madras. No serious attention was paid to the letter at the time, but when the Madras Council received instructions from London to open negotiations for a permanent settlement at Achin, it was decided to make preliminary enquiries concerning trade prospects not only in Achin but also in Kedah and the Straits area generally. Early in 1772 the Council wrote for information to the Madras firm which employed Francis Light. In reply the firm was able to refer to Light's information from Kedah, for by this time he had written to his employers that not only were there extremely good prospects for trade in cloth and opium at Kedah, but there was an excellent opportunity of establishing a settlement there if only they would 'act with spirit and authority', for the Sultan 'knows the English are capable of assisting him not only against Selangor but against Siam'. 'I beg of you not to let this noble opportunity slip of getting footing upon this coast,' he wrote. The Sultan was prepared to offer the port of Kedah itself and also the coastal strip southward as far as Penang Island.

Impressed by these considerations, the Madras Council wrote to London that it seemed likely that Kedah would be a more suitable site for a settlement than Achin, especially in view of its value for the China trade. Nevertheless, missions were sent to both Achin and Kedah in 1772. Both were unsuccessful. The leader of the

Kedah mission, Edward Monckton, was instructed 'to defend and protest against the Selangorians', but when the Sultan eagerly enquired when he 'would set out for Selangor', Monckton could only reply 'in general terms'. Evasion was the key-note of the Company's dealings with Kedah from the start. No arrangement could be accepted which would commit the Company to the complications and expenses of local warfare ; it could not agree to an offensive alliance, which, however, was precisely what the Sultan wanted. The Company would only undertake the duty of protection, which meant in effect that it would merely agree to protect its own settlement, and it hoped that territory for a settlement would be obtained in exchange for vague assurances. But the Sultan of Kedah had no intention of parting with territory except as a reward for positive military aid against his enemies. When it became clear that no such aid would be forthcoming, the Sultan recalled the fact that Siam had forbidden him to allow European settlement in his country, and the mission was dismissed. Visits to Trengganu and Riau met with no greater success.

Light continued to trade in the Malayan region and to nurse his scheme for a settlement. After a visit to Junk Ceylon or Ujong Salang in 1779 he suggested an establishment there on account of its good harbour and its tin trade. The final proposal in 1781 seems to have been that a settlement should be made as a private commercial venture but with the approval of the Company. However, this plan also came to nothing, mainly for the reason that war had now spread to Asia.

Britain had been at war with her American colonies since 1776. France came in on the American side in 1778, Spain in 1779. Dutch traders had been heavily engaged in smuggling tea and other goods into the colonies before the outbreak of war, and when war began strong pressure was brought to bear on the Dutch government to recognize American independence and enter into commercial relations with the new states. A draft of a commercial treaty with the Americans came into British hands, and war was therefore declared against Holland in December 1780. The naval defeat of the Dutch at the Battle of Dogger Bank in August 1781 left their merchant ships almost unprotected on the high seas, and during the next three years many Dutch vessels were captured on the way from the East Indies to Europe. In Asia the Dutch Company's possessions themselves might have been lost but for the presence of a French fleet in Indian waters. As it was, the Dutch stations at Negapatam on the Coromandel coast and at Trincomalee in Ceylon were captured by the British in 1780–1, and in South-east Asia a military expedition from Bencoolen seized the Dutch factory at Padang in Sumatra in 1781. No ships or troops could be sent from Holland to the Straits of Malacca until 1784. The opportunity was not lost by the Bugis at Riau to harry all shipping entering or leaving Malacca, which the Dutch could do little to prevent. A task-force sent from Batavia against Riau in 1783 was so inadequate that it was forced to withdraw, and the Bugis replied by bearing down on Malacca itself from both Johore and Selangor, so that the fortress was virtually besieged until the arrival of a fleet from Holland in 1784.

Holland remained at war with Britain for nine months after France and the United States had concluded peace, but when the Anglo-Dutch peace terms were signed in June 1784 the Dutch possessions, excluding Negapatam, were restored. But the war had shattered Dutch commerce and ruined the Dutch East India Company. Moreover, although Britain had restored the captured Dutch stations, she had secured the formal acknowledgment of her freedom to trade throughout island South-east Asia even as far as the Moluccas, hitherto the most closely guarded of the Dutch Company's commercial assets. The Dutch monopoly of trade in South-east Asian waters had at last been definitely broken.

The year 1784 therefore marks the rise of Britain as a South-east Asian and a Far Eastern power. The war had cost her the American colonies, but it had gained for her—after Rodney's defeat of the French fleet in the Battle of the Saints in 1782—an assured supremacy on the seas. It had ushered in a period of rapid development of overseas trade; between 1782 and 1790 the value of British exports and imports rose from less than £20 million to nearly £40 million. The balance of Britain's overseas interests and power was now shifting from North America to Asia, at a time when her expanding industries were demanding an increasing supply of tropical and semi-tropical raw materials. From an agricultural country, self-supporting in food, Britain was gradually being transformed into an industrialized country, seeking to exchange her mass-produced cloth and heavy machinery for food supplies and the raw materials of her industry. What her economic organization seemed to require now was not so much overseas colonies of her own people as free and open overseas markets everywhere. Asia offered a vast potential market for a country possessing, as Britain did, world leadership in the production of cheap manufactured goods. With her Manchester cottons, as well as with her Indian opium, Britain would be in a position to build up predominant control of the markets of India, South-east Asia and the Far East.

The China trade was already well developed, but after 1784 it expanded with extraordinary rapidity. It was greatly stimulated by the Commutation Act, passed by the British Parliament in 1784, which cut down the duties on tea from over 100 per cent to 12½ per cent. British trade with China was more than doubled in the next few years, and the exports of opium from India to China increased enormously. It was a good moment for Francis Light to reopen the project for a station on the China run.

The Dutch, released from their war-time isolation in Batavia and considerably reinforced by the arrival of a fleet from Holland in March 1784, were busy settling accounts with the Bugis. They first drove them off from Malacca, then invaded Selangor and expelled its Bugis Sultan. The Dutch fleet then proceeded to Riau and drove the Bugis out of there. In November 1784 the Malay Sultan and his ministers, having surrendered sovereignty over the whole of the dominions of Riau, Johore and Pahang, formally acknowledged themselves and their descendants to be vassals of Holland. The Sultan was left with administrative powers, but a Dutch Resident and garrison were stationed at Tanjong Pinang, capital of Riau. The traditional principles of the Dutch commercial system were reasserted without essential modification. The Company was to have full trading privileges throughout the Johore dominions and the exclusive right of purchasing tin for export. Restrictions were placed upon Chinese and other Asian traders at Riau so as to protect the Company's monopoly of the spice trade and its claim to the tin supplies of Banka Island. Johore vessels passing through the Straits must respect Malacca's traditional supremacy by putting in at that port for inspection and for permission to proceed.

In 1785, then, there were strong arguments in favour of Light's proposal for a settlement in Kedah. Such a settlement would provide both a useful port of call and supply on the China run, and a valuable *point d'appui* for British influence as a counterbalance to the renewal of Dutch control in the Straits. Light had kept up his trading contacts with Kedah and he was in favour with its new Sultan. But there had been no change in Kedah's standpoint with regard to the terms which it would accept as a basis for an agreement with the East India Company. As Light pointed out, the principal reason why the Sultan wanted an alliance was to obtain protection against his enemies. This was made perfectly clear in the draft of an agreement drawn up in August 1785 between Light and the Sultan, in which it was proposed that Penang Island should be ceded on condition that any hostile power attacking Kedah by land or sea should be automatically regarded as an enemy of the Company. Light delivered this draft to the Company at Calcutta in February 1786. The Governor-General had no doubt in his mind that the Sultan's main aim was British protection, but he noted in a minute that 'this protection . . . cannot be effectually given without involving us in disputes with the Burmans or Siamese'.

It was decided, however, to accept Penang and avoid the consequences. Delaying tactics in the negotiations, combined with an early show of force at Penang, should secure the island while postponing any formal agreement. The Company would agree 'always to keep an armed vessel stationed to guard the island of Penang and the coast adjacent belonging to the King of Quedah', but the Sultan's request for protection against attacks from the interior would have to be referred to London. Armed with a reply to this effect, and supported by a force of one hundred and fifty men, Light returned to Kedah. The Company's reply, even though backed by Light's personal assurances, fell far short of the formal undertaking which Kedah expected, but since the Company seemed fully prepared to go ahead with the occupation of Penang, the ruler and his ministers were ready to believe that reference to London was no more than a matter of form and that a treaty embodying their own proposals would soon be offered. Light, in any case, had now at last at his disposal the small force for which he had appealed in 1771, and he was not going to waste it. He took formal possession of Penang Island on 11 August 1786.

When weeks passed and no treaty of alliance was forthcoming, Kedah began to press Light for an indication of the Company's intention to offer something in consideration for the occupation of Penang. Light was driven to take refuge in evasions and delays. He informed the Governor-General in October 1786 that he had promised the Sultan that 'while the English are here they will assist him' but the reply from Calcutta in January 1787 made it clear that the Company would sign no formal undertaking of the kind. Again in the following May Light urged that 'there is a necessity for coming to some terms with the King of Quedah while the fears of the Siamese and Burmans are upon him', and added that he had every reason to believe that 'nothing will be acceptable without Government promising the King protection'. But it was no use; Light was informed (January 1788) that 'the Governor-General in Council has already decided against any measures that may involve the Company in military operations against any of the eastern princes'. This sounded very righteous, but it ignored the unpleasant fact that the acceptance of Penang had implied a willingness to enter into an alliance of some sort with Kedah. In their good time the Directors of the Company in London confirmed the policy of non-intervention; they resolved, in February 1793, that 'no offensive and defensive alliance should be made with the Raja of Kedah'.

Kedah had already abandoned hope of any such alliance. By the year 1790 nothing had been obtained in exchange for Penang beyond the offer of an annuity to the Sultan. Should Kedah now cancel the whole arrangement and take Penang back by force? The Bugis Sultan of Selangor had driven the Dutch out of his country in 1785, and the Malay Sultan of Johore had done the same in 1787, although in neither case was this a lasting achievement. At any rate in 1790, when an alliance was formed between the Bugis and the Malays of Johore, Siak and Indragiri to attack the Dutch north of Malacca, it was agreed that the allied forces should then assist Kedah to drive the English out of Penang. But

the fleet that sailed from Siak for these operations was intercepted
by Dutch naval forces and dispersed, and Kedah was left to fight
its own private war with the English. In April 1791 Kedah's forces
gathered for the attack at the Prai river, opposite Penang Island.
The Penang garrison, however, was not obliging enough to await
the attack, but crossed to the mainland and scattered the Malay
forces without much trouble. The time had now come to set a
legal stamp on the acquisition of Penang. By treaty of 1 May the
cession of the island was confirmed. The Sultan obtained an
annuity but, needless to say, no alliance.

The future of Penang (or Prince of Wales Island, as Light had
named it) was not yet, however, by any means certain. It rapidly
attracted settlers, so that by 1795 it had a population of some
twenty thousand, of whom about three thousand were Chinese.
But while the Company was fully aware of Penang's potential
value as a commercial possession, it was not entirely convinced of
its soundness as an investment from the strategic point of view.
Relations with Kedah so far had clearly shown that the danger of
becoming involved in local wars, with the possibility of ultimate
conflict with 'the Burmans or Siamese' in the background, was
likely to be lasting even if avoidable. The authorities would have
preferred a station which held Penang's commercial and positional
value without its political dangers. As a result of this uncertain
attitude Penang was very much neglected during the first twenty
years of its existence as a Company settlement. There was no
proper governmental establishment or provision for the administration of justice. Until his death in 1794 Light was left in sole
charge of the administration as Superintendent, and there was no
regular system of law-courts before 1805. An attempt to establish an
alternative settlement on the Andaman Islands was undertaken in
1792, but the scheme was badly organized and had to be abandoned
four years later. Opinions on the value of Penang were, however,
revised as a result of the renewal of war in the Eastern seas.

The French Revolutionary government's declaration of war on
Britain and Holland in February 1793 introduced the culminating
episode in a long series of struggles between England and France
for controlling influence in the Netherlands. By a successful

invasion of Holland in the winter of 1794–5, the French secured ultimate control of the Dutch fleet, Dutch financial resources, and the Dutch possessions overseas. As an enemy-occupied country Holland thus became ranged against Britain in the world war that lasted until 1815, and her overseas possessions became liable to attack by British naval forces. Before the fall of Holland, however, the Dutch Stadtholder William V had been evacuated to England with the nucleus of a 'free Dutch' government, and in February 1795 he issued a general order to all Dutch governors and commanders overseas not to oppose the admission of British ships and troops for protection against the French. British forces accordingly took possession of the Cape of Good Hope and Trincomalee later in 1795, and of Colombo in February 1796. In South-east Asia the Dutch commander at Malacca, and those on the west coast of Sumatra and at Amboyna, admitted British forces in 1795 without serious opposition. The Banda Islands were captured, but Ternate refused to surrender and succeeded in holding out until 1801.

The British occupation of Malacca in 1795 was carried out on behalf of the refugee government of the Dutch Stadtholder. A mixed Anglo-Dutch government was set up in the first instance, and for a time both British and Dutch flags flew over the fortress. This amicable arrangement was soon changed on the orders of the authorities in India, and a British Resident was appointed to take charge ; but throughout the period of British occupation to 1818 Dutch institutions and Dutch law continued to operate, and Dutch officials who declared loyalty to the Stadtholder remained in office.

The East India Company authorities in India and London, who regarded Penang as a doubtful asset at this time, looked upon Malacca as a positive liability. Its commerce had dwindled as a result of the long sequence of conflicts between Dutch, Bugis and Malays, and its occupation involved the Company in considerable financial loss. No attempt was made to assume the place, which the Dutch had tried to maintain, of commercial and political masters of the Straits area. The policy of isolation within the actual settlements, and avoidance of implication in political affairs outside, prohibited any dealings with Selangor, Perak or Johore. The Dutch themselves had decided to restore the Johore Sultan who had driven them out of Riau in 1787. He had appealed to the

English for assistance, but without success, and had fled from his capital. When the Dutch reoccupied Riau in 1788, therefore, they found that it had been abandoned by the Malay population and that its trade had disappeared. But it was the English who actually restored the Sultan at the same time as they removed the Dutch Resident and garrison in 1795.

Logically, the next step after the occupation of Malacca by the British should have been an advance against the headquarters of Dutch rule in Batavia, but that step was not to be taken until sixteen years later. The conquest of Holland, the establishment of a puppet republican government by the French, and the presence of the Stadtholder in England, had combined to produce a sharp cleavage of opinion among the Dutch in Java and in the East generally. As long as the war lasted they were faced by two almost equally unpalatable alternatives—French control or British occupation ; and Dutch opinion was divided on the choice of the lesser of those two evils. That the choice would have to be made in Java seemed more than ever probable after the defeat of Admiral de Winter off Camperdown in 1797, by which the Dutch navy was destroyed as a striking force. In Batavia one party favoured the English side, with which the royal house of Orange was associated, but there was also a strong pro-French and republican party. A British attempt to occupy Java would therefore be bound to meet with opposition.

Nevertheless plans were made. An expedition including five thousand British troops, an equal number of sepoys, and Colonel Arthur Wellesley, assembled at Penang in 1797 for an attack on Batavia and possibly also Manila—since by this time Spain had joined in the war. The expedition got no further than Penang, however ; the whole plan was cancelled and it was decided to concentrate the British forces in India. Wellesley, who was greatly impressed by what he saw of Penang, wrote a memorandum to his brother, the Governor-General, in favour of its retention as a strategic base. Another expedition against Batavia was being prepared at Trincomalee early in 1799, but again the demands of higher strategy caused a change of plan, and in April the force was earmarked for a combined attack on the French army in Egypt. Later in the same year the President of the Board of Control in

London had new plans for a move against Batavia under consideration, but they went no further, although Batavia was closely blockaded by a squadron of five British warships between August and November 1800, and the island of Ternate was captured in June 1801.

With the continuation of the war against France after the breakdown of the Peace of Amiens in 1803, the value of Penang came up for discussion once again. The British Admiralty now argued that the island would make an excellent base for naval operations in Eastern waters, as well as a useful shipbuilding and repair centre which would help to relieve both the pressure of work and the shortage of naval stores and large timber in English dockyards. The East Indies Command could be divided into two parts, one based on Bombay and the other on Penang, and at the same time the latter could be elevated to the status of a Presidency—on a par with Bombay and Madras—with a Governor and Council. These proposals were carried into effect in 1805. But although an elaborate and expensive administration suited to Penang's envisaged importance as a naval base and a Presidency was rapidly installed, the practical measures necessary to equip the island for building and servicing ships were postponed, curtailed, and finally abandoned. Even before the end of 1805 Penang was warned by the Indian administration that it need not expect as a Presidency to receive any considerably greater financial support than hitherto, and it was strongly advised to delay the construction of 'docks, warehouses or other expensive works'. But in fact there was little danger of such work being started, for Penang was entirely without the necessary technical advice until May 1806, when a solitary assistant engineer arrived. The sum total of Penang's output as a naval base was one thirty-six-gun frigate, launched in 1809. The Admiralty's enthusiasm for the whole scheme had soon evaporated. The victory of Trafalgar in 1805 greatly eased Britain's naval position and thereby relieved the strain on her shipbuilding resources. Penang, in any case, had not proved to be the ideal naval base it was pictured as in 1805. Great difficulty had been found in procuring suitable timber locally, and supplies of teak had to be ordered from Rangoon. But such difficulties might have been overcome, as Penang's Governor pointed out with some bitterness in 1809, 'had docks been constructed . . . or had we been assisted with proper professional advice'.

As part of the Penang scheme it had been decided to evacuate Malacca, demolish its fortress, and transfer the inhabitants to Penang. Penang, according to the Admiralty, would henceforth command the Straits, and from the Company's point of view the loss of Malacca would be good riddance of an expensive liability. Orders were issued to this effect in April 1805, but work on the demolition of the Malacca fortifications did not begin until August 1807. It was completed by November 1808. In that year Stamford Raffles visited Malacca on sick leave from Penang, where he held the post of Secretary. He wrote a memorandum to Penang urging that Malacca should not be abandoned, and in 1809 the Company decided to reverse its previous decision. By that time Penang had definitely ceased to begin to be a naval base, and the East Indies Command had been reunified. Besides, although after 1806 there was little danger of a large French fleet appearing in Eastern waters, Dutch squadrons were operating in the Java Sea and French frigates and privateers were prowling between Mauritius and the East Indies. Even though English naval forces had been blockading Batavia and patrolling the north coast of Java since 1806, and had penetrated the Straits of Madura and destroyed the last remaining Dutch warships at Grisek in November 1807, it would clearly be unwise to leave Malacca, even without its fortifications, undefended and unoccupied for any enemy force that chose to move in. Especially so since the arrival of the energetic Marshal Daendels at Batavia as Governor-General at the beginning of 1808; for he was working on a plan for organizing naval supply depots at various ports on the eastern side of the Bay of Bengal. Evidence of this was obtained in 1809 when a French emissary from Batavia was captured on the way to Achin and Burma, and sent under arrest to Penang.

When Holland was annexed to the French empire by Napoleon in July 1810 the Dutch overseas possessions came under direct French control. This led to the British invasion of Java in 1811. Already, in June 1810, Stamford Raffles had crossed to Calcutta from Penang and had interviewed Governor-General Minto, who agreed with him that Java was 'an interesting island', graciously adding that he would be happy to receive further information about it. 'From this moment,' Raffles wrote, 'all my views, all my plans, and all my mind were devoted to create such an interest regarding Java as should lead to its annexation to our eastern empire.' Annexation of enemy overseas territories was in the air in 1810. News of the capture of Bourbon by a British expedition from India reached Calcutta early in July. Mauritius was taken in December. In the same year the East Indian islands restored to the Dutch at the Peace of Amiens were recaptured ; Amboyna, the Bandas and Ternate all capitulated to British forces, and various ports in southern and northern Celebes were occupied.

In August 1810 the Company wrote from London approving the Governor-General's suggestion that the Dutch should be expelled from Java. In October Raffles was appointed as 'agent to the Governor-General with the Malay States' to prepare the way for an expedition against Batavia. Raffles chose Malacca as his headquarters, and there prepared a series of reports containing much miscellaneous information on Java and most of island South-east Asia. He advocated that the Governor-General of India should become Protector of the Malay States, explaining his interpretation of protection as 'a general right of superintendence over and interference with' the states. In May 1811 Governor-General Minto himself arrived at Malacca to take over the command of the Java expedition. After a satisfactory reconnaissance of the Kari-mata Channel between Billiton and Borneo, the first section of a fleet of 100 ships, including 57 transports with nearly 11,000 troops (half English, half Indian) under the command of Sir Samuel Auchmuty, sailed from Malacca on 11 June 1811. On 29 July Minto and Raffles, in the frigate *Modeste*, came in sight of Java.

The Dutch Company had never recovered from the effects of the 1780–4 war, in which convoying of merchant ships became almost impossible as a result of the Dutch naval defeat at Dogger Bank in 1781. But the real decline of the Company had set in well before then. The war dealt a fatal blow to an organization which had already been weakened internally by corruption and ineffi-ciency. Basically the trouble was that the Company was unable to undertake the capital outlay which might have made possible a reconciliation between its original commercial purposes and its developing political responsibilities. Drawn further and further into the interior of Java in an effort to increase profits by securing control of production over an ever-widening area, the Company found that in fact the resultant gains never outstripped the inevitable expenses. The policy of cutting expenses down to the minimum merely starved the whole organization, encouraged corruption and inefficiency, and reduced profits accordingly. Inadequate salaries, as in the old Portuguese empire and in the English Company in India, resulted inevitably in private trading. Poorly paid and ill-equipped military forces were incapable of supporting the Company's commercial aims to the full, and entailed excessive expenditure on military operations in the long run. Fortifications were inadequately garrisoned and supplied. The recruitment of officials from Holland completely failed to keep pace with the Company's expanding responsibilities in a period, from 1755 onwards, when the population of Java was beginning to increase as a result of the comparatively settled conditions created by the Dutch themselves. In Batavia, out of a population of about twelve thousand at the end of the eighteenth century there seem to have been less than three hundred Dutch. Portuguese was still the European language generally spoken and understood there. Health conditions in Batavia and in other cities were extremely bad. Generally speaking, Dutch officials in the East Indies had become demoralized by conditions of service, by a system in which lucrative posts could be purchased for money (the *ambtgeld* system), by the lack of sympathy between the man on the spot and the Directors in Amsterdam, and by the growing weakness of the Company's position in the world at large. And while many of the Company's servants were busy lining their own pockets, smuggling and contraband trade made serious inroads into the Company's monopoly.

The expiry of the Company's charter in 1774 drew attention in Holland to its unsatisfactory financial position and provided an occasion for general criticism of its monopoly. The charter was renewed provisionally for two years only ; and in 1776, although the renewal of the charter for a further twenty years was obtained, there was a strong demand for the setting up of a committee to

M

enquire into the Company's affairs. The regular payment of dividends to shareholders ceased in 1782, and a committee of enquiry was appointed in the following year ; but it accomplished nothing. Another committee started work in 1787 and issued a report in 1790. The report announced that the Company's balance-sheet showed a deficit of 85 million guilders, only partially offset by assets amounting to 20 million guilders in actual produce. It proposed a limited admission of private enterprise to the East Indies trade, the Company retaining its monopoly in spices, sugar, opium and tin. This half-measure, which was really no more than a recognition of existing conditions, was adopted by the Company in the following year.

In the same year, 1791, the States General appointed a commission to enquire into the Company's affairs and to recommend reforms. The commission dragged out its investigations in Java over three years, avoiding unpleasant decisions and yielding to the self-interest of local officials. It reported in 1795 that the Company was virtually bankrupt. The States General of the new French-sponsored Batavian Republic therefore decided to abolish the Company's Board of Directors and to replace it by a 'Committee for the affairs of the East Indian trade and possessions', a body of twenty-eight who mainly represented the commercial interests of the provinces of Holland and Zeeland. At the same time the Company's charter was renewed for a further four years to 1799. But before the end of that period the fate of the Company had at last been finally settled. As a result of legislation passed in 1798 the Company was dissolved on the expiry of its charter, and the State, acting through a 'Council of Asiatic possessions and establishments', took over the administration of its property. By this time the Company's debts amounted to 134 million guilders.

In the years which saw the final collapse of the Dutch Company the liberal principles of the French Revolution were in the air. The revolution in 1789 had proclaimed not merely the rights of Frenchmen but the rights of man, and had declared that 'men are born, and always continue, free and equal in respect of their rights'. This represented the logical extension and universal application of the doctrine of natural rights and natural law as expounded by John Locke towards the end of the seventeenth century. Although for that reason the majority of the British people may have felt that the rights of Englishmen were at least a hundred years older than the 'rights of man', yet the restatement of liberal individualist principles by the French revolutionaries had a profound effect in England as in the Netherlands, even though that effect was temporarily weakened when the revolutionary movement proved to be nationalist and aggressive, culminating in the dictatorship of Napoleon. On the political side, Locke's doctrine of natural freedom and natural rights had been translated into more concise, and more romantic, language by Rousseau earlier in the eighteenth century, and it had been adopted, more directly from Locke, by the American revolutionaries. On the economic side, the doctrine of a natural law had been elaborated by the French Physiocrats, who argued for the fullest freedom in the agricultural system—freedom of labour, of exchange, of contract—and the abolition of all special privileges and monopolies; and their arguments had been applied to the commercial sphere by Adam Smith. It was ideas of this kind—of economic implication—which particularly influenced liberal-minded European officials in Southeast Asia in the early years of the nineteenth century.

One such was Van Hogendorp, who had urged the Commission of 1791 in Java to abolish the Company system with its forced deliveries of produce and its control of agricultural labour, to put an end to slavery, and to introduce free labour and free trade, the protection of individual rights along with a fixed system of taxation for the natives, and a regular and adequate salary scheme for officials. Although his proposals made little impression on the Commission, Van Hogendorp continued to campaign for his ideas in Holland itself, where liberal principles were much advanced after the establishment of the Batavian Republic in 1795; and in 1802 (after the Peace of Amiens) he was given a seat on a new Commission which was to draw up a constitution for the government of the East Indies. But by that time the first era of liberalism was drawing to a close; in 1802 France under Napoleon cancelled her earlier extension of liberal principles to the government of colonial territories, and a similar reversion of attitude took place in Holland. It could be fairly argued, moreover, that the desperate need of the moment was to repair and restore the war-shattered

trade of the East Indies, a purpose more likely to be achieved by
known methods of mercantilist regulation and control than by
new and untried economic plans. A revival of the coffee trade,
which had accounted for an ever-increasing proportion of the
Dutch revenues in Java during the eighteenth century, and which
had collapsed with the virtual elimination of the Dutch fleet in
1797 and the consequent economic isolation of Java, seemed to
demand familiar methods rather than new experiments. Van
Hogendorp was unable to carry his views in the Commission, and
the reforms included in its proposed charter for the Indies in 1803
were administrative reforms within the existing system; monopolies, forced labour and compulsory deliveries of produce were all
retained.

Although this proposed charter was withdrawn in 1805 in
favour of a slightly more liberal constitution, many of its principles
were tested by Daendels during his Governor-Generalship, 1808–
11. He introduced a programme of administrative and judicial
reforms which foreshadowed the measures to be introduced during
the British occupation of 1811–16 for more direct rule in Java, and
on which Raffles was to comment that they established 'a much
more regular, active, pure and efficient administration' than had
ever existed in Java before. For administrative purposes Daendels
divided the north-east coastal region stretching from Cheribon to
the Bali Strait (hitherto a single province) into five prefectures,
which were subdivided into thirty-eight regencies. To all authorities within these administrative units, including the Javanese
regents themselves, was assigned the status of Dutch officials, with
military rank and appropriate salary. This whole north-eastern
area of Java had been for many centuries the great agricultural
production-centre of South-east Asia, supplying rice not only to
Java itself but also to most of island South-east Asia and to the
Malay Peninsula. During the eighteenth century the native regents
of the area had been made to serve as rice-agents to the Company,
furnishing fixed assessments of rice in the form of 'contingents',
as well as sharing responsibility for the compulsory cultivation of
coffee. Under Daendels' scheme this collecting system was to be
tightened up by bringing the regents more closely under Dutch
control. To reinforce this policy, as well as to offset the difficulties

of coastal communication by sea due to the British blockade, Daendels had a military road built from Batavia across to Surabaya. On the judicial side, Daendels established a system of separate courts for dispensing native law and custom in cases where Javanese alone were involved—a sphere of control with which the Dutch had not hitherto concerned themselves beyond the extent of laying down very general principles. Alongside the established courts (*raden van justitie*) in Batavia, Semarang and Surabaya, which would henceforth deal only with cases concerning Asian and European foreigners, Daendels now introduced provincial courts of Javanese law at Semarang, Surabaya, Cheribon and Bantam, minor courts in the prefectures and regencies, and itinerant courts in the coffee area of Priangan. In general, Daendels was the visiting efficiency expert of the time ; somewhat lacking in perception, determined to introduce honest, businesslike and rational methods into the old administration in Java, but at the same time inexperienced in the peculiar problems of such an administration.

Daendels was recalled after the annexation of Holland by France in 1810, and his successor Janssens, who had surrendered to the British at the Cape of Good Hope in 1806, arrived in Java in April 1811—just in time to face another British invasion. The British-Indian expeditionary force from Malacca made its first landing on August 4 some twelve miles east of Batavia. In a proclamation to the Javanese Lord Minto declared : 'The British come as friends.' Batavia was occupied without opposition, the Dutch forces having withdrawn to a fortified position at Meester Cornelis, seven miles to the south. On August 10 the British moved forward and drove the Dutch from an advanced post, and on the 26th they took the main enemy position at Cornelis. Cheribon was taken on September 3, and Semarang was occupied on the 11th. On September 18, at Semarang, Janssens signed his second capitulation to a British force. Java, Macassar, Timor and Palembang, with all establishments and military posts in the Indies, were surrendered. Raffles was appointed Lieutenant-Governor of Java and the dependencies, the whole area of the former Dutch dominions being subdivided into the four administrative units of

Malacca, Java, the west coast of Sumatra, and the Moluccas. Dutch law was to continue in force (with some softening of police methods and legal punishment), and the Dutch in Java were to retain trading facilities and elegibility for official posts.

All this went rather beyond the aims of the Java expedition as originally envisaged by the East India Company, which had instructed Lord Minto that it wished for nothing more than 'the expulsion or reduction of the Dutch power, the destruction of their fortifications, the distribution of their arms and stores to the natives, and the evacuation of the island by our own troops'. Although the Company seems to have had no conception of the vast resources and potentialities of Java, nor any real appreciation of the political and moral implications of the plan which it proposed, yet even had it been better informed in these matters it would probably have been no less unwilling to accept further responsibilities in South-east Asia. But to Minto and Raffles it was obvious that to overthrow the Dutch regime and leave nothing but anarchy in its place would be a morally indefensible step. Besides, they had more ambitious ideas. Raffles had hoped from the start that Java would become a permanent British possession, and Minto now declared himself greatly impressed by 'the face of prosperity which every part of the island wears'. They therefore agreed to set up an administration for the occupied territories and to await events. The Governor-General returned to India on October 19, and Raffles set to work to apply his political ideas to the complex conditions of the vast territory now under his rule.

Chapter Thirteen

THE ADVANCE OF BRITISH AND DUTCH INTERESTS

THE British occupation of Java from 1811 to 1816 provided an opportunity for experiments in administration along liberal lines similar to those proposed by Van Hogendorp in the last decade of the previous century. Raffles, like Van Hogendorp, was inspired by the liberal principles of the age ; moreover, there was a direct link between the two in the person of Muntinghe, who had been a supporter of Van Hogendorp and was now an adviser to Raffles in Java. Thus it came about that the reform programme of the Dutch liberal group was actually presented on the stage of Javanese administration by an English producer. This is not to say that Raffles derived his ideas from Van Hogendorp ; but rather that the liberal beliefs which Van Hogendorp, Muntinghe and Raffles all shared naturally led them to similar conclusions with regard to colonial policy.

The close similarity between the views of Van Hogendorp and those of Raffles is clearly illustrated by an extract from one of the latter's official statements of policy. Raffles outlined his aims as :

'1. The entire abolition of all forced delivery of produce at inadequate rates, and of all feudal services, with the establishment of a perfect freedom in cultivation and trade.

2. The assumption on the part of Government of the immediate superintendence of the lands, with the collection of the revenues and rents thereof, without the intervention of the regents, whose office should in future be confined to public duties.

3. The renting out of the lands so assumed in large or small estates, according to local circumstances, on leases for a moderate term.'

All this amounted to a political policy of direct rule, coupled with an economic policy of direct taxation. It involved sidetracking the Javanese rulers by the appointment of government officials as Residents and collectors, and the abandonment of the system of organized cultivation and collection of produce, with which the rulers had been associated, in favour of a revenue system based on money rents assessed on the value of land. The new government assumed the right of land-ownership, and it based its whole revenue system upon that right by levying taxation upon the peasantry in return for permission to use the land. These changes, it was believed, would benefit the government by carrying its administrative and fiscal control down through its collectors and the village headmen into the villages themselves, and by extracting a money revenue instead of a produce revenue from the land. At the same time the changes would benefit the peasant by setting him free from traditional feudal bondage and from the burden of compulsory cultivation, greatly reducing his liability to 'contingents' or forced sales of produce to the government, and enabling him, to a large extent, to grow what crops he wished and to sell them for what he could get. Economic freedom for the peasant would go hand in hand with economic advantage to the government, and, beyond the government, to the British war-time economy. For a money economy in Java would provide favourable conditions for the sale of British goods, which was a matter of much greater consequence to Britain than the acquisition of stocks of Javanese coffee. True, there was a most valuable market for coffee on the continent of Europe, which Britain continued to exploit even after the establishment of the Napoleonic blockade in 1806, but for coffee supplies for that purpose she naturally went to her own colonies in the West Indies.

The attitude of the British administration to the rulers, and to the former system of agricultural exploitation, was proclaimed in treaties of December 1811 with Surakarta and Jokjakarta. The English Company was acknowledged as the full successor of the Dutch administration; the rulers were forbidden to correspond with one another except through the Company; the system of compulsory deliveries was to be replaced by a free market for all produce. Later treaties displayed additional signposts on the road towards Raffles's goal of direct rule. The sultanate of Bantam was abolished in 1813 ; Cheribon was annexed in 1815. Surakarta and Jokjakarta were deprived of the right to maintain armed forces in 1813, the rulers becoming virtual pensioners, bound to accept the advice of the British government in the administration of their states. Direct control was similarly extended to the various regencies by means of the Resident system, combined with the institution of a corps of 'collectors' responsible for the collection of land rents from village headmen.

The details of the innovations introduced by Raffles during the British occupation of Java are of less interest than the attitude of mind and the political assumptions that lay behind them. As an early exponent of liberalism in colonial administration, Raffles in his Java policy foreshadowed to a considerable extent the colonial approach of later nineteenth-century liberal statesmanship. The allied conceptions of freedom, reason and progress formed the background of ideas in each case. As a child of eighteenth-century enlightenment, Raffles displayed a generous if naïve humanitarianism combined with a 'modern', realistic and rational approach to political problems, an approach which enabled him without hesitation both to sweep aside traditional institutions and tried methods in favour of the seemingly rational and progressive, and also, when necessary, to make use of morally doubtful means in order to gain his ends. His cheerful readiness to modernize, to make a clean sweep of the old (and probably partly, but not wholly, bad) in favour of the new (and probably partly, but not wholly, good), has formed, in a sense, a tradition of British—rather than of Dutch or French—liberal policy in South-east Asia ; for it would not perhaps be an unfair generalization to say that British rule in South-east Asia, up to most recent times, has been characterized by long periods of inaction and neglect, punctuated by sudden outbursts of drastic—sometimes catastrophic—modernization and reform. Raffles's policy in Java may be regarded as a kind of preview of nineteenth-century liberal colonial policy in so far as it was formed of a mixture of humanitarian theory, realistic practice, and an oversimplified view of the problems and techniques of reform. His rash application of the jury system to the process of Javanese law is a fair example of the liberal tendency to assume universal validity for the institutions and ideas of the 'colonial' power.

Raffles's policy of direct rule and direct taxation in Java was inspired, in fact, by a mixture of humanitarian and practical motives. He saw himself as the liberator of the simple peasant from the unenlightened despotism of Java's feudal rulers, and he tried to act at the same time as the efficient Company servant whose first concern was to ensure a financially self-supporting administration. His policy of direct rule was curiously similar in method—though not in aim—to that of Daendels. Daendels had curtailed the independent powers of the Javanese rulers for the benefit of the Dutch administration and in order to increase production; Raffles did the same for the benefit of the Javanese peasant, but in order to increase revenue as well. His policy of direct taxation bore close resemblance to the land revenue system in operation under the East India Company's administration in India.

While it may fairly be held that Raffles was inclined to an over-confident belief in the direct relevance of Western political ideas to Eastern political institutions, at the same time there can be no doubt of the fundamental humanity of his point of view, or of his essential goodwill towards the people over whom he had come to rule. He had come to Asia prepared to learn as well as to teach; he had spent five years studying the Malay language and the history and customs of the people of the East Indies. His specific attempts at reform may have been hasty and ill-judged; nevertheless the spirit of his administration in Java marked a real turning-point in the history of the relations between South-east Asia and the Western world. Before the time of Raffles the European trading companies had been concentrating on their purely commercial aims; they were essentially unaware of any responsibilities towards the inhabitants of the countries over which their control had gradually extended. They had not begun to understand, much less provide for, the peculiar social and economic needs of the indigenous inhabitants, and had remained aloof from their civilization and culture. Raffles was an outstanding representative of a new attitude of mind. Although he may have had an over-simplified conception of the means of achieving the welfare of the people of Java, he was at least conscious of the duty of providing for their welfare and of studying their needs. His work in Java pointed the way towards new aims and methods in colonial administration.

The collapse of French rule in Holland, in November 1813, after the failure of Napoleon's Russian campaign, and the proclamation of William Frederick of Orange as king, paved the way to the negotiations which culminated in the Anglo-Dutch Convention of August 1814. The terms of this agreement were evidence of the British government's policy of contributing towards a restoration of the balance of power in Europe and overseas by rebuilding the power of the Netherlands. Most of the Dutch overseas possessions taken by Britain since 1803 were to be restored. In accordance with this arrangement the British occupation of Java came to an end in August 1816, and that of Malacca in September 1818.

Apart from wider political considerations, Malacca, overshadowed by Penang, was regarded as virtually worthless, and Java was in fact a financial liability. Raffles had already been replaced in Java (March 1816), an indication of the Company's disappointment with the financial results of his administration. He had been largely responsible for selling the idea of the occupation of Java; he had been given full opportunity of proving the merits of the scheme; and the immediate result was, as his Directors complained, that his administration had caused 'financial embarrassment' to the British government. At the same time the East India Company as such was no less concerned to protect and develop its trade in the Straits area, and through the Straits to China, than to support the British government's diplomatic policy towards the Dutch; and the Company's government in Calcutta was inclined to sympathize with the view of Raffles, who had now become almost hysterically anti-Dutch, that steps should be taken to counterbalance the restoration of Dutch power in island South-east Asia by the establishment of a new British strategic and commercial base within the region. Raffles, who had returned to South-east Asia as Governor of Bencoolen, the English Company's station in Sumatra, in March 1818, was warned that the British government would not tolerate any independent measures that might provoke

Dutch opposition, but he persisted in his views, and a personal interview with the Governor-General in Calcutta in October 1818 left him satisfied that sufficient sympathy existed in that quarter to permit him to proceed with his plans. He landed on Singapore Island on 29 January 1819.

The prospect of the restoration of Dutch rule in island South-east Asia had already inspired diplomatic approaches to the Bugis Raja at Riau, the power behind the Malay throne of Johore, which included Singapore Island in its dominions. In August 1818 the English Company's government at Penang had arranged a com-mercial treaty, granting 'most favoured nation' conditions of trade, with Johore; and the British Resident at Malacca had recommended the occupation of Carimon Island in the Riau Archipelago—though this proposal received no definite support in Penang. Such attempts to counterbalance the restoration of Dutch control in the Straits area south of Penang were, in effect, neutra-lized by the transfer of Malacca to the Dutch in September 1818, which was immediately followed by the installation of a Dutch Resident and garrison at Riau. Acting independently of the Penang government, Raffles had now penetrated this sphere of Dutch influence and established a base on behalf of the English Company on the unconsidered island of Singapore. Taking advantage of the existing division between real and nominal rule in the Johore dominions, he secured the concession from one of the two sons of the previous Sultan.

Raffles's enterprise had succeeded; the Governor-General in Calcutta advised London that Singapore was 'exceedingly important' and should be retained; and the British government, while withholding its approval, decided to wait and see how the Dutch reacted.

The occupation of Singapore inevitably increased the growing tension in Anglo-Dutch relations in South-east Asia. Represen-tatives of the two home governments had already come together in order to review the position as it had developed out of the Convention of 1814. Other officials of the English Company in South-east Asia besides Raffles had been complaining to London that the Dutch were strenuously rebuilding an exclusive system of trade monopoly in the region; they made a point of underlining the contrast between the English policy of free trade competition and the Dutch policy of obstruction and monopoly. Raffles's action in Singapore added a fresh cause of dispute, which contributed to the prolongation of discussions until 1824. The English Company wanted to hold Singapore, mainly for the protection of the China trade; the British government, however, remained doubtful of the legal basis of the settlement; while the Dutch government was certain that it had no proper legal basis at all. Meanwhile, Singapore was deciding its own fate by its striking success as a centre of trade. The debate on the legal position was accordingly abandoned, and it soon became clear that the ruling factor in the negotiations lay in the financial weakness of Holland. In the end the British government accepted the Dutch factories in India and an additional £100,000 in settlement of Holland's indebtedness to Britain, and in return the Dutch concurred in the British claim to Singapore. Malacca was exchanged for Bencoolen, and rights over the island of Billiton (ceded to the English Company by the Sultan of Palembang in 1812) were transferred to the Dutch; the result being the demarcation of a British sphere of influence in the Malay Peninsula and a Dutch sphere of influence in island South-east Asia. The treaty of 1824, which incorporated these provisions, marked off the boundaries of the separate fields within which British and Dutch colonial activities were to operate in South-east Asia during the nineteenth century.

The extension of the English East India Company's interests to the three Settlements of Penang, Malacca and Singapore was, in intention, a strictly limited commercial liability which envisaged no acceptance of political responsibility in the Malay Peninsula; and for a time Malayan political conditions, and the restricted commercial interests of the Settlements, permitted the Company to remain generally aloof from the affairs of the Malay States. In Burma, on the other hand, political conditions drew the Company into intervention and war before the first quarter of the nineteenth century was out.

In 1784–5, during a brief interval in her wars with Siam, Burma had turned her attention westward to the independent coastal region of Arakan; that country had been quickly overrun by

Burmese forces, and reduced to the status of a province under a viceroy appointed by the court of Ava. The invasion of Arakan drove large numbers of its people across the border into the Chittagong district, which was under the nominal jurisdiction of the English Company's presidency of Bengal. From then on, the border region of Chittagong became a base for Arakanese resistance to Burmese rule, with the result that the frontier was crossed and recrossed again and again by Arakanese insurgents and by Burmese punitive expeditions. Here was a situation which seemed to call for some sort of consultation between the English Company and the Burmese government; and at the same time there was an additional motive for new diplomatic approaches to Burma in England's suspicion of French commercial and strategic intentions in that country. A series of English missions, all more or less unsuccessful, was sent to Burma between 1782 and 1811.

Unaffected by the course of these discussions, the frontier wars dragged on until 1815, and all the time the Burmese court remained convinced that Arakanese resistance was being prolonged as a result of English connivance or support. Then in 1817 a similar situation was created by Burma's invasion of Assam, when a resistance movement developed in the frontier zone between Assam and the Company's territory. The Burmese armies completed their conquest of Assam by 1822, and for a time there was a real danger that they would attempt to push forward into the Company's territory from that direction; but early in 1824 a new threat appeared on the Chittagong frontier, where the Burmese forces in Arakan began preparations for an invasion. The Company's government in India decided to take up the challenge, to forestall and outflank the Burmese offensive by a sea-borne invasion of southern Burma. In May 1824 Rangoon was captured without a struggle.

The fall of Rangoon marked only the first stage in a difficult campaign which had as its objective the Burmese capital of Ava. Operations northward from Rangoon and in western Burma were bogged down by temporary deficiencies of equipment and supply, as well as by the perennial difficulties of warfare in jungle country and rainy climate. But the occupation of Prome, in April 1825, provided the necessary base for a final advance against Ava; and in February 1826, when the British-Indian forces were approaching the capital, the Burmese court agreed to peace terms. By these, Burma surrendered her coastal provinces of Arakan and Tenasserim, agreed to enter into commercial treaty arrangements with the English Company, and undertook to accept a British Resident at Ava.

Thus by 1826 the English East India Company's interests were well committed in South-east Asia, but nowhere more deeply than in Burma, mainly as a result of that country's proximity to India. In Burma the Company had now undertaken a potentially vast political responsibility, a far heavier commitment than was involved in the territorially circumscribed and outward-looking Settlements of Penang, Malacca and Singapore, which, although combined under a single administration in 1826, remained in fact separate outposts on the fringe of the Malay world, divided not only by distance but also by the uneven commercial development that was giving to Singapore a predominant share in a somewhat artificial partnership. In Burma, by contrast, the Company had carried war into the country itself and had emerged from that experience as the administrator of large provinces.

The year 1826 marked the conclusion of the first stage in Burma's subjection to Western rule. In the same year the English Company managed with difficulty to obtain agreement from Siam for a limitation of the latter's right of action in the Malay States. Although the Company had successfully maintained its policy of avoiding political responsibilities in the northern Malay States, which were liable to Siamese suzerainty, this had been no easy matter ; it called for all the Company's powers of diplomatic dexterity and evasion. The Sultans of Kedah had hoped to strengthen their own position against Siam by securing English military aid, but the Company had succeeded in obtaining the cession of Penang in 1786, and also that of Province Wellesley (on the mainland opposite Penang) in 1800, without committing itself to a defensive alliance with Kedah. To have done so would certainly have drawn the Company into conflict with Siam (who maintained a traditional claim to suzerainty over Kedah), as was clearly demonstrated when Kedah was compelled to invade Perak in 1818 in order to bring that state under Siamese control. The delicacy of the Company's position was emphasized when Kedah itself was invaded and occupied by the Siamese in 1821 and its Sultan fled to Penang. The Company now decided to send a mission to Bangkok to discuss trade relations as well as the question of the exiled Sultan's future. The mission met with little success, and Siam refused to consider the restoration of the Sultan. However, another mission was sent in 1825, this time in the hope of forestalling a new invasion of Perak, which had thrown off Siamese control three years earlier. Agreement was reached in a treaty of 1826 by which Siam undertook to refrain from intervention in the Malay states of Perak and Selangor ; her position as overlord of Kedah, however, remained unaffected. Kedah was thus left to carry on her own struggle against Siamese occupation. She did so, with some temporary success in 1831 and 1838, but it was not until 1842 that Siamese troops and officials were withdrawn and the Malay Sultan restored.

The southward pressure of Siamese political authority upon the Malay States had been in effect counterbalanced by the establishment of the Straits Settlements. On the eastern side of the Indo-Chinese peninsula the balance of power lay between Siam and Vietnam, which were only nominally separated by the now subservient state of Cambodia. Siam had established a protectorate over Cambodia in 1786, but this was challenged in 1809 by a Vietnamese invasion ; and as a result Cambodian territory was virtually partitioned, Siam annexing the province of Battambang (which included the ancient site of Angkor), and Vietnam making a dependency of the remainder.

While the English Company was avoiding political and military undertakings in the Indo-Chinese peninsula outside Burma, it was pressing on with the development of its trade through the Straits and eastward to China. Penang—whose trade connections remained comparatively localized, with westward and northward radiations towards northern Sumatra, Siam and Burma—definitely yielded place after 1823 to the younger Straits Settlement of Singapore, better qualified by its convenient situation to inherit the historic position of exchange centre for the triangular trade between South-east Asia, India and China. Singapore rapidly became a collecting and redistributing centre for the produce of the

Straits and of much of island South-east Asia, as well as a forward base for the opium and cotton trade to China, which had steadily increased since 1782. Chinese merchants in Singapore directed the flow of goods and built up a reputation for straight dealing. Fleets of small Bugis sailing ships, converging on Singapore with 'Straits produce' from the islands, mingled in the harbour with larger 'country ships' from India, junks from China, and a growing number of vessels owned by Singapore Chinese and Arab merchants. The Bugis ships carried away cargoes of British cotton and iron goods, and Indian opium, for distribution among the widespread markets of island South-east Asia. Singapore, with its free port facilities and its expanding trade, seemed to symbolize Britain's commercial position in the East.

The growth of Singapore coincided with the emergence of the British policy of free trade. Even after the loss of her American colonies Britain had still retained the old principles of mercantilism. But the basis of her economic life was changing, and a new set of economic relationships between Britain and the rest of the world were beginning to call for some modification of the principles of mercantilism and of the old conception of empire as a closed economic unit. Britain was changing from an agricultural to an industrialized country, and her new economic organization, based upon large-scale production of manufactured goods, was demanding not a closed economy within a self-contained empire, but the opening up of overseas markets for the sale of her manufactured goods in all parts of the world. In response to these changing conditions there was a steady movement of thought in Britain away from the restrictive regulation of imperial and international trade and towards complete freedom of trade; and this conception naturally linked up with liberal conceptions of human freedom and progress.

The doctrine of free trade and free competition was based essentially upon Britain's growing confidence in her own ability to win in any open commercial competition. She could afford what might seem to other countries the luxury of liberalism in economic policy because she was industrially strong and becoming stronger. Free trade was the economic policy of the salesman with a powerful industrial machinery behind him. It was not, of course, a policy of economic impartiality or disinterestedness. It was no less a policy of economic advantage than was mercantilism or monopoly. As an economic theory, in the form of *laissez-faire*, it accorded with liberal philosophy, but as economic practice it was based not upon generosity but, very naturally, upon self-interest.

The restored Dutch government of the Netherlands East Indies could derive no material advantage from subscribing to the principle of free international trade. The post-war years had brought the restoration of Dutch rule but not a revival of Dutch trade in the East Indies. Although the English Company had handed back political control, British trade and British-Indian shipping continued to dominate the area, and after 1819 Singapore began to overshadow Batavia as the central exchange market for island South-east Asia. The comparatively meagre output of Netherlands textiles, and the serious shortage of Dutch shipping, meant that a market for Dutch goods in the East Indies could hardly be maintained without protection from the powerful competition of British and British-Indian goods. Even with such protection, as provided for in 1819, the import of Dutch cloth into the East Indies reached only a fraction of the total cloth import. In 1824, with the surrender of their factories in India under the Anglo-Dutch treaty, the Dutch lost all direct share in the import of Indian textiles into the East Indies. In the same year they erected a higher protective wall around Java, imposing a 25 per cent duty on all imports of foreign textiles, with an additional 10 per cent duty on such goods if they came from any port that lay to the east of the Cape of Good Hope. This measure, combined with the formation of the Netherlands Trading Company in 1824 and a marked increase in Dutch shipping, helped to stimulate Dutch imports into Java after 1825.

The Dutch were now mainly concerned with the protection and development of their commercial interests in Java, for that island provided the most profitable market for Western products as well as the highest production of peasant agriculture. While Dutch control had steadily extended over Java during the eighteenth century, it had diminished in the outer territories of the East Indies; and there was no marked change in this respect until after the middle of the nineteenth century. Outside Java, therefore, the Dutch had less reason for putting obstacles in the way of free competition in the seaports. They made Riau a free port, as a counter-attraction to Singapore, in 1828, hoping to draw Bugis trade back to its old headquarters in the Straits. In the Moluccas the Dutch retained a formal claim to the monopoly of the spice trade until 1863, but the monopoly had in fact lost much of its value since the British occupation of the islands during the war and the consequent dispersal of clove and nutmeg plants. Penang and Singapore, for example, took up spice planting, and carried it on—though rather fitfully—during the first half of the nineteenth century.

Within Java itself the Dutch attempted at first to apply liberal economic principles in the sphere of production. They retained the policy which Raffles and Muntinghe had pursued during the British occupation, the policy of replacing the old system of compulsory tribute of agricultural produce, collected through the Javanese rulers and chiefs, by a land-tax based upon the assessed value of the village fields and collected through the village headmen. In this way, while a revenue would be ensured for the government, peasant agriculture would be liberated from direct exploitation by government, and production would be based upon free enterprise. In conformity with this policy of free enterprise the Dutch in 1818 were prepared to allow unrestricted development of plantation with European capital. The Priangan district, however, was excluded from the operation of the new liberal policy; coffee production there continued to be carried on by the old Company method of compulsory cultivation, and, as part of the system, the regents retained their feudal powers almost undiminished.

In practice the assessment of land-tax presented a tremendous problem, requiring a long period of land surveying and a large staff of efficient collectors; and during the short period of British rule the system had not had enough time to show results. But after 1816 it began to justify itself; the land revenue showed a steady increase, and liberal economic policy seemed to be a paying proposition.

While retaining his principle of direct taxation, the Dutch departed to some extent from Raffles's policy of direct rule, which had involved the displacement of the Javanese rulers from their traditional feudal status. After 1820, although Dutch Residents remained as official advisers at the royal courts, the rulers obtained some restoration of their judicial and administrative authority over district chiefs and village headmen.

Such measures, however, could not suffice to restore the old equilibrium of Javanese society, which had been gravely upset when, as a result of the policy inaugurated by Raffles, the traditional world of feudal relationships and services had been invaded by the cash nexus and by the free play of new economic forces. Although under restored Dutch rule payment of land revenue might be made in money or in kind, the Javanese peasant, set free from compulsory labour, was inclined to produce little more than was necessary for the subsistence of his family, and had recourse to borrowing whatever money was required for the payment of land-tax. Thus the ultimate effect of the new economic policy in Java was to deliver the peasant out of the hands of his feudal and royal masters and into the hands of Chinese and Arab moneylenders. To some extent it also delivered him into the hands of the district chiefs and village headmen, who, with the moneylenders, were the main beneficiaries of the new system.

It was not for such reasons, however, that the Dutch were to abandon their liberal economic policy in Java. Although the land revenue rose steadily up to 1823 it did not meet the expense of administration ; other sources of income were failing, and there was an annual deficit from 1819 onwards. In 1823 there was a slump in the price of coffee, the commodity which provided government's most important source of revenue ; the value of Dutch exports from Java declined, and production itself began to fall off. The foundation of the Netherlands Trading Company (*Nederlandsche Handelmaatschappij*), with headquarters at The Hague, in 1824 was an attempt to stimulate Dutch trade by the application of capitalist and monopolist organization to the distribution of East Indies produce, but by itself it could not stimulate production. The formation of the Company, however, marked the beginning of the end of the economic experiment that had been carried out in Java since the governorship of Raffles ; it represented a move in the direction of positive measures for planning general economic development. The foundation of the Java Bank in 1827 was another step in the same direction.

Java since 1816 had been the scene of the first attempts of a Western power to shape colonial policy over a large area of Southeast Asia in accordance with new aims and ideas arising out of the fundamental economic changes that had been taking place in western Europe. For some fifteen years the Dutch experimented with new methods of organizing production, methods which largely conformed to the principle of *laissez-faire*, but they found that these methods did not pay. By 1825 the financial position of the government in Java had become so unsound that a new direction of policy was called for. The outbreak of war in Java in the same year, and the continuance of serious disturbance until 1830, further undermined the financial position to such an extent that a new direction of policy became imperative. The war, which hinged upon the personality of Dipa Negara, a prince of Jokjakarta and a practical mystic, was partly a reaction against the whole sequence of disturbing experiments in administration which had been going on since the end of the Company's rule ; like the mutiny against British rule in India in 1857, it was a kind of blind, instinctive protest against the disintegration of a traditional society that had resulted from the well-meaning interference of Western administration. For both Jokjakarta and Surakarta the practical results of the war were loss of territory and further subjection to direct Dutch rule.

It had cost the Dutch some 20 million guilders to fight the Java war, and by 1830 the public debt of the East Indies administration reached 30 million guilders. In Europe the revolt of the Belgian provinces in 1830 began a nine-years period of heavy financial loss for the Dutch. The financial position, both for the administration in Java and for the home government, was saved by the *culture system*, the new system of organizing production which was developed in Java after 1830.

The culture system was not in essence an innovation ; it was rather the old system of compulsory cultivation and tribute readjusted to meet new and increased demands, and reshaped by more effective and more direct methods. It signalized the abandonment of the policy of free enterprise in production and a whole-hearted return to the former Company system, a system which had never, in fact, been fully superseded. It represented a reversion from liberal to mercantilist ideas. The plan of the system in its new form was based upon the government's claim to one-fifth of the produce of arable land (in place of the land-tax inherited from Raffles) or, as an alternative, sixty-six working days a year from all heads of families. This led on in course of time to the closest control and direction of commercial agriculture ; and the exploitation of labour and production thus secured was accompanied by the fullest possible monopoly of Java's exports and imports by Dutch shipping. Java became virtually a vast State plantation the produce of which was consigned for export solely to the Netherlands Trading Company, and as production expanded under the new system the Netherlands government collected an increasing revenue and the Company was transformed into a most powerful commercial concern.

The main crops cultivated and developed under this system of State compulsion were coffee, sugar and indigo ; subsidiary crops were tea, tobacco, cotton and pepper. Coffee was already well established in the Priangan highlands as a forced culture ; it now became extended as a compulsory crop to other areas, but, unlike sugar and indigo, it nowhere infringed upon the rice-lands nor did it involve a factory system. The cultivation of indigo, which encroached on the rice-lands most of all, was developed with greatest intensity between 1834 and 1840 ; thereafter it gradually diminished, while the cultivation of sugar and coffee correspondingly increased. Production as a whole was at its highest, and the profits of the system were greatest, between the years 1840 and 1848. The large-scale organization of labour and production which the system involved did not require any considerable investment of capital ; it was based upon the co-operation of rulers, district chiefs and village headmen in the exploitation of the industry of a subservient peasant population, and the co-operation of those authorities was cheaply bought by allowing them a small percentage of the huge profits of peasant industry. Nor did the culture system induce any serious attempts to improve methods of cultivation, at any rate during the first ten years. There were expensive failures in all crops except coffee during this period, but it was the peasant and not the State who paid for failure, since the peasant was rewarded not for his labour but only for its results.

As a by-product of the culture system there was some progress in road construction in Java after 1830. Roads were primarily designed to assist collection and export of produce and were built generally by forced labour. But otherwise Java derived little permanent benefit from the great wealth created by the industry of its people during this period. The Netherlands, on the other hand, obtained an enormous cash return from Java ; the amount received between 1831 and 1877 (when the culture system had already been nominally abandoned) was 823 million guilders. Besides this, Holland's shipping and her general position in world commerce were greatly strengthened by the culture system ; her mercantile marine became the third largest in the world, surpassed only by those of Britain and France.

The economic plan of full exploitation of peasant production in Java was paralleled by an administrative policy of indirect rule. Although the Resident system was retained, the native rulers or regents were restored to their former position of prestige in Javanese society, since the combination of feudal authority and direct financial interest which they represented was a most useful support to a system of compulsory cultivation. In the districts and villages, although the government's Controller (*opziener*) exercised a general supervision over native affairs as well as cultivation, in practice the native chiefs and headmen retained unrestricted local power as long as the government's demands for produce were satisfied. The culture system also left the Chinese in power as middlemen, dominating the growing internal trade of the country, and providing the management and skill in factories where sugar and indigo crops were processed for export.

The practical result of the operation of the culture system—in a country whose population was rapidly increasing in response to peaceful and comparatively prosperous conditions—was an enormous expansion of agricultural production, especially after 1850. The indirect results of the system are more difficult to assess. It strained, though it did not dislocate, the peasant village organization by subjecting it to the purposes of commercial agriculture.

It clearly placed a heavy burden of compulsory labour on the population, and in some areas and for some periods it seriously curtailed rice cultivation and caused famine. And it allied the regents and village leaders to what must have been, on the whole, a demoralizing system of human exploitation.

For Holland the culture system was a financial lifebuoy. But although it showed enormous profits, the system did not encourage a healthy development of Dutch trade with Java, because it was inevitably bound up with the maintenance of exclusive commercial privileges by the Netherlands Trading Company. The fence of monopoly by which the culture system was thus protected induced an attitude of complacency and prevented the development of a commercially progressive outlook. Whereas the abolition of the English East India Company's trade monopolies with India (1813) and China (1834) had released a flood of British commercial enterprise in the East, and had also been followed by major developments in British shipbuilding in response to a demand for increased speed, Netherlands trade with the East Indies remained largely reserved to monopolist control, and Netherlands merchant shipping failed to keep pace with world developments. The Dutch were slow to improve the design of their sailing ships, and for too long they neglected to develop the steamship. In these circumstances, and in view of the proximity of Singapore, the Dutch were likely to lose an increasing proportion of the Java trade. In fact the value of Dutch manufactures imported into Java fell considerably between 1840 and 1850, whereas the value of English imports—mostly cottons—rose during the same period.

The end of the culture system came after the Netherlands States General had succeeded in establishing some control over colonial policy. By the Dutch constitution as revised in 1814, ministers of state were responsible to the king alone in colonial matters, and there was no major change in this respect until 1848. In that year the constitution was revised in accordance with liberal principles, and parliament obtained the right to receive an annual report on the administration of the East Indies. For some years these reports were generally uninformative or evasive, and colonial questions remained very much in the background of Dutch politics. Liberal principles were gradually applied in minor matters of policy in

Java, but it was not until 1860, with the publication of *Max Havelaar* by 'Multatuli' (D. Dekker), that the whole question of colonial policy was brought into the foreground, and attention focussed on the working of the culture system in Java. From then on compulsory cultivation was gradually abandoned in favour of free agriculture. The culture system lingered on, however, in respect of sugar and coffee, although the conditions of labour were improved ; State cultivation of coffee did not end until shortly before 1920. The feudal services that had formed part of the machinery of the system were reduced and finally removed in 1882, being replaced by a poll-tax ; and the Dutch officials most closely identified with the system, the Controllers, were incorporated in the civil service.

Chapter Fourteen

THE BEGINNINGS OF THE NEW COLONIALISM

ALTHOUGH Dutch control was widely extended over Java in 1830, elsewhere in South-east Asia Western interests were still confined to seaports and to certain limited coastal regions. But during the next forty years, up to 1870, there were indications of an intensification of commercial activity, and of an increasing rivalry between the various Western commercial interests, which would lead to a deeper penetration of the South-east Asian countries by the combined economic and political purposes of a new 'colonial' system. The conscious aims of the Western countries, however, remained essentially commercial. The political implications of their developing commercial needs had not yet become fully apparent; or if they had, it was still possible to hope that they could be avoided or at least carefully restricted. Outside the Dutch sphere in South-east Asia, Western policy at this time meant largely British policy, and up to 1870 it was the policy of Britain to develop free markets everywhere while avoiding as far as possible any new political responsibilities. Free trade was Britain's commercial religion, and it taught that rule over overseas territory was an unnecessary expense when all that was needed was free commercial access to overseas markets. However, the gentle economic theories of Manchester were liable to be rudely shaken by the harsh reality of direct action in the East. In general the period between 1830 and 1870 was one of transition, in which commercial interest was more than once promoted—in effect if not in intention—by the use of armed force, so that the foundations of colonial rule were being surely if unconsciously laid, and a theoretical distinction between commercial and political interests was becoming more and more unreal.

Western powers might remain officially uninterested in the acquisition of colonial territory, but, as the nineteenth century

wore on, their widening commercial interests were steadily carrying them along the road that was to lead to the consolidation of
colonial rule over large areas of South-east Asia, areas which for
hundreds of years previously had been only lightly touched by the
pre-industrial West. Signs of this process were already beginning
to appear in the eighteen-thirties. Britain, with two of Burma's
coastal provinces in her possession, was seeking to establish friendly
business relations with the remainder of the country. But although
Burma had admitted a British Resident to Ava in accordance with
the terms of the treaty of 1826, she was not prepared to go further
than that. The Residents met with no success in their prolonged
efforts to obtain a commercial treaty; indeed they met with so
little co-operation of any kind that in 1840 the Residency was
abandoned. Siam showed herself rather more responsive after 1825.
An Anglo-Siamese treaty in the following year not only defined respective spheres of influence in the Malay Peninsula but also allowed
for freedom of British trade in Siamese territory. In 1833 the legal
status of American citizens in Siam was regulated by agreement.

In the Malay Peninsula British interests were still confined to
the Straits Settlements; but although the hinterland was for the
most part unknown and unwanted, Chinese settlers, sometimes
backed by Chinese merchants in Singapore, were beginning to
work pepper and gambier plantations in the Malay state of Johore
from about 1835. Chinese were working tin mines on the island
of Banka as they had done since early in the eighteenth century,
but now under Dutch supervision. Banka had formed part of the
dominions of the Sultan of Palembang; Raffles had acquired it
after deposing the reigning Sultan; but in 1814 it was restored to
the Dutch, and they took over direct ownership of the tin mines in
1816. The island of Billiton, which reverted to Dutch rule in 1824,
was found to contain tin about the same time, but not (it was
believed) in great quantity; the full exploitation of Billiton tin
did not commence until after 1850.

The tentative advance of Dutch authority along the east coast
of Sumatra during the eighteen-thirties revealed both the growing
tendency to reach out for new markets and the latent antagonism
between competing Western interests in South-east Asia. Sumatra
had been placed entirely within the Dutch sphere of control by the

Anglo-Dutch agreement of 1824, but the British Straits Settlements retained valuable trade connections with the Sumatran ports on the opposite side of the Straits and were the natural entrepôts for their produce. Besides, the treaty of 1824 had left the authority of the Dutch along the east coast of Sumatra in a rather equivocal position, for it had included an undertaking on their part to respect the independence of Achin (whose trade was of importance for Penang), and the extent of Achin's direct and indirect jurisdiction in Sumatra was by no means clearly defined. At the same time Achin had incurred the anger of Western commercial interests in general on account of the organized piracy which operated from her coasts against passing vessels of all countries. British and American warships, called upon to protect shipping in the Straits, had shelled Achinese coastal villages. For all that, British commerce did not welcome the extension of Dutch control along the Sumatran coast of the Straits, against Achinese opposition, during the eighteen-thirties. Penang and Singapore feared the loss of their Sumatran trade, and they appealed to the British government. Anglo-Dutch relations became more and more strained on this score until 1841, when the Dutch decided to postpone further action on the east coast of Sumatra.

During the eighteen-forties Britain's commercial, political and strategic interests were becoming more and more closely combined in action in the Far East. The impact of the West on China began in earnest in 1839 with the outbreak of the 'Opium' War, which was followed by the cession of Hong Kong to Britain in 1842 and the opening up of Shanghai to foreign trade in 1843. This new phase of British relations with the Far East began at a time when the steamship was making its first appearance in Eastern waters, and when coaling stations were consequently becoming important links in the trade-routes. A Dutch attempt in 1836 to start a steamship service between Holland and the East Indies was unsuccessful, but the British P. & O. Company established a regular service between the Red Sea and India in 1840 and extended it further eastward soon afterwards. The island of Labuan, off North Borneo, was acquired by Britain in 1846 as a coaling station between Singapore and Hong Kong.

Gold, diamonds and pepper had attracted the Dutch and English East India Companies to Borneo in earlier centuries, but attempts to maintain regular trade had never lasted long. Western traders had found Javanese settled along the south and east coasts, and Malays along the west, with Buginese interspersed among them generally during the eighteenth century, and Chinese gold-miners and pepper-planters on the west coast after 1750. The Dayak people of Borneo had mostly been driven inland. The Dutch maintained fairly constant trade in pepper with Banjermassin in the south, but on the west coast their diamond trade had failed early in the seventeenth century, and an attempt to develop regular trade with Pontianak between 1778 and 1791 was unsuccessful. Commercial contacts with southern Borneo were renewed after the war period in 1818, but Borneo and the 'outer territories' generally received little attention from the Dutch as compared with Java.

James Brooke, an adventurer who had himself obtained the territory of Sarawak in 1841 in return for military assistance to the Sultan of Brunei, presented Labuan to the British government in 1846. The Dutch protested against this as being an infringement of the treaty of 1824, but in the end they acquiesced in the extension of British influence in North Borneo and turned their attention to coal-mining within their own sphere of influence in the remainder of the island.

The Dutch government offered mining concessions in the East Indies to private enterprise in 1850; the first concession to be taken up was for the mining of tin on Billiton Island. In the Malay Pensinsula tin-mining at this time was entirely a matter of private enterprise on the part of Chinese prospectors and miners. There was a marked expansion of mining in the Malay States after 1850; but although the Chinese miners of Perak, Selangor and Negri Sembilan were more or less closely linked with Chinese merchants in the Straits Settlements, depending on them for capital and supplies, the government of the Settlements showed no interest in the possibilities of developing trade with the sparsely populated hinterland. There was no response to the beginnings of pressure from mercantile interests in the Settlements for the extension of British influence in the peninsula, such as was expressed in 1858 in a petition to Parliament from the citizens of Singapore, who complained that 'the cultivation of friendly relations with native states and chiefs has been neglected, and Government does not possess that influence in the Indian archipelago which the interests of British commerce require'.

In Burma, on the other hand, there was a large population offering a vast potential market for the sale of British cotton goods. The acquisition of the provinces of Arakan and Tenasserim in 1826 had been an encouragement for British trade, but the country's main seaports remained under the jurisdiction of Burmese royal officials, whose attitude to the operations of foreign traders was generally either noncooperative or positively obstructive. The Government of India received frequent complaints of oppressive treatment of British merchants in Rangoon, and in 1851 Governor-General Dalhousie decided to support a specific charge of wrongful arrest which had been brought by two British sea-captains against the Burmese Governor of Pegu. A warship was sent to Rangoon with a demand for compensation. The commodore of the vessel, unable to obtain satisfaction, blockaded the port, exchanged fire with the Burmese shore batteries, and destroyed Burmese shipping. This action was followed by the despatch of a full expedition with a demand for an increased amount of compensation. Ava remained unresponsive, and the second British invasion of Burma began. Rangoon was occupied in April 1852; by November Prome had been captured and the main body of the Burmese army defeated; and in December Pegu was proclaimed a British province. Three years later, with the end of guerrilla resistance in the new province, the whole of Burma's coastline had been brought under British control. Relations with the court of Ava improved from this point, although the British mission which was received there in 1855 failed to establish those relations on a treaty basis.

British approaches to Siam in the same year, 1855, were more successful. Both British and American envoys had been refused a treaty in 1850, but the accession of King Mongkut in the following year introduced a new spirit of co-operation with Western aims. The new king, studious and intelligent, favoured a policy of gradual westernization for his country, and in 1855 he agreed to revised treaty terms with Britain, including provision for a British consul at Bangkok with extra-territorial jurisdiction, and the regulation of duties on imports and exports. Similar treaties were obtained soon afterwards by the U.S.A. and France.

It was to the eastern part of the Indo-Chinese peninsula, however, that France's revived interest in South-east Asia was being drawn. The murders of several French missionaries in Vietnam in the eighteen-forties provided some justification for official and forcible intervention in 1858, as a result of which France obtained half of Cochin-China (southern Vietnam) in 1862. Having thus secured a firm foothold on the coast, France next obtained by treaty a protectorate over Cambodia. Immediately afterwards Cambodia, vaguely hoping to satisfy all claims, confirmed the protectorate which Siam had re-established over her in about the year 1844. The publication of this agreement started a series of Franco-Siamese discussions which continued until 1867, when Siam consented to surrender her rights over Cambodia. In the same year France obtained from Vietnam the remaining half of Cochin-China.

Meanwhile, on the western side of the Indo-Chinese peninsula, Britain was developing her position in the coastal provinces of Burma and seeking to establish official commercial relations with the remainder of the country. In 1862 the three British provinces were amalgamated in a single administrative unit in charge of a High Commissioner under the Crown, the Company organization having come to an end in 1858. In 1862 also the Burmese court (now at Mandalay) agreed at last to receive a British Resident and to allow unrestricted trade between the two parts of Burma. Pegu, with its port of Rangoon, was the real heart of British Burma, and there the effects of Western rule were beginning to be most clearly shown. The introduction of a money economy and Western commercial methods was stimulating rice production and the sale of newly-imported consumer goods from Europe. There was an all-round increase of material prosperity. Although growing numbers of Indian immigrants were being attracted to the towns, the traditional Burmese ways of life and labour in the villages were hardly disturbed by the new regime before 1870.

But while Britain valued Burma itself as a market for the sale of her manufactures, she had an equal interest at this time in developing trade through Burma with China, where a much larger market for British goods was hoped for. Northern Burma was regarded by Britain—just as northern Indo-China was coming to be regarded by France—as a tradesman's entrance to south-west China. Attention had been drawn to the existing overland trade after 1826; observers had noted the large imports of raw silk from China; and the vision of an immensely profitable trade along the route from Bhamo in Upper Burma to the Chinese south-western province of Yunnan had captured the imagination of British merchants. The realization of their hopes seemed to come nearer with the conclusion of a new treaty between Britain and Burma in 1867. British subjects in Mandalay were now to come under the extraterritorial jurisdiction of the British Resident, British vessels were allowed free navigation of the Irrawaddy river, and a commercial agent was permitted to reside in Bhamo.

These various moves marked successive stages in the increasing penetration of the Indo-Chinese peninsula by Britain and France; and each move added to the growing rivalry and suspicion between the two powers in that area. There was suspicion, too, between Britain and the Netherlands, arising out of the renewed expansion of Dutch authority along the east coast of Sumatra after 1850, a move which was itself largely inspired by fear of the intrusion of other European interests there. The establishment of a Dutch protectorate over Siak in 1858 alarmed Britain; it also disturbed Achin, although the Dutch succeeded in negotiating a treaty of friendship with the Achinese in the same year.

Meanwhile the age-old means of communication between the different parts of South-east Asia were being revolutionized by the techniques and aims of the West. After 1850 European-owned steamships began the gradual process of taking over the bulk of the inter-port trade from Bugis sailing-boats and Chinese junks. A Dutch-sponsored steamship service operated between the west coast of Sumatra and the Moluccas, serving Singapore, Batavia, the west coast of Borneo, and Macassar. A British firm obtained the contract for this service in 1865 and continued to operate it until 1890. A regular steamer service between ports of the Malay Peninsula was started by a group of Malacca Chinese in the eighteen-sixties; it later developed into the Straits Steamship

Company. The Burma Steam Navigation Company was founded in 1854, to become the British India Line in 1862.

The contract for the first railway in Java was granted in 1864. Java's first telegraph line was opened in 1856, and in 1859 Batavia was in telegraphic communication (though only temporarily) with Singapore. These developments were stimulated by the speeding up of communications with Europe. In 1850 there was a regular monthly mail to India via the Middle East; after 1857 it was weekly. The first overland telegraph line between Europe and India was opened in 1865. Cable lines had been laid along the existing steamship routes to India in the eighteen-sixties, and in 1870 the British Indian Telegraph Company completed the first direct cable between Britain and India, whence it was continued to Singapore and Australia. The telegraph not only increased the command of European business over Asian markets; it also increased the control of European states over the actions of their colonial governments, and so tended to bring colonial policy into line with changing international situations.

The many-sided development of communications accompanied, and was also partly responsible for, the political and commercial developments which constituted the beginnings of the new colonialism in South-east Asia between 1830 and 1870. But it was the opening of the Suez Canal in 1869 that made possible the great modern expansion of Western rule and trade, and thereby brought about the economic and social revolution which has created the South-east Asia of today. The year 1870 is the real dividing-line between medieval and modern in the history of South-east Asia.

Up to 1870 the bulk of the merchandise and most of the passengers between Europe and Asia still travelled in sailing-ships round the Cape of Good Hope. Steam had by no means displaced the sail on the long sea-routes; coaling stations were still a problem; coal took up a large amount of space on board the steamer, and it was believed that certain delicate goods, such as tea, would be ruined by coal-smoke. Besides, while steam was more expensive than sail, it was not necessarily faster, though certainly more regular, before 1870. But the effect of the opening of the Suez Canal after 1870 was to increase the advantage of steam, to stimulate

o

technical improvements in the steamship, and to reduce the value and importance of the sailing-ship. Cargoes of heavy goods could now be carried between Europe and Asia via the Middle East in one shipment, and also much faster than by the Cape route.

The Canal thus enormously facilitated and accelerated the opening up of Asian markets to European trade. Other European countries besides Britain and the Netherlands were encouraged to build modern merchant fleets and to develop their own direct trade with Asia. Whereas Britain had held an almost complete monopoly of the world's shipping in the eighteen-fifties and 'sixties, and most of Asia's exports to Europe went first to Britain in British ships before being re-exported to other European countries, after 1870 direct trade was opened up between Asian and European ports. The Suez Canal strengthened Britain's hand in Asia, but at the same time it sharpened the challenge of other European states to her leading position as an industrial country, and assisted the development of a new international competition for overseas markets and colonies.

After 1870 there was also an increase in the number of steamers employed in the inter-port trade of South-east Asia. During the 'eighties the sailing-ship was definitely ousted as Chinese and Arab as well as European ship-owners turned to steam.

In South-east Asia generally after 1870 there was a further extension of Western rule, with a parallel expansion of mainly European and Chinese private enterprise, which was accompanied by a gradual and general shift of emphasis from trade to production. A new stage began in the development of the natural resources of the whole region.

In British Burma this development remained for some years largely in the hands of the Burmese themselves. The opening of the Suez Canal created a wide market for rice and thus greatly stimulated rice production; good prices encouraged the peasant cultivator to produce a surplus over and above his immediate needs, and thus the agricultural economy expanded naturally within its traditional framework. But it was not long before the growing demands of an uncontrolled economic expansion found the methods and resources of the Burmese peasant inadequate. The profits of an expanding export trade sent the Indian middleman and moneylender into the countryside to provide the cultivator with the capital for increased production, to market his crops, and often in the end to gain possession of his land. The shadow of an absentee, alien landlord soon lay over many a rice-field of Lower Burma. The immigration of Indians was directly encouraged by the British administration after 1874 in order to satisfy the economic demand for an industrial and agricultural labour force, as well as to provide subordinate staff for its own departments. At the same time it attempted, without much success, to assist the Burmese rice cultivator by providing loans at easy rates, and later it promoted the co-operative credit system for the same purpose. But although the position of the individual Burmese cultivator might have deteriorated, the production of the country as a whole increased steadily, and at the end of the nineteenth century Burma was exporting more than double the amount of rice she had exported in 1870, and for about double the price, while she was importing nearly four times the quantity of cotton goods.

Upper Burma, like Siam and Vietnam, still retained her independence, but none of these countries could remain unaffected by the economic and social expansion taking place in adjacent areas under European rule. Certain administrative reforms were introduced by the Burmese crown, but the traditional royal monopoly of trade remained. Siam had held steadily to its policy of a gradual adoption of Western techniques since the accession of King Mongkut in 1851. During his reign progress was made in the construction of roads and canals and in shipbuilding ; and under his successor Chulalongkorn (who succeeded in 1868 as a minor and took up active rule in 1873) the process of reform continued with the help of foreign experts and advisers ; it affected the systems of administration, revenue, law and education ; it abolished slavery and introduced the railway. In Vietnam, on the other hand, the emperor tended to share the Chinese official indifference towards the West and a steady dislike of foreigners in general.

Siam, sandwiched in between the main area of British power in Lower Burma and that of French power in southern Indo-China, retained her independence throughout the period of Western colonial expansion, but Upper Burma, largely as a result of Anglo-French colonial rivalry, lost her independence in 1886. Siam sought to preserve her independence by playing off Britain against France, and she succeeded ; Burma did the same and failed. Vietnam sought the protection of her traditional suzerain, China, against the French advance, but this failed to preserve her independence.

France had fully established herself in Cochin-China in 1867, but her real interest was in the development of trade with the south-western provinces of China by way of the Red river in Tonkin, and from 1874 onwards she used a combination of armed force and diplomatic pressure in order to gain control in northern Indo-China. China responded with an explicit assertion of her suzerainty over Vietnam in 1881, and Chinese 'volunteer' forces entered Tonkin by the Red river. This did not deter the French from sending an expeditionary force into Tonkin, placing a Resident over the province, and declaring a protectorate over the whole of central and northern Vietnam in 1883. Inevitably these steps led to a state of war between France and China, and some fighting took place in Tonkin ; but the Chinese imperial government responded readily to renewed diplomatic approaches from the French, and in 1884 an agreement was reached whereby China abandoned her claim to suzerainty in Indo-China and sanctioned trade between Tonkin and her south-western provinces, in return for a French guarantee to respect the boundary between Indo-China and China. Misunderstandings arose over the withdrawal of Chinese forces from Tonkin, resulting in a renewal of hostilities in 1885, but later in the same year the whole matter was cleared up and a final settlement reached. In 1887 all the Indo-Chinese territories under French control were amalgamated into a single administrative unit under a Governor-General.

The French penetration of the Indo-Chinese peninsula had given rise to growing suspicion in Great Britain about French intentions with regard to Upper Burma. At the same time Britain's own relations with Upper Burma had deteriorated since the accession of King Thibaw in 1878. His accession had been accompanied by serious disturbances, and the British Residency at Mandalay had closed down for safety at the end of 1879.

Thibaw decided to gamble on the dangerous game of playing off the French against the British. In 1883 he sent a mission to Europe, hoping to obtain arms from France. His approaches to the French government found some response after a forward policy in South-east Asia had been decided upon by Jules Ferry, and in January 1885 it was announced that a treaty had been concluded between France and Burma; it was described as a purely commercial arrangement, and it provided for a French consul at Mandalay. It now seemed quite possible that Upper Burma might be incorporated into the French sphere of the Indo-Chinese peninsula. The difficulties of trading with Upper Burma, on account of royal restriction and unsettled conditions, had already provoked European and Chinese mercantile interests in Rangoon to demand British annexation of the country, and their demands were now supported by the fear that the French would get there first.

Then King Thibaw himself provided the British with grounds for strong action. He called upon a British timber firm, which held a lease of the teak forests, for a loan of £250,000, and when this was refused the firm was summoned before the High Court and fined precisely the same amount. The matter was taken up by the Government of India, but Thibaw naturally refused to allow any further appeal in the case outside his own country. If, however, he had relied on French support in the case of a showdown he was unfortunate in the timing of events, for the French were still involved with China over Tonkin. Britain therefore took the opportunity to increase pressure upon Upper Burma, demanding the full acceptance of a permanent British Resident in Mandalay, facilities for trade with the Chinese province of Yunnan, and the right to supervise Burma's foreign relations. The rejection of these demands was followed by the British invasion of Upper Burma in November 1885. Mandalay was quickly occupied, though guerrilla warfare continued for some time in the remainder of the country. Burma now became a new province of India and it was administered directly from India until 1897.

Siam survived as an independent state because it served as a buffer between the two spheres of British and French control that had become clearly separated out by the end of the century. Even so, Siam lost some of her border territories to both France and Britain. In 1893 the French put forward a claim to the Siamese provinces on the east of the river Mekong on the grounds that these had properly belonged to Vietnam. After a brief show of force Siam gave way, though the settlement of the frontier required further adjustments in 1904 and 1907. Laos, however, became a French protectorate in 1893, though it was in fact governed by direct rule except for the kingdom of Luang Prabang.

Meanwhile the main direction of French commercial interest continued to be towards south-west China. An agreement was obtained from China in 1895 by which the French were to have a major share in any development of the mineral resources of Yunnan, Kwangsi and Kwangtung. In 1898 France obtained the right to build a railway from Tonkin to Yunnan-fu (the present Kunming), capital of Yunnan province; the actual concession was granted to a French company in 1903, and the line, one of the world's great feats of engineering, was completed in 1910.

The main sphere of Dutch expansion after 1870 was in Sumatra. An agreement with Great Britain in 1871 gave the Dutch a free hand in that island by removing any British objection to the extension of Dutch control over Achin. But Achin was subdued only after a long and expensive guerrilla war lasting from 1873 to 1899; control of the sultanate and of the capital did not in this case give command of the country, and the war had to be fought out against local forces led by district chiefs and religious leaders.

One of the major developments that occurred in South-east Asia after 1870 was in the overall growth of population; another was in the increase of the foreign Asian element in the population of each country. British rule attracted Indians to Burma from the start and especially after 1880, but from the middle of the century there had also been an increasing flow of Chinese into Burma, and into other South-east Asian countries as well. The rapid growth of the Chinese population of South-east Asia in modern times is directly linked up with the expansion of Western rule and economic enterprise. The urge to Chinese emigration was already there; it arose especially from the pressure of population on the land of China's southern provinces of Kwangsi, Kwangtung and Fukien;

but the establishment of Western rule in its modern form in South-east Asia had the effect of releasing a flood of southern Chinese which poured into the comparatively empty lands of this region after 1870. This infiltration of Chinese into South-east Asia was in general a voluntary, instinctive movement which owed nothing to the direct encouragement of governments ; indeed there was an official ban on Chinese emigration until 1894. At first it was not so much a migration of people as a movement of labour, for it was a movement of individuals and not of families ; until well into the present century it was a movement of male Chinese, a fair proportion of whom not only intended to return to their homeland but actually did so.

Most of the new Chinese in South-east Asia settled more or less directly under the protection of the Western colonial governments. The British Straits Settlements had attracted Chinese from the start, and indeed Singapore and Penang owed much of their commercial prosperity to the enterprise of these immigrants. By 1860 the population of the Settlements included some hundred thousand Chinese, among whom there was now an important nucleus of 'Straits-born' whose economic interests were entirely bound up with the commerce of the Settlements. But there were also many thousands of Chinese living inland in the Malay States, whither the profits of tin-mining had attracted the bolder types who were prepared to live in difficult and dangerous conditions. Tin-mining in the Malay States had by now largely become an extension of Chinese economic enterprise in the Settlements ; Straits Chinese had direct interests in mining development, supplying goods, equipment and labour as well as money.

The workers in these mining settlements formed small and often rival pioneer groups, deprived of the traditional restraints and conventions of family and village life, but retaining the intense group or clan consciousness of the Chinese in their home land. This group solidarity inevitably became all the more powerful in face of the harsh conditions of life in the Malay States, promoting the growth of the secret society, the band of confederates who were a law unto themselves, which has been a special characteristic of the Chinese in Malaya. Rivalry between the early mining groups over land and concessions was intensified by the confusions and uncertainties of the system of land-ownership among the Malays, and consequently by competition for the personal patronage of Malay rulers and chiefs. After 1860 these rivalries engendered a permanent condition of warfare in the state of Perak. In 1867, after years of fighting among the Chinese in the Larut district of that state, disturbances broke out in Penang among corresponding groups of Chinese financial backers and supporters there. A serious increase in piracy, which had always been a normal hazard in the Straits of Malacca, resulted from the extension of the land war to the coasts of Perak and Selangor, and in 1871 a British naval vessel exchanged fire with Malay forts at the mouth of the Selangor river.

Up to this point the British government had held to its original policy of non-intervention in the affairs of the Malay States. The peninsula appeared to have been safely neutralized by the limitation of Siam's suzerainty in the treaty of 1826, with its counterpart containing a formal assurance of British protection to Perak in the same year. This policy of non-intervention was maintained after the Settlements had become separated from the India Office and created a Crown Colony in 1867. It was maintained up to the end of 1872, at which time the Straits administration explicitly refused to accept any responsibility in the Malay States, informing the Singapore Chamber of Commerce that the business speculations of British citizens there were no concern of the government.

However, in November 1873 a new Governor arrived at Singapore with instructions to enquire into the disorders in the peninsula and to report whether any steps could be taken to restore peace and to protect trade. Interpreting this as authority to take direct action in Malaya, the Governor first persuaded the leaders of the rival Chinese groups in Penang to submit their disputes to arbitration, and then concluded a new treaty with the Malay state of Perak. By the Treaty of Pangkor (January 1874) Perak accepted a British Resident, whose advice was to be followed in all matters of general administration. The treaty was confirmed by the British government in the hope that peace and order would lead to an 'unrestricted growth of commerce' and a steady increase in the wealth and material prosperity of the Malay States; it furnished the model for later treaties with other states of the peninsula. The

Malays at this time numbered about 300,000 in the whole peninsula. The 1947 figure was 2,500,000.

The four central states of the Malay Peninsula, Perak, Selangor, Negri Sembilan and Pahang, which had accepted the guidance of British Residents, agreed in 1895 to form a federation. This was a federation in name only, for no attempt was made to define the respective powers of federal and state governments. The only change it effected in the relationship between the British administration and the Malay States was that it permitted the maintenance of a unified policy of development throughout the four states from a central point under the direction of a Resident-General in Kuala Lumpur. The federation was, in effect, an administrative union from the British point of view.

In North Borneo a group of British merchants obtained a lease of territory from the Sultan of Brunei in 1877. Five years later the European company system reappeared in one corner of South-east Asia when this territory was taken over by the British North Borneo Company. In 1888 North Borneo came under British protection, though it remained under Company government, and in the same year the Sultan of Brunei agreed to British control over the foreign relations of his remaining territory. The boundaries between British and Dutch Borneo were finally defined by treaty in 1891. In 1906 Brunei accepted a British Resident who was in practice a member of the Malayan civil service ; under him were a number of European officers at the head of the various government departments ; in fact, Brunei's relationship to Britain was very similar to that of one of the Malay States.

There had thus been a very definite quickening of the pace of Western penetration of the South-east Asian countries after 1870, along with a considerable increase in immigration from the densely-populated neighbour countries, China and India. Britain had brought the whole of Burma under control and had extended her protective power over the Malay Peninsula and North Borneo. Holland had finally added the whole of Sumatra to her East Indian possessions. France, re-entering the South-east Asian scene after 1860, had laid the foundations of modern colonial development in Indo-China.

Chapter Fifteen

CAPITAL AND DEVELOPMENT

THE real significance of the expansion of European rule and influence in South-east Asia during the last quarter of the nineteenth century lay in the economic and social changes that ensued.

The liberal economic policy of the time, which was shared by British and Dutch administrations (and only less so by the French), aimed at the removal of all internal restrictions on trade and enterprise so as to enable the free play of economic forces to bring about the material development of the new colonial areas. It was assumed that free economic development would inevitably bring a general increase in prosperity and welfare. Development, however, required capital ; and although a large, if unknown, amount of Chinese and Indian capital investment (especially in the form of moneylending) was employed before and after 1870, European capital was at first slow in following up the extension of European rule. The amount of European capital employed in South-east Asia before 1900, except in the case of Java, was comparatively small.

In the Malay States up to 1890 it was almost entirely Chinese enterprise and the revenue derived from Chinese tin mines which provided the financial resources available for development. Revenue from import duties on opium, from the licensing of gambling-houses and pawnshops, and from export duties on tin, provided the funds with which the British Residents were able to lay the foundations of a complex modern administration in each state. The federation agreement of 1895 helped to attract British capital to the peninsula because it suggested stability and permanence. It had the practical merit of facilitating the adoption of similar methods of administration and a concerted policy of development in all the states.

In Burma up to 1890, apart from the long-established exploitation of the teak forests, the attention of British capital was practically confined to the export trade in rice. Rice cultivation remained, of course, in native hands, but the rapid growth of the export trade since 1870 had been followed by the establishment of a number of European-owned rice mills. British capital was really only beginning to develop the mineral resources of Burma when the century ended ; it was early in the present century when the Burmah Oil Company introduced methods and equipment for large-scale production ; and the lead and silver mines were developed later. Up to the end of the nineteenth century British enterprise in Burma was in fact essentially commercial ; it was not yet concerned with the exploitation of natural resources, but was content to encourage native production of rice for export and to develop the market for British imports. The modernization of communications was regarded as the one necessary spur to economic expansion. The Rangoon to Prome railway was opened in 1877 ; railway service was extended to Toungu in 1884 and to Mandalay in 1889. But the British administration in Burma maintained in general a policy of *laissez-faire* with regard to development ; apart from improving and developing roads and other means of communication, it limited itself to maintaining conditions favourable to free economic enterprise ; it established peace and order, and maintained the rule of law.

In Indo-China the French administration also confined itself at first to the development of communications. Although the major purpose of railway construction at the beginning was to develop trade with south-west China, railway building began in fact in Cochin-China in 1881, and in Tonkin not until 1890. This early railway construction was on a small scale, and it was largely financed from internal capital resources. It was not until after 1895 that major projects of railway construction were begun with funds subscribed in France and with materials provided by French capital. The canals built by the French in eastern Cochin-China were also intended in the first instance to form a transport system ; in fact they performed an even more valuable function in facilitating the irrigation and drainage of previously uncultivated lands in the Mekong delta, thus promoting human settlement and the

production of rice and corn in new areas. The exploitation of
natural resources by French capital began a little before 1890
with the development of the coal mines of north-east Tonkin,
but there was no real development of tin mining until after
1900. The first sizeable plantations under European management
—for coffee growing—were started about the end of the century. The French official policy towards economic development in Indo-China at this stage was therefore one of indirect
encouragement, while French capital was as yet extremely timid
in its approach.

In Java, on the other hand, the Dutch had for long been engaged
in the direct promotion of agricultural production, which had been
steadily developing since 1850. As the culture system by which
the government had organized production was gradually abandoned, the private planter took over the leasehold and management of estates. Apart from rice cultivation, which, as elsewhere in
South-east Asia, was left to the native population, the main crops
grown in Java in 1870 were still coffee (not yet released from the
culture system), sugar, indigo, tobacco and tea. There was a
marked increase in the production of commercial crops after 1870
as a result of the new Dutch policy of free enterprise, combined
with the stimulating effects of the opening of the Suez Canal and
the general boom conditions of world trade.

The Dutch had all along been concerned with the exploitation
of Java as a source of valuable tropical produce rather than with its
development as a market for imported goods. After 1870 they
adapted liberal principles to their old policy—principles similar to
those which had been advocated at the end of the eighteenth
century ; they accepted the idea that production would be increased by the removal of restrictions on enterprise, and that
increased revenue from customs duties, land rents and the like
would more than offset the loss of revenue from direct cultivation.
One of the purposes of the Agrarian Law of 1870 was to allow full
scope for the development of estate agriculture by private capital ;
it provided for long leases of uncultivated and unoccupied land for
periods of seventy-five years, and thus opened the door to the
private capitalist. The result was seen in a great expansion of sugar
cultivation, though tea and tobacco production also increased.

Sugar production in Java doubled between 1870 and 1885. But world demand for sugar fell away from 1880 onwards ; there was a slump in prices, and the individual capitalist, unable to hold out until business improved, gave place to the limited company with headquarters and shareholders in Holland. Investment of external Dutch capital in Java began in earnest from about 1890, much of it going into the sugar industry.

Tin mining had been carried on in Banka and Billiton for many years, and coal had been mined in Borneo since 1846, but the modern development of mineral resources only began in 1883 with the granting of a petroleum concession on the east coast of Sumatra. In general, although external capital was more active in the Netherlands Indies than in other parts of South-east Asia in 1900, it was still small in amount compared with what it was to become after 1900, and it was still mainly directed to investment in Java. Economically the other islands of the Indies were linked, by trade and by small-scale but widespread capital investment, with Singapore rather than with Batavia. The opening of the Suez Canal had strengthened Singapore's position as an exchange port. The foundation of the Dutch Royal Packet Company (the K.P.M.) in 1888 signified the beginning of an attempt to regain predominance in the inter-port trade of the Indies, but no great progress was made by the Dutch in this direction until after 1900.

The changes of the last quarter of the nineteenth century may be seen as the beginning of a general process by which the other countries of South-east Asia were brought into line with Java by being shaken out of their ancient self-sufficiency, by being impelled to increase their production for export and thus to become dependent upon world markets. It was the beginning of a general change-over from a subsistence economy to a commercial economy. That change involved the large-scale expansion of traditional crops or the development of new commercial crops ; it was stimulated by the introduction or expansion of a money economy, the flow of capital and the development of land and sea transport ; and it was supported by Western technology, methods of administration and systems of justice

This whole process, based at first upon uncontrolled economic enterprise, swept away a medieval world which had contained good institutions as well as bad. The free, individualist spirit of Western rule and commerce cut at the roots of traditional social life, undermining the corporate strength of family and village. But the most serious direct threat of the new economic forces was to the peasant's ownership of his land. Expanding economies, new money taxes and cheap imports meant better business than ever for the money-lender, whose position was protected by Western law. Many peasants became ruined by debt and lost their lands. Indebtedness and debt slavery were not new in South-east Asia ; the latter was fairly soon stamped out, but the former now became much more widespread than before, especially in Burma and Indo-China, resulting in the creation of a landless proletariat. Action was taken to prevent the loss of personal freedom (for example in the Netherlands Indies and in the Malay States), but only the Dutch took adequate steps to protect the peasant against the loss of his land. The Netherlands Indies Agrarian Law of 1870 had the dual purpose of allowing expansion of estate agriculture by European capital and of preventing that expansion from taking place at the expense of the peasant's rice-lands. In the Malay States, too, the rice-lands were well protected. In Burma, on the other hand, the government did little to curb the expropriation of the peasantry.

The present century has seen a rapid economic development and a great expansion of production in the South-east Asian countries. Although fluidity of foreign capital between the various countries has been permitted to a limited extent, and although there has been a limited degree of co-operation between different governments with regard to production and supply in more recent years, economic development under the separate Western colonial powers has moved generally along national lines. The international trade competitions of the modern world have been projected into South-east Asia, accentuating the differences and distinctions between the European administrations, and in the end helping to create separate national consciousness among Asians.

The direction as well as the pace of this economic development in the colonial or protected areas of South-east Asia has been primarily determined by the overriding economic interests of the imperial powers. Even in Siam, where political independence was preserved, economic dependence upon European capital resulted in the creation of a characteristically 'colonial' economy. The agreement between Britain and France in 1896 to respect Siam's independence reserved that country, in effect, mainly as a field of development for British capital. At the same time Siam's ability to 'westernize' (that is, to create the political and legal conditions in which foreign capital could operate efficiently) was a factor as important as her buffer position between British Burma and French Indo-China for the maintenance of her independence. The abandonment of extraterritorial jurisdiction by Western powers (Great Britain in 1909, the U.S.A. in 1922) was a measure of Siam's achievement in westernizing her legal system. In 1909, when the outstanding question of the frontier between southern Siam and the British-protected area of the Malay Peninsula was settled by Siam's abandonment of suzerainty over Kedah, Perlis, Kelantan and Trengganu, the agreement also provided for a British loan of £4 million for the development of Siam's railways. But while the Siamese government made what contribution it could towards economic development by bringing law and order and social services into line with Western practice, it had to leave development itself to European and Chinese capital and enterprise. European interests were in shipping, tin, teak, the exchange trade, transport and banking. British investment amounted to £13 million by 1938. Chinese immigrants took over light industry and wholesale and retail trading almost completely. In 1931 95 per cent of Siam's industry and commerce was in European or Chinese hands.

British capital played an important part in the economic development of Burma, but it was not directly applied to the tremendous expansion of agricultural production which has taken place in that country in the present century. British companies developed mineral resources (oil, lead, silver, tungsten and tin); British investments in trade, banking and transport amounted to some £50 million by the nineteen-thirties; but most of the capital that swelled the production and export of rice in Lower Burma was provided by Indian moneylenders, who had invested some

£50 million in that province by 1930 and had acquired ownership of half its occupied land by 1938. The acreage under rice in Lower Burma rose from 3 million in 1880 to nearly 10 million in 1930, and about two-thirds of the crop was exported. During most of that period the main part of the export crop went to India. Manufactured goods and machinery came from Britain, but cotton goods were imported mostly from India. Economically, Burma was India's colony rather than Britain's.

Development in Malaya during the present century has been the most spectacular of all the South-east Asian countries. It has been based upon a rapid expansion of tin production, due in the first instance to Chinese skill and enterprise, and of rubber production, in which European capital and initiative have played a prominent part.

The establishment of Penang, and the high prices that English traders were prepared to bid against the Dutch, stimulated tin production in Perak ; but although the Chinese mining groups in the Malay States increased after 1850, production remained comparatively low until after British intervention in 1874. Malaya's output in 1870 was still less than that of Cornwall. Tin was a Chinese industry before and after 1874, and even as late as 1912 Chinese-owned mines produced 80 per cent of the total output. The entry of European capital into the field at the end of the last century led to the abandonment of the old 'open-cast' method of mining and the adoption of mechanical methods in Chinese as well as European-owned mines. European companies alone had some £14 million invested in the mining industry in 1936, by which time the Chinese share in production had fallen to 36 per cent. Production had risen from 26,000 tons in 1889 to over 70,000 in 1936. There was also some development of gold mining under European management and of iron mining by Japanese.

Unlike tin mining, rubber planting in Malaya owed its origin to British initiative. The industry began slowly, exports in 1905 amounting to only 200 tons, but the coming of the automobile age created an immense world demand, and by 1920 exports had risen to 196,000 tons. Investments of external capital (about three-quarters of which was British) in the Malayan rubber industry amounted in 1936 to nearly £55 million. At the same time small-scale peasant cultivation of rubber had become very general, so that more than half the total acreage under rubber belonged to the smallholder or the small Asian company. Total production in 1948 reached nearly 700,000 tons.

Rubber planting was taken up by the French in Indo-China comparatively late, but this gave them the advantage of being able to learn from the experience of the industry in Malaya and the Netherlands Indies. The earliest plantations in eastern Cochin-China began to produce in 1912. The unit of cultivation was small until after 1924, for external French capital was shy of investing in rubber before then, and the capital investment of some 40 million francs that had gone into rubber planting by the end of 1921 had been largely found among the French in Indo-China itself. External capital other than French was excluded by the provision that only French citizens, or members of subject or protected states, might be granted concessions of land; this effectively excluded Chinese as well as foreign Europeans from estate ownership and kept the rubber industry in French hands. There was some participation by the native smallholder in rubber production, but to nothing like the extent prevailing in Malaya and the Netherlands Indies. It was not until 1938 that the quantity of rubber produced in Indo-China became sufficient to meet the requirements of France's own industry.

French industrial interests played a major part in determining the pace of economic development in Indo-China. In the early stages of French penetration liberal ideas prevailed, and trade with Cochin-China was for the most part free to all; but opinion changed with the successful expansion northward into Tonkin, and the apparent intention of the 'assimilation' principle accepted by the French Parliament in 1892 was to create a closed economy within which the exports of France and Indo-China would each have free entry into the other country, whereas a uniform scale of duties would apply to foreign imports in each case. In effect, however, the advantages of this arrangement were all on the side of French industry, for goods imported into France from Indo-China were in practice subjected to almost as heavy duties as those from foreign countries. French industry was interested in Indo-China's consumption but it did not care to encourage her production, and

P

French capital did not wish to build up industries that might compete with those of either France herself or her other colonies, or to
see foreign capital do so. As a result the economic development of
French Indo-China was comparatively slow until after the 1914–18
war.

It was not until after 1924 that external French capital was attracted to Indo-China in considerable amount. Between 1924 and 1930
some 2,870 million francs were invested in various concerns. Much
of this investment went into new rubber companies, since rubber
production was now seen to fit most neatly into the imperial economic scheme. A large share of capital also went into rice plantation
under French management in Cochin-China, and rice continued
to be the major export commodity. Large-scale tea plantation also
developed. A pause in development due to the world economic
depression of 1929–31, which severely affected the whole South-
east Asian region, was followed by a new influx of capital from
1936. After the depression, and with the resulting tendency towards autarchy and imperial preference, there was a much greater
demand in France for Indo-China's rice and a new demand for her
maize, the latter becoming the second largest export product in 1932.

External Dutch private capital had been drawn to Indonesia (as
the old Netherlands East Indies may now conveniently be termed)
from about 1885 onwards ; thereafter many new companies were
formed to carry on plantation agriculture. During the present
century international capital has been attracted to the islands,
again mainly to plantation but also to oil production. In Java itself
the various plantations were developed for the most part by Dutch
capital, but in the Outer Provinces there was a much higher
proportion of non-Dutch (e.g. British and American) capital. A
considerable amount of non-Dutch as well as Dutch external
capital had flowed into Indonesia by 1940. The basic sugar
industry, in its modern form, was almost entirely developed by
Dutch investment, but probably about half the investment in
rubber, tea and tobacco plantation was non-Dutch. On the east
coast of Sumatra in 1939, for example, Dutch capital represented
only slightly over half the total amount of foreign investment ;
there were large amounts of British capital invested in rubber and

THE SINGAPORE WATER FRONT

Straits Times (Singapore)

tea, American in rubber, French and Belgian in rubber and palm-oil, and German in a variety of undertakings.

From the beginning of the present century official Dutch policy in Indonesia definitely abandoned *laissez-faire* and took up a programme of active economic and social construction. The government assisted economic progress not only in agriculture (by the construction of a modern irrigation system, for example) but also in mineral production and in industry and commerce. State or public capital investment now began to play a major part in promoting a general development of agricultural and mineral resources, not only in Java but also in the Outer Provinces of Indonesia. Such development was greatly favoured by the fact that there was a general rise in world prices of tropical produce between 1900 and 1910. The first fourteen years of the century brought the sugar industry in Java to the height of its prosperity ; production rose from 700,000 tons in 1900 to 1,400,000 tons in 1914. During the same period tea production increased five times and that of tobacco by half, while oil production rose from 360,000 to 1,540,000 tons. The production of rubber (first intro-duced in 1883 and planted mainly in Sumatra and in south and west Borneo) rose from almost nil in 1900 to 15,000 tons in 1914. By 1925 Indonesia was producing one-third of the world's supply of rubber, in 1927 almost a half.

A notable feature of the economic development of Indonesia during the present century has been the increasing share of the Outer Territories in production. The value of Indonesia's exports doubled in the period 1900 to 1914 ; but although in 1900 only one-third of this export came from the islands outside Java, the contribution of these territories had risen in 1914 to 50 per cent of total exports. Their main export commodities were pepper, coffee, copra, rubber, sugar, tea, tobacco, tin and petroleum. It was the rubber boom of the nineteen-twenties which gave the Outer Provinces their definite lead in production over Java. The eco-nomic boom of the 'twenties seemed to provide final justification for the opening up of Indonesia to world trade by the Dutch. Between 1920 and 1930 Indonesian production and general pros-perity were far greater than they had ever been. Production of sugar and tea rose during the ten years by 100 per cent, copra by

50 per cent, and rubber by 200 per cent. In mineral production, tin increased by 50 per cent, coal and oil by nearly 100 per cent.

This tremendous expansion of production was checked by the economic depression which began in 1929. Nevertheless, strenuous efforts were made in Indonesia to counter the depression and to meet the changing conditions of international trade. Faced with a fall in world prices and all-round increases in international tariff protection, the Dutch after 1931 encouraged the development of local industry in Java for the manufacture of cheap consumer goods. There was a rapid expansion of industrialization in the late 'thirties. In fact the Dutch in the decade 1930–40 'were progressively welding Indonesia into a functional economic unit, with considerable inter-insular trade in foodstuffs and a concentration of manufacturing industries in Java, which was also becoming more and more the managerial nucleus for the whole system'.[1]

Yet Indonesia's economy as a whole remained substantially unchanged by either State or private capitalist enterprise. Indonesia remained first and foremost an agricultural country; her major problem continued to be the production of sufficient crops to feed her dense population, and in the Outer Provinces agricultural production for export was still the main occupation. For Indonesia as a whole the vast increase in agricultural production during the present century has been the most important result of the stimulus of external capital. With the application of modern engineering skill to land development the artificially irrigated area of Java was increased from 450,000 acres in 1895 to $3\frac{1}{2}$ million acres in 1939, at a cost of 250 million guilders. The prevention of soil erosion was another major task undertaken by the Dutch in Java, entailing the maintenance of State-controlled forests which covered nearly a quarter of the island.

The Indonesian peasant-farmer was responsible for almost the entire production of food crops, but he also had a large share in agricultural production for export. In 1938 native growers supplied as much as 48 per cent of exported rubber.

In the Philippines in 1900 large-scale production for export had not yet begun. Almost up to the end of the nineteenth century the

[1] C. A. Fisher, in East & Spate: *The Changing Map of Asia*, 1950, p. 211.

Philippine Islands remained virtually untouched by the changes that had drawn other countries in South-east Asia into the sphere of international trade and politics. The Filipino peasant in Luzon under Spanish rule was normally a tenant-farmer on a large feudal estate, cultivating tobacco and hemp as well as food crops, though in no great quantity. Foreign traders had been calling at Manila more frequently, especially since 1870, but the weakness of Spain's international position since the end of the eighteenth century had left the Philippines unaffected—for the time being—by the expansion of Western commercial interests in Asia, and uncommitted to the aims of a modern colonial power. The old paternalistic and monopolistic system of Spanish rule had in fact passed away, but nothing positive had taken its place; there was a temporary vacuum. The vacuum was filled by a Western power new to Asia, the United States of America. Spain and the United States were at war in April 1898, and on 1 May a Spanish fleet was defeated in Manila Bay. Spain surrendered the Philippines, and American civil government was proclaimed over the islands in 1902.

Economic expansion under American rule in the Philippines did not really get into its stride until after 1914. American capital was at first deterred by the clause of the cession agreement with Spain by which commercial legislation favouring the United States vis-à-vis other countries was barred for ten years. In 1909, however, the 'assimilation' principle was introduced; the Philippines were brought within the United States tariff system and their economy thus became tied to the American. This opened the door wide to American capital and technical skill. From 1914 onwards there was a rapid expansion in food production and in the export of commercial crops such as hemp, tobacco, sugar and copra, with a corresponding development of processing industries.

This expansion of agricultural production was achieved without superseding the tenant-farm unit; indeed it was American policy in the Philippines to prevent the growth of new estate plantation by a strict limitation of the amount of public land that might be taken up by individuals or companies. Rubber plantation was restricted in this way, and American rubber concerns were diverted to Malaya and Indonesia. In fact certain aspects of the mercantilist attitude of Britain to her North American colonies in earlier centuries had a modern counterpart in the commercial relations between the United States and the Philippines. American sugar and tobacco interests supported the limitation of large plantation industry in the Philippines; they had opposed admission of the islands into economic union with the United States in the first place, and later they were to lend strong support to the movement in favour of granting independence (without benefit of free access to United States markets) to the Philippine people.

Firmly rooted in the land, and sheltered behind the United States tariff wall, the export trade of the Philippines was a healthy, rapidly-growing plant, but its early growth depended almost entirely upon the sunshine of the American market. It was therefore considered to be one of the main prerequisites for a genuine independence that the Philippines export trade should be slowly and gently conditioned to the competitive world of international trade. Hence the device, adopted after 1935, of subjecting Philippines imports into the United States to an increasing proportion of the normal duties payable on goods of foreign origin; a gradual 'hardening-off' process.

Chapter Sixteen

POPULATION AND WELFARE

THE economic expansion of the previously underdeveloped countries of South-east Asia, which began about the year 1880 and which has still far to go, was made possible by the introduction and circulation of capital. But capital would have been useless without labour, enterprise and modern technical skill. The latter was inevitably lacking within South-east Asia until Western educational programmes became well advanced, and it remains seriously inadequate. The supply of labour, however, has been generally more than adequate for the requirements of economic development, but it has not everywhere been furnished by the indigenous peoples (in spite of considerable increases in their numbers), and has been maintained in most cases by the immigration of Asians from outside the region, from India and from China. Commercial and industrial enterprise, again, has been mainly furnished by elements from outside, especially European and Chinese.

The last hundred and fifty years have witnessed a remarkable increase in the indigenous population of South-east Asia. Java, the major example of a country developed under Western rule, has shown by far the largest population increase. Having apparently remained more or less stationary during the eighteenth century, Java's population grew from less than 4 million in 1800 to 28 million in 1900 and 48 million in 1940. The island has become one of the most thickly populated agricultural areas of the world, with a population density of over 900 per square mile. Though it contains less than 7 per cent of the total land area of Indonesia, Java holds over two-thirds of the total population of some 90 million.

The tremendous increase of population in Java poses an exceedingly difficult problem for any government. It has tended to offset the most strenuous measures for welfare and development

by reducing agricultural holdings to dwarf proportions, by
increasing the class of landless agricultural workers, and by producing further indebtedness and food shortage. The Dutch began
to tackle the population problem in the nineteen-thirties by
promoting industrialization, an extremely long-term policy, and
by encouraging migration to the Outer Islands, a task which was
rendered no less difficult by the fact that conveniently accessible
areas of fertile soil (e.g. in Sumatra, Bali and Lombok) were already
densely populated. The system of shifting cultivation (*ladang*),
widely practised in the Outer Islands, formed another obstacle to
the opening up of new areas for permanent (or *sawah*) cultivation
by immigrants from Java.

Vietnam is another South-east Asian country which contains
areas of unusually high population density. Its overall increase
of population (from probably 7 million in 1800 to 23 million in
1940) has not been as spectacular as that of Java, but Vietnam's
Red River delta region of Tonkin sustains more persons than any
equivalent area of Java, its population density being as high as
1,000 per square mile. Vietnam's other great delta region, that of
the Mekong in Cochin-China, has the comparatively low density
figure of something over 250 persons per square mile.

The population of Siam (Thailand) increased from perhaps 6
million in 1800 to about 16 million in 1940, and there was a closely
similar increase in the Philippines. Population growth in Burma
has also been on roughly the same scale, reaching over 16 million
in 1940. The number of Malays in the Malay Peninsula in 1800
was probably well under half a million; in 1947 there were
2½ million. These, however, now formed but one element in a
total population of 6 million.

The demographic position of the Malays is a striking illustration
of the fact that, along with a rapid increase in the indigenous people
of South-east Asia, there has been in some cases an even more rapid
increase in other Asian elements of the population. The presence
of these elements has created the difficult economic and political
problems of the 'plural society', problems which have been
especially acute in South-east Asia, though not, of course, peculiar
to it. Basically the plural society is no new thing in South-east

Asia, since the region has always formed a kind of social laboratory in which much interaction between diverse peoples and cultures has taken place. The modern problem of the plural society is really an old problem in a new and enlarged form. Naturally the peculiar features of the basic problem differ in the various South-east Asian countries today ; in some they are very much more complex than in others.

The emergence of the plural society of South-east Asia in its modern form has been closely linked with the expansion of Western administration, commerce and capital during the last hundred years, and especially since 1870. Chinese and Indian immigrants were attracted to most South-east Asian countries by the opportunities for material advancement offered by expanding money economies combined with stable administrations. If South-east Asia's geographical situation, intermediate between India and China, has been a permanent factor making for social and cultural complexity in the region throughout its history, the combined effect of the wide extension of Western rule in South-east Asia, and of population pressure within the great neighbouring countries, has been an unprecedently powerful contributory factor in the last hundred years.

The indigenous peoples of South-east Asia in general showed little desire to compete for the prizes offered by this brave new world. They shared indirectly, in varying degrees, in the general increase of material prosperity, but they did so for the most part in their traditional role of subsistence agriculturists. They left direct participation in industry and commerce to immigrant Chinese and Indians, better equipped for success in a competitive money economy by their experience of the struggle for existence in their own homelands. For this reason, the new economic forces and incentives introduced from the West resulted in a violent disturbance of the social and economic balance of South-east Asia. They attracted new immigrants to the region, and at the same time they had the effect, broadly speaking, of creating a cleavage between the indigenous and the immigrant, and between the two different ways of life which they represented, the old way and the new. On the one hand, the new economic forces tended to cause disintegration of the traditional life and customs of the old societies; on the other hand, the same forces called into existence new communities of men uprooted from their homelands but unrooted in their adopted countries, thereby creating the unbalanced plural society with its lack of cohesion or common purpose. For not only were the typical class divisions of Western society reproduced, as well as a division between urban and rural interests, but those divisions were accentuated and complicated by racial differences.

The social disintegration which accompanied economic expansion has not, of course, spread evenly throughout the whole Southeast Asian region. For one reason or another some countries have managed to survive economic regeneration without too severe a loss of social cohesion. And where disintegration has taken place, there is reason to suppose that in the long run of history this will prove to have been a transitional stage, if also a painful one, in social evolution. Nationalism now seems likely to provide the reintegrating force which is needed to transform the plural societies of South-east Asia. Nationalism itself, however, depends upon a sense of common purpose. And in the complex societies of Southeast Asia this means that many divided loyalties have somehow to be reconciled or superseded.

In a general sense the immigrant Asians in South-east Asia have formed a new middle class between the native rulers and European administrators on the one side and the indigenous peasant peoples on the other. Class divisions, however, do not necessarily correspond everywhere in the region to ethnic differences. In Malaya, for example, there are clear divisions of class, among both Indians and Chinese, between the merchant and the plantation or mine worker. And there are wide contrasts in occupation among members of the same ethnic group in different parts of South-east Asia, as, for example, the Chinese rice-exporters of Siam and the Chinese subsistence farmers of west Borneo. At the same time there has been considerable social fluidity, especially among the Chinese; for class has been based almost solely upon wealth, so that it has been possible for the enterprising individual to rise rapidly in the social scale.

Most of the South-east Asian Chinese came from original homes in China's south-eastern provinces of Kwangtung, Fukien and

Kwangsi. Their number in South-east Asia has been estimated as not more than 15 million out of a total population of some 180 million; but the part they have played in the economic development of the region has been a much more important one than mere numbers would suggest. Both their numerical and their economic relationship to the indigenous people among whom they have lived is perhaps most strikingly illustrated by the record of their position in Indonesia.

Numbers of Chinese settled temporarily or permanently in Indonesia throughout the Dutch period, mostly Hokkiens during the seventeenth and eighteenth centuries, with some Hakkas in west Borneo. With the development of mining and plantation agriculture in the second half of the nineteenth century there followed a period of large immigration of Chinese labour, especially to the east coast of Sumatra and the islands of Banka and Billiton. This period lasted until the end of the nineteen-thirties, by which time the flow of immigration had greatly diminished as increasing numbers of Indonesians came to work on the new estates, and deterrent legislation had been introduced against imported labour. Many of these immigrants returned to China as they had originally intended, but others established a place for themselves in Indonesia as artisans, small traders or shopkeepers, thus joining the ranks of the resident Chinese community which had been established, with its headquarters in Batavia, for many generations. But although the number of Chinese in Indonesia (including locally born and immigrant) was more than doubled in the first thirty years of the present century, in 1930 they still amounted to a mere 2 per cent of the total population.

The importation of Chinese labour into Indonesia was a temporary expedient to meet the requirements of capitalist methods of production at an initial stage. When this wave of immigration died away, and increasing proportions of the Chinese of Indonesia were permanently resident and locally born, their unity as an economic class was largely restored; as a group they reverted to their traditional role of middlemen in Indonesian society. Especially in Java, where the plantation worker was Indonesian and where ownership of agricultural land by non-Indonesians was forbidden, the Chinese stood between the Indonesian village and the outside world as the purchaser and provider, the general agent, and the moneylender. In the cities and towns he was the wholesale merchant, the shipper, the banker, the businessman, the technician or the artisan. Almost the whole of the industry and internal trade of the country was in Chinese hands.

The stratification of society in Burma was another indication of the way in which the Asian immigrant could adapt himself to Western-style economic and administrative techniques, and could interpose himself between ruling class and indigenous population. This middle class was almost everywhere created, sustained and enriched by Western rule; at the same time, without it the machinery of Western rule could not have turned, its purposes could not have been achieved. The British administrative structure in Burma was largely built out of Indian experience and with Indian personnel. The government relied upon the services of Indian officials and clerks, engineers and doctors. 'Whatever was not English in the new administration was Indian.'[1] Indians also predominated in commercial life as merchants and retailers; they controlled most of Burma's foreign trade, about three-quarters of which was with India. Over half the external capital in Burma in 1941 was Indian, and over a third of the cultivated land of Burma was Indian-owned. Agricultural and industrial labour was largely Indian.

The Indian middle class and Indian labour in Burma, like the corresponding Chinese immigrants in Malaya, were mostly temporary and transient settlers. Members of the middle class would return to their homeland when they reached retiring age; much of the migration of labour was seasonal. Over 5 million Indians arrived in Burma between 1911 and 1927, but 4½ million left the country during the same period. Again as with the Chinese in Malaya and other parts of South-east Asia, a considerable proportion of the earnings of Indians in Burma was sent out of the country in remittances to their homeland.

The Chinese in Burma took second place to Indians in the commercial life of the country; in 1941 there were altogether perhaps 250,000 Chinese as compared with about a million

[1] Furnivall, J. S., in *South Asia in the World Today*, 1950, p. 6.

Indians. They, too, appeared as merchants, especially in the rice and timber trades ; as shopkeepers ; and in the mines as industrial workers. Forming a comparatively small immigrant group, the Chinese in Burma tended to merge more fully into the rest of the community than they did elsewhere in South-east Asia.

In Malaya, by contrast, the Chinese in 1947 amounted to about 45 per cent of the total population, whereas Indians accounted for only 10 per cent. The Straits Settlements had attracted a number of Indian merchants before the separation from India in 1867, and Chettiars had acquired much of the most valuable land. When the Malay States were opened to rubber plantation in the present century, there was a steady flow of temporary labour from India and back again, and Indians became numerous in government services. The working conditions of Indian labour in Malaya were closely supervised by arrangement between the governments.

Immigration of all foreigners into Malaya was unrestricted up to 1930, and the Indian community included a growing number of Chettiar and Sikh moneylenders ; but the ownership of rice-lands was secured to the Malay. After 1933 the Straits Settlements had power to restrict the numbers of immigrants entering Malaya through the main ports ; locally recruited labour, Chinese and Indian, was now becoming more easily available ; in other words, labour was becoming less transient. A ban on emigration from India in 1938 had the effect of emphasizing this trend as far as Indian labour was concerned.

Chinese labour in Malaya had been no less transient than Indian. Although an estimated 5 million Chinese arrived in Malaya during the nineteenth century, and a further 12 million between 1900 and 1947, there were only something over $2\frac{1}{2}$ million there at the latter date. Chinese were to be found at every economic level, from that of coolie or squatter to that of capitalist employer or banker, but in general they formed a commercial middle class. With the increase in the proportion of female Chinese entering the country after about 1920, the rhythm of ebb and flow between China and Malaya slowed down ; Chinese family life became more widespread and more continuous in Malaya, and settlement became more permanent.

In Siam the Chinese, forming more than one-fifth of the total population, held an unchallenged position as an economic middle class. They owned most of the rice mills and controlled the rice market. They planted and marketed rubber. They were the moneylenders as well as the tin-miners and market-gardeners.

Chinese, along with Indian Chettiars, were also moneylenders in Indo-China. When northern Vietnam was being opened up by the French, Chinese labour was employed on railway construction and in mining, but the majority of Chinese immigrants by-passed the northern provinces of Tonkin and Annam, with their comparatively crowded and industrious Sinicized population, and entered the more economically receptive southern regions of Cochin-China and Cambodia. By 1941 these latter contained about 85 per cent of the total Chinese population of the country. The greatest concentration of Chinese was to be found in the city of Cholon-Saigon in Cochin-China. There they were the buyers, millers and exporters of rice; they also owned sawmills and sugar refineries. Outside the cities there were Chinese market-gardeners, rice-growers, and (along the Gulf of Siam) pepper-planters.

There was rapid immigration of Chinese into North Borneo after the British North Borneo Company had been established there in 1882. Once again the immigrants formed mainly trading and artisan sections clearly separated from the mass of native peasants.

In the Philippines, Chinese and mixed Spanish-Chinese formed part of the dominant economic class as landowners and merchants. In 1947 slightly less than one-third of the foreign trade of the Philippines was in Chinese hands.

The expansion of commerce and of commercial agriculture in South-east Asia after 1870, and the corresponding enlargement of the field of colonial administration, had also brought a considerable increase in the number of Europeans temporarily resident in the region. These, of course, formed only a tiny fraction of the whole population, but they held key positions in commerce and banking, and, as government servants, they planned and directed the various public services essential to development along Western lines. They introduced and managed new systems of transport, public health, education and law.

Paul Popper, Ltd.

THE SHWE DAGON PAGODA, RANGOON

The construction of roads and railways was primarily designed to assist production for export. In Malaya, for example, the modern transportation systems which replaced river transport helped to attract external capital to plantation and mining by ensuring that produce would be carried swiftly to the main ports of Singapore and Penang. In Burma, Siam and Vietnam, however, where the ports were directly served by large river systems, water transport was supplemented, not displaced, by railways and roads. River and ocean shipping met, and export produce was therefore conveniently transhipped, at the Vietnamese ports of Saigon and Haiphong for example. Haiphong was the outlet for the river system of Tonkin as much as for the French-built railway that wound its way down 6,000 feet from the Chinese province of Yunnan to the sea. Saigon was the outlet for the Mekong river and the focus of the waterways of the Mekong delta ; its immense export trade was fed by water transportation of the rice and corn of Cochin-China and Cambodia.

Public health services, apart from the humanitarian considerations involved, were a necessary adjunct of economic development in tropical areas. Generally speaking, welfare and development were parallel aims in colonial policy. Medical and other social services were financed out of a part of the revenues resulting from economic expansion. For example in Malaya, where economic progress (though limited in direction) was especially rapid, there was a very heavy expenditure on public health ; full advantage was taken of the latest discoveries in the science of tropical medicine, and an Institute of Medical Research was set up in Malaya itself.

Again, the new educational systems were generally designed at first to meet the requirements of economic expansion. It was when the economic need for systematic instruction along Western lines had fully arisen that government departments of education were set up in the various South-east Asian countries. But, from the start, education was inevitably a powerful agent of social and political change as well as of economic development ; and as time went on educational policy became more consciously shaped by these wider considerations.

In Burma the new educational system entered into competition not only with Western missionary schools already founded, but with a long-established indigenous system of education in the Buddhist monastic village schools. The latter, to Western eyes, were too closely associated with organized religion to be suitable as instruments of a State-controlled education, and they therefore found no place in the new system. Vernacular schools, sponsored but not directly controlled by the government, were established under the management of district councils ; as a whole, however, these schools were badly equipped and poorly attended ; they had little or no value as avenues to success in the new economic environment. The main direct concern of the government was with the establishment and development of mixed schools—in which vernacular instruction led on to instruction in English—and of purely English schools ; these were the training-grounds for the many clerks whom government offices and commercial houses required. A university was founded at Rangoon in 1923 for training administrators, teachers, doctors and engineers.

As in other South-east Asian countries, many children of immigrant Chinese took advantage of these new educational facilities. But the Chinese as a community preferred to establish and maintain their own independent schools, which would be free to follow the direction of educational policy and practice in China itself. After the Chinese revolution of 1911, education in these independent Chinese schools of South-east Asia became increasingly imbued with a nationalist spirit that was directed to the homeland rather than related to the countries in which they were situated. Such schools therefore tended to emphasize and to perpetuate the social and political detachment of the Chinese from the South-east Asian societies in which they lived.

In the Malayan Straits Settlements educational policy was less obviously linked with economic need than it was elsewhere. Government responsibility for education began comparatively early—the Straits Settlements Department of Education was founded in 1870—so that economic considerations did not predominate when the foundations of the educational system were being laid. The original purpose was to establish a system of free Malay vernacular schools, leaving English schools largely to private enterprise. But when an educational system was being extended to the Federated Malay States both English and Malay schools were established under government control. Vernacular instruction remained the basis of the educational system in Malaya, but it was English schooling that had the greater economic value. At first the governments provided vernacular instruction in the Malay language only; later they opened schools for Tamils. The Chinese were able to take care of their own vernacular education; and although Chinese students predominated in the English schools, a great many more attended the independent vernacular schools which were run almost entirely as if they were in China itself. In 1938 there were over 91,000 children in these Chinese schools as compared with less than 27,000 in government and government-sponsored English schools.

Thus in Malaya, while Western-controlled and Western-inspired education slowly but inevitably instilled the idea of nationalism, the actual pattern of educational organization tended to obstruct the development of a broad-based nationalism by accentuating the racial, linguistic and social divisions that had already arisen within the country. To break down the barriers of social pluralism was fundamentally an educational problem, but it was a problem that had been rendered all the more difficult by the early effects of education itself, which tended to underline pluralism.

Colleges and universities for higher study were also founded in various South-east Asian countries in conformity with Western ideas. The degrees of the Medical College in Singapore, founded in 1905, were recognized by the British General Medical Council in 1916. Malaya had an arts and science college (Raffles College, Singapore) in 1928 and an agricultural college in 1931. But the main emphasis everywhere was on elementary and technical instruction. In Vietnam, for example, half a million children were attending the lower elementary schools in 1939; of these only 10 per cent would go on to higher elementary schools, and only 1 per cent to secondary schools.

Siam travelled an independent road towards westernization, but the luggage that accompanied her, in the shape of educational and other Western-inspired institutions, was very similar to that which was carried by the dependent countries of South-east Asia. Her modern system of education, introduced after 1891, allowed for instruction in English as well as in Thai. But, unlike the British system in Burma, the new educational structure in Siam incorporated the old tradition of elementary education in the Buddhist monastic school. The student was gradually introduced to the study of English and of Western school subjects in the primary and secondary schools. Alongside these were a number of private English schools, run mostly by American missions. From the schools a student might proceed to institutions for technical or professional instruction, such as a medical college, a teachers' training college or, after 1917, the Chulalongkorn University at Bangkok. As elsewhere, the Chinese had their own schools where Chinese was the medium of instruction, and where much of the instruction was devoted after 1911 to the glorification of the Chinese republic.

Similar Chinese schools existed in Indonesia. There, however, the Dutch had also provided government schools for Chinese since 1908. The Dutch were comparatively slow in introducing systematic vernacular education, but when they did so (after 1907) they provided separate educational facilities for each ethnic group —Indonesians, Chinese and Europeans. As with the Malays in Malaya, only a small proportion of Indonesian children went beyond the elementary vernacular schools; other races predominated in government primary and secondary schools. There were over 2,300,000 children in elementary schools in 1939, but only 53,000 in primary or intermediate schools; while a mere 777 students passed out of the secondary schools. In the same year there were 1,100 students attending the university that was centred in Jakarta.

The American administration in the Philippines, like the British in Burma, was guided in educational matters by the principle of the separation of Church and State. The Spanish Catholic schools, although they had in fact brought the educational standards of the Filipinos to a comparatively high level, were virtually superseded by government schools designed for more strictly secular ends. In 1939 nearly 2 million students were attending State schools, and it was expected that by 1950 the number would be nearly doubled.

Modern education in South-east Asia has aimed primarily at

adjusting the child to a changing economic environment; it has been primarily an instrument of economic change, only secondarily one of political change, and only to a limited degree one of social change. Equally, education has been regarded by parents and students in South-east Asia (rather more generally than in other parts of the world) as first and foremost an economic asset. Educational systems have been provided from above, mostly by Western administrations, as part and parcel of a process of change in which economic aims have predominated. From the South-east Asian point of view, education has been regarded as a kind of machine from which, by diligent attention and by carrying out a sequence of clearly defined instructions, one might eventually obtain a ticket of admission to the happy world of economic gain that the West had created. Education has been associated with making a living rather than with life ; all the more so as Western educational methods and curricula often bore little relation to life as it was being lived in South-east Asia. But the educational problems of South-east Asia were of the kind that belong inevitably to a period when cultural change is slowly following in the wake of economic change.

Modern education, and the economic progress with which it has been associated, have been confined to only a small proportion of the population of South-east Asia. The vast majority of the inhabitants of the South-east Asian countries were, and still are, small peasant farmers. Before the revolutionary economic changes of modern times, the typical South-east Asian was the peasant who was whole or part owner of the land he cultivated. He was a subsistence farmer, primarily concerned with producing from his land enough to maintain his family and no more. He could be virtually self-sufficient in food, clothing and shelter. If he occasionally sold some of his produce it was usually in order to meet a temporary need for money—when he had to pay rent or taxes, or to repay an instalment on a loan, or when he wanted to buy something that came from outside the village, such as salt, iron, or manufactured cloth. His life centred in the village and was surrounded by the laws, customs and beliefs that the village embodied and upheld.

In some ways the economic changes of modern times improved the lot of the South-east Asian peasant. He might participate, even if only to a minute degree, in the profits of commercial agriculture. He might acquire a kerosene lamp, a bicycle, or a sewing machine. But in other ways the new economic forces were a threat to his existence and to that of the village community. The new intrusive economic forces demanded freedom of competition, but the old social institutions of the country, if they were to survive, needed not freedom but protection. The introduction of a money economy, unaccompanied by adequate credit facilities or social protection, tended to place the native farmer at the mercy of the small capitalist—sometimes a European entrepreneur, but much more often a Chinese or Indian moneylender. In the new economic conditions the peasant would easily fall into debt ; he might finally lose his land and become a landless, seasonal wage-earner. Work on estate agriculture might take him away from the village and from its traditional customs, habits and restraints. Indeed the whole spirit of the new economic system, with its emphasis on the individual and on free competition between individuals, struck at the roots of the traditional group institutions—the family and the village, upset the balance of native society, and produced a wide-spread social *malaise*. Western law and order gave the peasant more physical security in his home, but also helped him to lose his social security by upholding the sanctity of the moneylender's contract in the name of freedom of enterprise. The economic freedom that the West admired often meant for South-east Asia freedom for acquisitive immigrants—European, Chinese or Indian —to exploit the economic weakness and the social conservatism of the native peasantry. Western rule brought wealth, but it also brought wide contrasts in wealth ; it created new classes—the wage-earner, the entrepreneur, the educated élite—but comparatively few of the native inhabitants succeeded in moving out of the peasant class into a better one ; it brought about tremendous economic development, but it usually left the native inhabitant a poor man in a newly rich country.

Many of the native institutions of Burmese society were under-mined when the country came under direct British rule. There had been a kind of indirect rule through a graded system of hereditary headmen, each of whom was responsible for the 'circle', or group of villages, under him. The villages themselves had been left to run their own affairs as social and economic units. Under British rule, however, the headman was put aside, the 'circle' was broken down into its component villages, and each village became an administrative unit directly subject to government regulations for the maintenance of order and the collection of revenue (1885–90). The village thus lost much of its self-reliance, its individuality and its social significance.

The new economic forces at work in Burma had a contributory effect in their tendency to cause social disintegration and to dissolve family and village ties. Rural community life was largely undermined by peasant indebtedness which was associated with the presence of Indian tenants and cultivators. Neither the British administration's loan scheme for peasant cultivators (1883–4), nor the Co-operative Credit movement that began at the beginning of the present century, did much to help matters.

The position of the Buddhist monks in the religious and social life of the community was also greatly weakened under British rule. The British administration, acting on the principle of *laissez-faire*, did not wish to interfere with Buddhism, but neither was it prepared to grant official recognition to the Buddhist ecclesiastical code, or to find a place in the new educational system for the traditional Buddhist monastic school which every Burman boy had attended as a matter of course.

The growth of rural indebtedness was a problem common to all the South-east Asian countries after the introduction of money economies, but some governments took more effective steps than others to ensure that indebtedness did not lead to the loss of the peasant's land. Not enough was done in Burma. In French Indo-China, although positive measures to check the growth of rural indebtedness were largely ineffective (e.g. the Agricultural Credit organization which was developed after 1914), there was some attempt to protect native ownership of land both from the grasp of the moneylender and from the encroachment of commercial agriculture. Some large-scale agriculture in Indo-China was established on land purchased from native cultivators, but most was based

either on land subject only to shifting or *ladang* cultivation by
natives, or on public land leased from local authorities or the
central government.

There was considerable indebtedness among peasant cultivators
in Malaya, but the Malay was assured of undisturbed ownership in
the rice-lands. His immediate position as a cultivator was not
prejudiced by the development of rubber plantation, indeed he was
able to supplement his income by becoming a rubber grower
himself in a small way; but the improvement in his economic
position was far behind the material progress of the country as a
whole.

The Dutch in Indonesia took early measures to protect the
peasant proprietor from the worst effects of the impact of a money
economy and capitalist enterprise. They showed that an economic
policy of *laissez-faire* need not preclude measures for safeguarding
the structure of native society. Legislation passed in the eighteen-
seventies prevented the alienation of land to non-Indonesians.
Land for tea and rubber plantation had to be obtained on long lease
from the government; it was unsuitable for wet rice cultivation,
and often had to be first cleared of tropical forest. Land for sugar
and tobacco (which amounted to roughly one-eighth of the total
area of plantation agriculture) was generally obtained on annual
lease, and at government-controlled rents, from the villages.
After 1900 the Dutch 'ethical' policy strove to protect the peasant
from the moneylender by the institution of government pawnshops, credit banks, and village banks—the latter providing the
cultivator with seed and equipment against repayment in rice.

Besides safeguards of this kind, there were constructive measures
for restoring the social strength of the Indonesian village community. A hundred years earlier the village was still a self-
contained and self-governing unit. It governed itself, according to
the long-established principles of *adat* or customary law, through
its own headman and council, with the help of various other
officials who were elected and supported by the community as a
whole. But the village had been greatly weakened by the culture
system, for under it the headman and his fellows inevitably
suffered a reduction in social status from that of elected leaders of
the village to that of nominated agents of the central government.

Added to this, the economic forces of the post-1870 era also had the effect of loosening the traditional bonds and loyalties of village life. The conscious purpose of the Village Act, passed by the Dutch in 1906, was therefore to restore to the Indonesian village its independence and its social solidarity. This was not an attempt to revive an 'old world' village mentality or to preserve the village as a kind of museum piece. It was rather an attempt to awaken in the village a sense of its responsibility and importance in the whole process of modernization. The village council was to be encouraged to develop as an elected local authority, not only managing the traditional affairs and the property of the peasant community but also carrying into local effect the new schemes for increasing responsibility and welfare. For if the ideas and methods imported from the West were to have any real success, they would have to be adapted in and by the village community. Adaptation, as opposed to assimilation, was the keynote of Dutch policy.

For the native peoples of South-east Asia in general, however, exclusion rather than adaptation was the reality of their position under Western rule. Economic progress left them behind. Wealth was created around them, but they were able to acquire only a minor share in the distribution of wealth. Their welfare did not keep pace with economic development, because the kinds of economic development that took place under the impetus of external capital did not greatly affect them, and therefore did not bring about a *general* rise in the level of economic welfare. The employment of external capital did not bring about a general rise in the level of production, and, for that reason, did not create a widely distributed social capital. The 1940–1 report of the High Commissioner for the Philippines stated the point clearly with reference to the local conditions. 'The bulk of the newly-created income has gone to the government, the landlords, and to urban areas, and has served but little to ameliorate living conditions among the almost feudal peasantry and tenantry.' Facts such as these disproved the easy assumption that free economic development would automatically bring about a general increase in prosperity and welfare.

Chapter Seventeen

THE GROWTH OF NATIONALISM

WESTERN rule created revolution in South-east Asia. This does not mean merely, or even primarily, that Western rule created revolt against itself; but rather that, by introducing powerful new economic and political forces and concepts, it set in motion a whole revolutionary process—a process that was, in a sense, a renaissance. For South-east Asia's revolt against Western rule was not the only, or even the most important, symptom of revolution; at least equally significant was the revolt of South-east Asia against its own past. From the viewpoint of history this was simply the latest—though certainly likely to be at once the most rapid and the most far-reaching—of the series of revolutions that South-east Asia has had to undergo as a result of the impact of external commercial and cultural forces. The really significant aspect of South-east Asia's history in modern times is to be found not so much in the dependent or colonial status of the countries concerned, as in their speedy emergence, under the drive of irresistible forces, from a medieval into a modern world.

The growth of nationalism was one of the symptoms of this revolution in South-east Asia. The spirit of nationalism grew inevitably with the spread of education, which not only instilled the political ideas implicit in Western culture but also stimulated individual criticism, comparison and ambition. In urban areas especially nationalism became widely felt, if not clearly understood, as a result of the spread of literacy and the development of the press. But political consciousness was confined to what was after all a small minority, so that nationalism in South-east Asia could not properly be equated with democracy. The peasants of South-east Asia's villages, largely illiterate, retained their traditional conception of government as some mysterious and inscrutable power that might have to be placated but could not possibly be controlled.

Within South-east Asia itself the spirit of nationalism fed upon discontent engendered by the wide contrasts between economic progress and general social welfare, between the 'liberty' of Western literature and the 'authority' of colonial life, between the decisive political power of a handful of Europeans and the lack of political influence of the growing body of educated Asians. From outside there came the influence and example of national self-assertion in the neighbour countries of Asia, also inspired by political ideas drawn from the West. In India the National Congress Party was founded in 1885, and after 1906 its declared aim became *swaraj* or self-government for India. The Japanese, after attacking a Russian fleet at Port Arthur in 1904, completely defeated the main fleet which the Russians had then despatched to the Pacific, in the battle of Tsushima in May 1905. Japan's victory created a deep impression on the minds of the people of Asia and contributed most powerfully to the growth of national consciousness. The Japanese had shown that an Asian people were perfectly capable of learning, and indeed improving upon, the techniques of the West. For other Asian countries, westernization might be the road to liberation from Western control. Japan's example stimulated Chinese nationalism and strengthened the growing demand for a radical change in China's political system, a demand which outpaced the constitutional reforms introduced by the Chinese Court during the first ten years of the present century and which finally swept the country into revolution. China's revolution of 1911, in its turn, greatly impressed the South-east Asian countries, though its first effect there was to arouse in the immigrant Chinese communities a national consciousness that was directed outwards to the homeland, so that for long it remained detached from, and at times even antagonistic to, nationalist movements that arose from within the South-east Asian countries themselves. The victory of the Allied powers in World War I, widely represented as a vindication of the rights of small nations, added a further stimulus to the growth of nationalism in Asia. Finally, Japan's powerful influence came into full play once again in World War II, stimulating South-east Asian nationalism both directly by her slogan of 'Asia for the Asiatics' and by her military success against Western colonial powers, and indirectly by the reaction

which her own ruthless and self-interested rule soon brought
against herself.

The governments of the South-east Asian countries responded,
each in its own way, to the development of nationalist feeling.
Where the feeling was weak, the response was also weak; where
the feeling was strong, the response was not always equally strong.
But at one stage or another in every case the growth of nationalism
was met, if not exactly greeted, by constitutional and administrative
changes intended to satisfy or to soften both the general aspirations
of a people and the particular ambitions of outstanding individuals.

Nowhere in South-east Asia was nationalism met with a more
conscious air of cordiality than in the Philippines under the rule of
the United States of America, themselves historically an outgrowth
of colonialism. Spanish rule had conceded little to nationalism
before the coming of the Americans in 1898. Because education
was well advanced in the Philippines, nationalist feeling was
awakened comparatively early. It was also at first comparatively
mild. The Young Filipino Party, led by José Rizal, was gradualist,
constitutional and intellectual in outlook. But when the Spanish
government had shown itself reluctant to concede even moderate
reforms this party lost control of the nationalist movement to
another group, the Katipunan, pledged to direct revolutionary
action. As a result of the armed struggle that broke out in 1898,
Rizal paid for his earlier leadership with his life; but the new
revolutionary leader, Aguinaldo, suffered no worse a fate than
exile, and a temporary exile at that. For after the outbreak of war
between Spain and the United States in 1898, and the destruction
of the Spanish fleet in Manila Bay on 1 May, Aguinaldo returned
from exile, by arrangement with the Americans, to proclaim the
renewal of the national struggle against Spain.

American forces occupied Manila in August 1898, and in the
following February the American Senate formally accepted peace
terms that included the surrender of the Philippines by Spain. The
United States had become a South-east Asian power. As such she
had now to deal with South-east Asian nationalism in a country
where it had begun to manifest itself early and violently. The
revolutionary nationalists fought on against the new occupying

power, and it was not until 1901 that Aguinaldo gave in and guerrilla resistance began to collapse. A civil government, the Philippine Commission, then took over from the military administration, and proceeded to carry through a series of projects for the rapid modernization of public works, hygiene, transport, education and justice. The system of paternalist autocracy thus created was modified in 1907 by the addition of an elected legislative assembly with the right to advise and to warn, but without executive powers. This made it practical policy for the nationalists to revert to constitutional methods; a new Nationalist Party took up the political struggle for independence. It met with an increasingly sympathetic response after the Democratic victory in the U.S. elections of 1913; and in 1916, in a wave of war-time enthusiasm for the principle of self-determination, representative government in the Philippines was carried a stage further towards responsible government. Filipinos obtained a predominant, though not yet a final, voice in the Commission as well as in the Assembly; the United States promised at the same time to recognize their independence as soon as a stable government could be established.

Between 1913 and 1921 Filipinos held an increasing proportion of the appointments in government services, and the Filipino-dominated legislature pursued a radical, if somewhat reckless, policy of economic nationalism and nationalization. With the return of the Republican party to power in the United States in 1921 there was a considerable cooling-off in American enthusiasm for Philippine independence. But after the world slump of 1931 American economic interests found reason for supporting the aims of Filipino nationalism in the expectation that the gain of political independence for the islands would fairly entail the loss of special economic advantages in the American market, so that Philippine products (sugar, tobacco, and coconut oil for example) would no longer be able to compete on equal terms with American products or continue to operate against purely American commercial interests in other ways.

In 1935 the Philippines obtained a new constitution which conferred self-government but not yet full independence. There was to be a further ten-year period of preparation for the responsibilities of political independence, with at the same time a gradual exposure of the islands to the rigours of economic independence through the slow removal of their economy from under the sheltering wall of American tariff protection. This period of preparation brought some disillusionment. The constitution was purely and serenely democratic in theory, but the Filipino Nationalist Government under the presidency of Manuel Quezon was thoroughly oligarchic in practice. The achievement of a measure of political independence did not diminish, but rather underlined, the extent to which the Philippines depended upon American trade, investment, and technical and managerial skill. Some adjustments were found necessary to meet the realities of the economic situation. The United States agreed in 1939 to slow down the pace at which duties on imports from the Philippines were to be raised, and undertook to do so without prejudice to the grant of full political independence that had been promised for 1944. Before that year arrived, however, the Philippines had found themselves within the Japanese sphere of 'co-prosperity'.

The economic dependence of the Philippines in 1939, after a lengthy period of clearly avowed preparation for self-government, was in striking contrast to the economic independence which Indonesia had achieved as a result of Dutch colonial policy. In 1939 only 18 per cent of Indonesia's foreign trade was with Holland. Indonesian nationalists may have had a harder struggle than those of the Philippines, but in the end they inherited a sounder economic basis for national independence.

As in the Philippines, nationalism in Indonesia was at first a moderate and gradualist movement confined to a small group of Western-educated idealists. It was a movement of thought which developed slowly into an organized political movement with the spread of Western education and the growth of urbanization after the opening of the present century. It was greatly stimulated by the example of Japan's progress, which was interpreted as proof that energetic modernization along Western lines could enable an Asian state to assert itself internationally and to gain the respect of the Western powers. This point was brought home to the educated Indonesian when, in 1899, Japanese citizens were accorded equality of status with Europeans in the East Indies; it was emphasized again in 1909, four years after Japan's victory over Russia, when a Japanese consulate was opened in Batavia.

Westernization was the declared aim of Indonesian nationalism in its first organized form, the Budi Utomo or 'Glorious Endeavour', an association mainly composed of Western-educated Javanese officials, which took shape in 1908. This group was primarily concerned with training its members for social and educational leadership ; its battle was to be against poverty and ignorance rather than against 'imperialism' ; its aim was a gradual and general advance, under the guiding hand of Dutch rule, towards Western standards of living and of social and political conduct. But if the basis of Indonesian nationalism were to be broadened, its aims would need to have a more popular appeal than those of Budi Utomo.

Such an appeal was found in the developing aims of the Sarekat Islam movement which began in 1911–12. This movement gained early popularity by its ability to present economic progress as a social and religious necessity for Indonesians. It appealed to religious and racial emotions by pointing to the contrast between the economic strength of the Chinese in Indonesia and the economic weakness of the Indonesians themselves. It emphasized the need for active co-operation amongst Javanese in order to remove the hold of the Chinese middleman on the internal trade of their country. Drawing its real support thus from the villages rather than from the intelligentsia, Sarekat Islam gradually developed into a national movement ; and as it did so its earlier aims merged into the wider aim of national independence.

Until the First World War, it was generally expected that independence would be gained by easy stages and by peaceful methods. But nationalism in Indonesia assumed a more aggressive and impatient attitude, as it did in India, after the war. The wartime emphasis on self-determination and the post-war claims of nationalism in Europe made educated Indonesians—and especially Indonesian students in Dutch universities—more vividly and painfully aware of a sense of national injustice and personal frustration.

Yet up to this point, and for some years longer, there was much common ground between Dutch and Indonesians on the question of self-government. Dutch 'ethical' policy was, in broad aspect, a preparation for Indonesian self-government. But it remained always the Dutch contention that the 'self' that was to govern must be the genuine self of Indonesia, that modern democratic institutions should and could be built up slowly and cautiously upon the basis of traditional institutions, that new political ideas must be adapted to old forms and forces in Indonesian society. The municipal and district councils inaugurated by the Dutch in Java from 1903 onwards were intended to be instruments of education in local self-government. Although for a long time these councils contained Dutch majorities, the Dutch were there as free citizens and not as 'official' members bound to support government policy in everything. The Village Act of 1906 was intended to encourage the full development of local responsibility ; it aimed at using the villages as training-grounds in practical democracy, and so adapting the traditional spirit of village self-government to the larger and more complex requirements of a modern state. Dutch administration in the larger territorial divisions, in provinces and residencies, was carried out generally on the principle of indirect rule, which allowed for a certain measure of non-democratic self-government by native rulers under the benevolent supervision of Dutch Residents. Indirect rule aimed at reconciling traditional forms with modern purposes by preserving the old customary law of the country and respecting the hereditary status of the native regents, while training up a native civil service on modern lines to carry out a wide scheme of modernization throughout the country. To complete the skeleton structure of self-government, a national parliament, the People's Council (*Volksraad*), was instituted in 1916 and first opened two years later. The composition and powers of this body reflected once again the Dutch faith in slow political evolution. It was essentially an advisory body, and for the first ten years of its existence it contained a majority both of Dutch members and of nominated members. But the Netherlands did not fail to make its ultimate political purpose clear. The Minister of Colonies in 1918 declared the aims of Dutch colonial policy in Indonesia to be 'to call as much as possible on the Indies' own forces in developing the country's resources ; to raise the population to such a level that they will be capable of attending to their own affairs and ruling their own country, and by so doing to lay the foundations for complete self-government'.

But good intentions were not enough. Indonesian nationalists in their post-war mood were beginning to demand something more than slow political evolution and assurances of goodwill. Besides, there appeared to them, during the decade 1920–30, to be too wide a discrepancy between political concession and economic progress. These were the boom years during which there was a spectacular expansion of production and a general rise in the level of prosperity in Indonesia. But increased prosperity brought no lull in nationalist activity. For a major effect of the economic expansion of the boom years, in the eyes of the Indonesian nationalist, was to entrench Dutch interests in Indonesia more firmly than ever. The boom brought not only a considerable expansion of the resident Dutch population (the 'blijvers') in Indonesia, but also a large increase in the numbers of Dutch civil servants, businessmen and technicians (the 'trekkers'), who came out from Holland for a period of service of anything up to thirty-five years. To the nationalist this seemed to mean that while the Dutch were conceding the forms of popular government with one hand they were strengthening their grip on the realities of administrative and economic control with the other. It seemed to show that whatever promises the Dutch might make, they had no intention of permitting any real shift of power during the lifetime of the present generation of Indonesians.

Not only did the First World War bring a revitalized nationalism to Indonesia ; it also brought the doctrines of international socialism and communism. The new political attitudes were reflected in the composition of the Sarekat Islam Party, and there followed a struggle for power within the party to decide which element would control policy. In 1923 the more radical revolutionary elements were expelled, and not long afterwards this left wing took off in independent flight as the Indonesian Communist Party, leaving the nationalists—an essentially middle-class group of lawyers, teachers and small professional men—in control of Sarekat Islam. The communists worked through labour groups and organizations, stirring up a series of disputes and strikes which culminated in a full-scale communist rising in 1926–7. The rising was rigorously suppressed; but though the communists had failed in revolution they had succeeded in discrediting the whole nationalist movement. Dutch sympathy with the idea of self-government almost evaporated, and by 1934 the chief nationalist leaders—Sukarno, Hatta and Shahrir—had been interned. For the hour of their release they had to wait until 1942 and the coming of the Japanese.

After the boom of the nineteen-twenties came the depression and the slump of the 'thirties. All the South-east Asian countries, with their heavy concentration on production for export, were badly hit by a rapid falling off in foreign buying. At the same time Japan began an economic invasion of South-east Asia with her cheap mass-produced goods. The Dutch administration in Java made a spirited attempt to meet the situation by establishing a quota system on imports and exports and by encouraging local manufacture of cheap consumer goods. One consequence of the developing international situation in the 'thirties was to bring out the tendency of the Dutch government in Java to treat Indonesia as a self-contained administrative entity whose interests might often be independent of those of Holland. The idea of independence was taking on new shades of meaning; the Dutch in Indonesia felt a renewed sense of partnership with Indonesians as the country weathered the depression and began to experience a revival of trade and production after 1936. That sense of partnership became deeper with the outbreak of World War II; and deeper still when Holland became cut off from her overseas colonies by German invasion.

In Malaya up to the nineteen-thirties the British administration was not called upon to make concessions to a nationalist movement, for no such movement existed. The reasons for delay in the awakening of Malayan nationalism were various; together they might be summed up as the combined effect of pluralism and prosperity. There was the political and administrative pluralism that arose out of the division of the Malay Peninsula into three Straits Settlements and nine Malay States. The Straits Settlements of Singapore, Penang and Malacca constituted a Crown colony under a Governor. But the Malay States had remained, in theory

and to some extent in practice, self-governing units under their
native rulers ; their relations with Britain were based on treaty
and not on conquest ; they were protected states and not colonies.
British protection over them was maintained in practice through
the Governor of the Straits Settlements in his other capacity
of High Commissioner for the Malay States, and through the
separate British Residents or Advisers who were attached to each
state.

But the nine Malay States did not all stand in a similar treaty
relationship with Britain. There was a further constitutional and
administrative distinction between the four states that had formed
a federation in 1895, and the five that were classified negatively, and
perhaps somewhat accusingly, as the Unfederated States.[1] The
rulers of the latter had separately agreed to be guided by British
Advisers, but they were not prepared to enter into a formal
association through which British guidance might be more easily
able to achieve uniformity among them in policy and administration. The Federated States had also undertaken by treaty to
accept British advice in all matters except those concerning religion
and custom. It could be said that all the Malay States had therefore
surrendered a considerable part of their independence, whatever
the constitutional theory of their relationship with Britain might
be. In fact, however, the Malay rulers and people were not disposed to think of the situation in terms of independence or
sovereignty. In practice there was co-operation and consultation
on both sides. Both sides doubtless took for granted the reality of
ultimate power that lay behind British protection, but persuasion
rather than power was the influence at work in Malaya.

A federal system inevitably required that the component states
should hand over to a central power the authority to act in certain
wide matters of common concern. But the absence of a clear
definition of such matters in the federation agreement of 1895
virtually placed the centre outside the circle ; it resulted in an
unusually unstable type of federal balance in which a British

---

[1] Federated States : Perak, Selangor, Negri Sembilan, Pahang.

Unfederated States : Kedah, Perlis, Kelantan, Trengganu, Johore, of which
the first four exchanged Siamese for British suzerainty in 1909 ; Johore accepted
a British Adviser in 1914.

R

Resident-General with undefined powers was in a position to draw
an increasing amount of initiative and direction to himself at the
centre. That was the tendency at first, so that the federation
appeared to be shaping towards a union. The establishment of a
Federal Council in 1909 served to emphasize this trend; being
composed of the British High Commissioner as President, the
Resident-General (soon renamed Chief Secretary), the four Malay
rulers, the four British Residents, and a small nominated unofficial
minority, it dwarfed the separate State Councils which had existed
since before federation, leaving them little room for independent
action. After 1930, however, there was a reaction in favour of
decentralization within the federal framework; the State Councils
were made more representative and were given separate authority
over certain matters—such as agriculture and education—within
their own borders.

The Malay States thus retained the forms of independent rule
along with the reality of separate though restricted legislative and
executive powers. But although the Malay people may therefore
have felt a sense of political gain rather than loss under British
protection, constitutional and administrative arrangements probably did not have the most important bearing on the slow development of political consciousness in Malaya. A more significant
factor was the pluralism that had rapidly become such a prominent
feature of the social pattern of the Malay Peninsula under British
rule and protection. In a population so racially diverse and
including so many transient elements, the development of a single
national consciousness, if possible at all, was bound to be extremely
slow. Within such a social pattern, if there were grievances among
the Malays they were economic rather than political grievances; if
there was patriotism among the Chinese it was patriotism for China
rather than for Malaya. As in all South-east Asian countries, the
local interests of the Chinese as a whole were capitalist or commercial rather than nationalist.

Besides all this there was general satisfaction with the British
regime because the economic prosperity that it brought, though
neither evenly shared nor steadily maintained, had transformed the
whole country. Malaya's foreign trade soared rapidly during the
boom years of the nineteen-twenties, reaching a peak value of

£264 million in 1926. The depression of the early 'thirties hit the country hard, but by 1938 the value of Malaya's trade stood at £121 million, which was more than the total value of New Zealand's trade and more than half the value of India's.

More so than in Malaya, official policy in Burma set great store by constitutional development along the historic lines of the British colonial system—a process of evolution from the simple Governor-in-Council type of rule through representative government to the ultimate possibility of responsible government. This was a policy that tended to concentrate on creating the forms rather than the spirit of constitutionalism; it involved much constitutional contrivance and administrative ingenuity. The process itself was a slow one in Burma up to 1923. Between 1897 and 1922 the Legislative Council included no more than two elected members out of thirty. But there was no political demand for a faster pace of constitutional advance. Burmese national sentiment had barely begun to recover from the shock of British conquest; it was quickened by Japan's victory over Russia in 1905, but it was not until after the First World War that it sprang suddenly and fully into new life at the time when fresh constitutional reforms for India were being proposed and debated.

The constitutional device of 'dyarchy' was applied to Burma in 1923, two years after it had been introduced in India. This amounted to a first instalment of parliamentary democracy on the British model. In the new legislature 80 members out of a total of 103 were to be elected by 2 million out of a population of 11 million. Certain fundamental matters (law and order, revenue, finance, irrigation) remained under the control of the Governor-in-Council, but other matters such as education, agriculture, public health and public works were placed under the control of ministers responsible to the legislature alone.

Burma received her next instalment of parliamentary government in 1937, at the time when her administrative connection with India was finally severed. There was now a legislature of two houses—a Senate, with one half its members elected and the other half nominated, and a fully elected House of Representatives. There were still certain reservations of authority to the Governor-in-Council (in matters concerning foreign relations, defence, currency, and the special areas containing the Shans, Karens and other hill people), but otherwise executive authority was vested in a full cabinet of ministers chosen from the political party holding a majority of seats in the parliament. The right to vote in parliamentary elections was granted to all males at the age of eighteen and to all females (subject to a literacy test) at the age of twenty-one. This was an unusually wide democratic franchise, even allowing for the comparatively high literacy rate (over 70 per cent among males in 1931), which Burma owed largely to her Buddhist schools.

It was hardly to be expected that the mere installation and setting in motion of constitutional machinery would satisfy the aspirations of Burmese nationalism. There was a growing demand for something more than representative or even responsible government. Burmese wanted to regain full independent control of their own political and economic life. They were inclined to regard the period of British rule as a kind of surgical operation, painful but necessary in order to bring modern Burma out into the world. They were not disposed to feel particularly grateful to the surgeon; it was his profession, and after all, they felt, he had drawn a fairly handsome fee. But they positively resented the presence of the horde of Indian assistants who were placed under him and who together derived considerable profit from the whole arrangement. They longed for the day when Burma would be able to leave the convalescent ward, to be free of the surgeon and the whole nursing staff, and to enjoy the pleasure of standing on her own feet.

Siam, with her flair for national survival, had escaped formal inclusion among the politically dependent territories of South-east Asia. Inevitably, however, she had been carried along in the general movement towards westernization, and in the process she had developed a degree of national awareness. Nationalism in Siam had no reason to manifest itself in antagonism towards the domination of an external power; it turned instead against internal powers within the state, against the economic domination of the Chinese community and the political domination of the Siamese monarchy.

The attack on the economic domination of the Chinese was bound to be largely ineffective ; it was a symptom of nationalist feeling rather than a practical economic proposition. It expressed itself in the imposition of a poll-tax on Chinese which led to rioting in Bangkok in 1910, and in later discriminatory legislation, but it never became a fully articulated or sustained national policy. The small middle class of Siamese saw little hope of winning economic power in their own country; for that reason they cherished all the more lively ambitions for political power.

Much of the actual achievement of westernization in Siam had been due to the judicious personal initiative of her kings ; they had appointed European specialists to advise on the modernization of various departments of state and the public services, and they had identified themselves closely with the whole process of reform. But in the end the monarchy was overtaken by the movement which it had itself begun. Associated with King Chulalongkorn (1868–1910) and his successors in the government of the country were an Executive and a Legislative Council, but membership of those bodies was restricted to royal princes, the king's ministers and foreign advisers, and nominated members of the aristocracy. The king retained absolute discretionary power in all matters ; he might be a benevolent despot in practice, but he remained a despot none the less. Thus the small group of Western-educated Siamese who longed for a share in political power were able to represent themselves as the party of constitutionalism as opposed to absolutism. In June 1932, with the backing of army and navy officers, they successfully carried through a *coup d'état* as a result of which the king consented to the restriction of his powers under a democratic type of constitution. But this bloodless revolution did not in fact bring democracy to Siam ; it merely widened the basis of oligarchy. It established a Council of Ministers and a People's Assembly, but it was the former that held real authority ; the politicians who belonged to it were the small group of men who had gained power through the revolution and who intended to keep that power to themselves. There was indeed little real basis as yet for national democratic institutions in Siamese society. As with the Malays of the peninsula, the great mass of the

Siamese were peasant cultivators whose minds were undisturbed by political ideas.

There was every likelihood that the political ideas of the West would be absorbed more rapidly by the inhabitants of French Indo-China than by those of other countries in South-east Asia. It was the French Revolution of 1789 that had provided the ideological basis for nationalism in Europe in the nineteenth and twentieth centuries, and political association of any kind with the French people was likely to result in a spread of liberal ideas. Not that French colonial policy as such consciously fostered nationalism or intentionally prepared dependent territories for self-government ; assimilation—in the economic and the cultural as well as in the political sense—rather than independence was the general purpose of French colonial rule. At first sight it might appear that in the particular case of Indo-China association rather than assimilation was the principle. The states of Cambodia, Laos, Annam and Tonkin were protectorates, not colonies, and French rule over them was indirect ; native rule and indigenous custom and institutions were modified but preserved. But, as elsewhere in South-east Asia, a façade of indirect rule was not incompatible with an inner reality of centralized imperial power, and the association of native with French administrators in the government of Indo-China was in practice extremely limited.

At the same time, Western-type education was likely to have more profoundly disturbing political effects in Indo-China than elsewhere for the reason that the major ethnic group, the Vietnamese, were above the average for South-east Asia in mental and physical ability. Among these people, who numbered about three-fourths of the total population of Indo-China, was a middle class whose economic position was based upon rice plantation and moneylending ; it was members of this class who were most affected by Western education and whose longing for political authority was largely frustrated by French paternalist policy. The political tensions of French Indo-China arose out of the reaction of a comparatively intelligent people to the apparent conflict between liberal-revolutionary theory and conservative colonial policy.

Education as a key to the whole process of modernization figured prominently among the aims of the early Vietnamese nationalists; indeed the demand for instruction in Western political and social techniques preceded the development of a revolutionary nationalist movement. The fact that the Chinese empire turned to the West for principles of constitutional and social reform during the decade following the Boxer Rebellion probably counted for more with the Vietnamese than Japan's example of successful westernization and her victory over Russia. If China could learn from the West, then indeed the West must have something to teach that was worth learning. The example of the Chinese revolution and the founding of the Kuomintang directed Vietnamese aims more consciously towards national independence.

Before the First World War, however, there were only minor skirmishes between Vietnamese intellectuals and students and the French administration. Vietnam nationalism as a movement really dates from the 1914–18 war; it gained much of its support, and derived some of its communist colouring, from the hundred thousand Vietnamese who had been brought to France as soldiers and workers during the war and who returned to Indo-China after 1918. During these vital post-war years the dissatisfaction of educated Vietnamese also grew as they remained largely excluded from administrative and political responsibility. Nationalism inevitably became more radical.

But nationalists at the same time became more divided. There were various parties and groups which more than once changed their name if not their programme. Of them all the left-wing revolutionary group, which had a Russian-trained leader—Ho Chi Minh—after 1927, showed most tenacity of purpose. A terrorist campaign was started in 1929; in the following year a Tonkinese garrison was incited to mutiny at Yen Bay and insurrections broke out in various parts. Order was quickly restored by the French; nationalist leaders of diverse revolutionary categories were arrested or fled the country. Ho Chi Minh fled to Hong Kong and was imprisoned there, but his communist group maintained continuity in organization and survived to form the core of the new party of Viet Minh which came into being in 1939. For the leaders of this party the Japanese occupation of Vietnam in 1941 was an intervention which appeared to brighten their prospects of becoming the ultimate heirs of French colonial power.

The idea of nationalism had been the most dynamic of Europe's exports to South-east Asia. If the experience of European rule had taught one clear lesson, it was that when a dependent people are brought into contact with ideas of self-government they must sooner or later be given self-government. But that lesson could not by itself provide a solution to the problem of nationalism; it could only define the approach to a solution. For it left unanswered the questions : how sooner ?—how later ?—and, what is the 'self' to which self-government is to be given ? To these questions each of the countries of South-east Asia has had to seek its own answers ; some have still to find them.

Chapter Eighteen

NEW NATIONS OF SOUTH-EAST ASIA

HARDLY had the South-east Asian countries emerged into the modern world before they found themselves caught up in the maelstrom of world war. And when it came, war swept the Western colonial and protective administrations almost completely away, leaving the native peoples alone to endure the years of Japanese occupation. The ultimate effects of that experience were to intensify nationalist sentiment and to accelerate the pace of independence movements everywhere.

The story of invasion, occupation and liberation between the years 1941 and 1945 need not be recounted here. It may be useful in these concluding pages, however, to attempt a rapid survey of some of the main changes that have taken place since the end of the Pacific war.

British rule in Burma, overthrown by the Japanese invasion in December 1941, was never to be fully restored. Nominal independence was conferred by Japan in 1943; and although the Japanese-sponsored Burma National Army welcomed the return of the British in 1945, its leader, Aung San, was determined to work on politically for real and full independence. He and his chief supporters were taken into the Governor's Executive Council in October 1946, and in January 1947 agreement was reached for the election of a constituent assembly which would determine the political future of Burma. This body resolved that Burma should become an independent republic. Aung San did not live to see his aims achieved, for he and six of his colleagues were assassinated soon afterwards. But the discussions with Britain were brought to a successful conclusion by others, and on 4 January 1948 Burma, with U Nu as Prime Minister, became fully independent.

British forces not only liberated Burma and moved into Malaya after the Japanese surrender in 1945. They also took over in Indonesia and in Indo-China, since neither the Dutch nor the French were in a position to send troops immediately to their pre-war colonial territories. In Java the British were faced with a difficult and dangerous situation, with some two hundred thousand Dutch prisoners of war and civil internees in camps throughout the island, and an organized, armed and potentially violent Indonesian republican movement in being, prepared to oppose the re-establishment of Dutch rule. The situation was met first by according *de facto* recognition to the republican leaders— Sukarno and his colleagues—and then attempting to bring the Dutch and Indonesians together to discuss the future political status of Indonesia. From the Dutch point of view the British attitude towards the republicans compromised the whole position from the start; but, apart from the wider international reasons for the weakness of the Dutch as negotiators, their statesmen were themselves unable to hold to one consistent attitude on the Indonesian question. They failed to make a firm choice between two broad alternatives of policy—either to refuse to deal with the republican leaders and revert to the pre-war programme of gradual preparation for Indonesian self-government at a pace controlled by themselves, or to accept the *de facto* position of the self-styled republican government and offer it immediate constitutional authority. Dutch policy wavered between these two alternatives; negotiations dragged on, with outbursts of fighting, until the Indonesian republic had succeeded in establishing itself in world opinion as an organized political entity, and the whole problem had been taken up on an international level by the United Nations. The final outcome was that full sovereignty over the former Netherlands East Indies, excluding West New Guinea and adjacent islands, was transferred in December 1949 to the republican government of Indonesia. West New Guinea was later transferred to United Nations interim administration in October 1962.

The French post-war position in Indo-China was particularly weak because the colonial administration there had already submitted to Japanese military occupation before the actual outbreak of war in the Pacific. The Japanese had moved into northern

Vietnam on the fall of France in 1940, and into the southern part of the country after the German invasion of Russia began in the following year. Thus by December 1941 the Japanese in Indo-China were poised for the swift descent upon Malaya that synchronized with their attack on the American Fleet in Pearl Harbour.

Like the Dutch in Indonesia, the French had to leave it to other forces to take over from the defeated Japanese in Vietnam—to the British in the south and centre, and to the Chinese in the north. Nevertheless the French were able to open discussions with nationalist leaders as early as October 1945, and there appear to have been opportunities for reaching a reasonable agreement. But the Viet Minh nationalist party, which had declared an independent republic and set up a provisional government in August 1945, could not be won over, and early in 1947 fighting began. It was over seven years later (May 1954) before France was finally compelled to admit military defeat, but by that time Vietnam itself had become divided into two separate parts, with a communist Viet Minh government in the north, and the government of the French-sponsored 'associated state' of Vietnam in the south. This division between north and south was formally acknowledged in the cease-fire agreement reached at Geneva in July 1954. French forces finally withdrew from the north in October of that year, and from the south two years later. In 1955 South Vietnam was declared an independent republic, but North Vietnam remained a separate communist state.

In Malaya there was no organized nationalist movement in existence when war ended. But Britain's post-war proposals to replace the traditional machinery of separate Malay states by a unified system of government for the whole country met with unexpectedly strong opposition from the Malay leaders, and soon had the effect of arousing a new political consciousness among the people in general. The British proposals were withdrawn in 1948 in favour of the pre-war federal system in a modified form. But in the same year Malaya found herself at war against an army of communist guerrillas operating from within the dense jungle. It was another twelve years (1960) before this communist bid for power was finally defeated. Meanwhile Malaya's political evolution went forward slowly but steadily; indeed the war against the communists helped to create a growing sense of common purpose. In August 1957 Britain withdrew from her protectorate over the Malay States, and Malaya became an independent nation.

The island of Singapore, historically a colony as distinct from a protected state, and with a predominantly Chinese population, obtained internal self-government in 1958 under a separate agreement with Britain. But political, economic and geographical considerations all pointed to the need for some form of merger between Singapore and Malaya, most likely within a wider association which would include the three predominantly Malay-peopled territories of northern Borneo. Of these, the British-protected state of Brunei had become the wealthiest since the discovery of oil there in 1929. Sarawak, ruled by the Brooke family from 1841, was ceded to Britain in 1946; and in the same year North Borneo was transferred to the British government from the chartered company which had administered the territory since 1882.

The question of the post-war political status of the Philippines was a straightforward one, since the United States had explicitly promised that the islands would receive full independence in 1946. The presence of President Quezon and his cabinet in Washington during the war made it only more certain that America's promise would be fulfilled. Although Quezon himself died in 1944, the independent republic of the Philippines came into being, with Roxas as president, on 4 July 1946.

For the newly-independent countries of South-east Asia self-government meant the end of old sources of political conflict, but it meant also the beginning of new ones. These countries had won a new international status, but they had yet to achieve national unity. During the first decade of independence the authority of Burma's government was challenged by Karens, by communists and by general lawlessness. The Indonesian government was faced with guerrilla warfare, by armed communist revolt, by political extremism combined with religious fanaticism, and by separatist movements in the various island territories and among the diverse populations that made up the new republic. The government of the Philippines had a communist-agrarian revolt on its hands until 1957. Vietnam was tragically partitioned into two separate states. Malaya had inherited the unresolved problem of balancing Malay political authority and Chinese economic power. And in all these countries the old problem of the overseas Chinese assumed a new significance in 1949 with the establishment of a communist regime in China.

Nor did independence necessarily bring democracy, even where democratic machinery existed. Army leaders held the keys to power in Burma, where they took over the government itself in 1958 and 1962. In Thailand, the one independent state of South-east Asia before the war, a series of post-war *coups d'état* left almost unchanged the oligarchic pattern of government established by the revolution of 1932. The people of Cambodia, Laos and Vietnam all lived under personal or party rule of one political label or another. In Indonesia a system of guided democracy left effective power in the hands of one man, President Sukarno, who was closely associated with the military leaders. Only in Malaya, Singapore and the Philippines could democracy be seen in operation as a working system. In general throughout South-east Asia, the peasant village communities had not been greatly affected by the achievement of national independence. Even where an electoral system functioned, there was hardly any political link between village and parliament. Nor was there anywhere a middle class sufficiently large and sufficiently educated to form the basis of a genuine democracy in the western sense. Everywhere there was a wide political gap between the ruling class and the mass of the people, such a gap as had existed in South-east Asia in medieval times and since. Even in the Philippines, politically more mature than the other countries of the region, political as well as economic power was in the hands of a ruling class which formed hardly more than 5 per cent of the total population.

Above all, political independence had brought no speedy solutions of the economic problems that beset the countries of South-east Asia. The main problems which they all shared were the creation of capital and the increase and diversification of production. After the war and until the middle of 1953 there was a world shortage of rice, and the main rice-exporting countries of South-east Asia—Burma, Thailand and Vietnam—were able to obtain high prices. But by 1954 there was an increasing world surplus of export rice, and prices fell. Similarly, post-war world demand for South-east Asian tin, rubber and copra reached a peak in the boom year of 1951, but the following year saw a drop in demand and a rapid fall in prices. South-east Asia's extreme dependence upon a fluctuating world demand for her agricultural and mineral exports thus remained a constant feature of the region's economy.

For a long-term solution to the problem of South-east Asia's dependent economic status, statesmen and leaders in general were looking more and more to the development of a degree of industrialization as the path to a more diversified production. An industrial revolution, they felt, would be necessary in order to win the economic welfare which political revolution by itself could not achieve. But industrialization would require investment capital as well as the technical and managerial skill which the South-east Asian nations could not of themselves yet provide. Their immediate problem was how to obtain foreign capital and economic aid without reopening the door too wide to foreign political influence. In countries where national independence meant the removal of colonial rule it was understandable that there should be a tendency to equate capital with capitalism and imperialism, but it remained inescapably true for all South-east Asian countries that, as the 1952 conference of the United Nations Economic Commission for Asia and the Far East declared, 'foreign capital and foreign aid are still needed on a basis of mutual agreement in developing agricultural and industrial resources'. Yet material progress in South-east Asia would everywhere depend in the last resort upon the efforts of the people themselves. What they needed in the post-war world, more perhaps than foreign aid, was energy, enterprise, and faith in the future.

Looking back over the past, the new nations of South-east Asia could see the colonial era as a comparatively short phase in their long history. But it was during that phase, and especially during the short space of seventy years between 1870 and 1940, that the South-east Asian countries were started off on the road to an economic, social and political transformation which amounted to a revolution. It remained an unfinished revolution, one which the new nations must now carry forward alone and in their own way ; they could not turn back.

For centuries prior to the colonial era the countries of South-east Asia were often at war with one another. Had their common experience of colonialism created new bonds of sympathy between them ? The future historian may be able to show that colonialism not only brought the countries of South-east Asia out into a wider world, but also brought them closer together than ever before. Evidence of growing co-operation between them might be seen in the participation of Burma, Cambodia, Laos, Vietnam, Malaya and Indonesia in the Colombo Plan, originated in 1950 ; in the South-east Asia Treaty Organisation, founded in 1954 for mutual defence, and including Thailand and the Philippines as members ; in the Association of South-east Asia for economic, cultural and scientific co-operation, founded in 1961 by Thailand, Malaya and the Philippines ; in the movement towards a Greater Malaysia comprising Malaya, Singapore, Sarawak, Brunei and North Borneo ; and in the joint plans for the development of the lower Mekong river by Thailand, Laos, Cambodia and South Vietnam. Examples of co-operative action such as these seemed to indicate a growing sense of unity and common purpose among the new nations of South-east Asia.

BOOKS FOR FURTHER READING

A select list of modern works

GENERAL

Coedès, G. *Les états hindouisés d'Indochine et d'Indonésie.* Paris, 1948.

Du Bois, C. *Social Forces in Southeast Asia.* Minnesota/London, 1949.

Emerson, R., Mills, L. A., and Thompson, V. *Government and Nationalism in Southeast Asia.* New York, 1942.

Fifield, H. R. *The Diplomacy of Southeast Asia, 1945–1958.* New York, 1958.

Furnivall, J. S., *Colonial Policy and Practice.* Cambridge, 1948, 1956.

Hall, D. G. E. *A History of South-East Asia.* London/New York, 1955.

Kahin, G. McT. (ed.) *Governments and Politics of Southeast Asia.* Ithaca, 1959.

Landon, K. P. *Southeast Asia, Crossroads of Religions.* Chicago, 1949.

Mills, L. A. (ed.). *The New World of Southeast Asia.* Minneapolis, 1948.

Purcell, V. W. *The Chinese in Southeast Asia.* London, 1951.

Vandenbosch, A. and Butwell, R. *Southeast Asia Among the World Powers.* Lexington, 1958.

BURMA

Cady, J. F. *A History of Modern Burma.* Ithaca, 1958.

Donnison, F. S. V. *Public Administration in Burma.* London, 1952.

Hall, D. G. E. *Europe and Burma.* London, 1945.
        Burma. London, 1950.

Tinker, H. *The Union of Burma.* London, 1961.

Woodman, D. *The Making of Burma.* London, 1962.

THAILAND

Blanchard, W. (ed.). *Thailand.* New Haven, 1958.

Graham, W. A. *Siam.* London, 1924.

Ingram, J. C. *Economic Change in Thailand since 1950.* Stanford, 1955.

LAOS

Lebar, F. M. and Suddard, A. *Laos.* New Haven, 1960.

CAMBODIA

Briggs, L. P. *The Ancient Khmer Empire.* Philadelphia, 1951, 1955.

Coedès, G. *Pour mieux comprendre Angkor.* Paris, 1947.

Groslier, B. and Arthaud, J. *Angkor: Art and Civilization.* London, 1957.

Steinberg, D. J. (ed.). *Cambodia.* New Haven, 1957, 1959.

VIETNAM

Buttinger, J. *The Smaller Dragon.* New York, 1958.
Cady, J. F. *The Roots of French Imperialism in Eastern Asia.* Ithaca, 1954.
Hammer, E. *The Struggle for Indochina.* Stanford, 1954.
Robequain, C. *Economic Development of French Indo-China.* Oxford, 1945.

MALAYA

Kennedy, J. *A History of Malaya, 1400–1959.* London, 1962.
Mills, L. A. *British Malaya, 1824–1867.* London, 1925.
          British Rule in Eastern Asia. Oxford, 1942.
Moorhead, F. J. *A History of Malaya and her Neighbours, Vol. I.* London, 1957.
Swettenham, Sir F. *British Malaya.* London, 1948.
Wheatley, P. *The Golden Khersonese.* Kuala Lumpur, 1961.
Winstedt, Sir R. *Malaya and its History.* London, 1949.
          The Malays, a Cultural History. London, 1950.

BORNEO

Irwin, G. *Nineteenth-Century Borneo.* The Hague, 1955.
Runciman, Sir S. *The White Rajahs.* Cambridge, 1960.
Tregonning, K. G. *Under Chartered Company Rule.* Singapore, 1958.

INDONESIA

Allen, G. C. and Donnithorne, A. G. *Western Enterprise in Indonesia and Malaya.* London, 1957.
De Graaf, H. J. *Geschiedenis van Indonesië.* The Hague/Bandung, 1949.
De Klerck, E. S. *History of the Netherlands East Indies.* Rotterdam, 1938.
Furnivall, J. S. *Netherlands India.* Cambridge, 1939, 1944.
Kahin, G. Mc. T. *Nationalism and Revolution in Indonesia.* Ithaca, 1952.
Palmier, L. *Indonesia and the Dutch.* London, 1961.
Van Leur, J. C. *Indonesian Trade and Society.* The Hague, 1955.
Vlekke, B. H. M. *Nusantara.* The Hague/Bandung, 1959.

PHILIPPINES

Corpuz, O. D. *The Bureaucracy in the Philippines.* Manila, 1957.
Forbes, W. C. *The Philippine Islands.* Cambridge, Mass., 1945.
Hayden, J. R. *The Philippines.* New York, 1942.
Phelan, J. L. *The Hispanization of the Philippines.* Madison, 1959.
Rosinger, L. K. *The Philippines.* New York, 1948.
Zaide, G. F. *Philippine Political and Cultural History.* Manila, 1957.

INDEX

A

Abdul Fatah Agung, Sultan, 110
Achin, 23, 52, 62, 64, 79, 80–3, 86, 89, 96, 98, 99, 102, 107–9, 116–18, 153, 163, 192, 196, 202
Aguinaldo, E., 238, 239
Airlangga, King, 31
Alaungpaya, King, 145, 148, 149
Amaravati, 15
Amboyna, 72, 75, 89, 95, 96, 99, 100, 102, 106, 113, 114, 124, 131, 132, 160, 164
Amiens, Peace of, 162, 164, 167
Amsterdam, 87, 88, 89, 115, 127, 165
Anauratha, King, 37, 38
Andamans, 159
Angkor, 28, 32–5, 40, 46, 78, 180
Anglo-Dutch Convention (1814), 175, 176
Anglo-Dutch Treaty (1824), 177, 182, 192, 193
Annam, 47, 49, 150, 226, 250
Arabs, 12, 42, 53, 110, 126, 181, 184, 198
Arakan, 78, 177–9, 194
Auchmuty, Sir Samuel, 164
Aung San, 253
Australoids, 4
Austronesians, 4, 5
Ava, 76, 120, 121, 124, 144, 145, 178, 179, 191, 194
Ayuthia, 40, 76, 77, 78, 98, 102, 122, 123, 145, 146

B

Bacsonian culture, 5
Balambangan, 143, 144
Bali, ix, 7, 30, 88, 93, 109, 138, 140, 168, 220

Bandas, 42, 52, 62, 63, 72, 89, 96, 97, 99, 100, 101, 102, 113, 114, 124, 160, 164
Bandon, Bay of, 36, 46, 76
Bangkok, 123, 146, 180, 194, 230, 249
Banjermassin, 98, 142, 193
Banka, 24, 118, 142, 156, 191, 209, 223
Bantam, 62, 88, 89, 94, 95, 96, 98, 100, 101, 102, 104, 105, 110, 111, 124, 125, 129, 139, 140, 169, 173
Barbosa, Duarte, 64
Bassein, 123, 148
Bataks, 5, 8
Batavia (see also Jacarta, Jakarta), 23, 101, 102, 103, 106, 109, 110, 111, 112, 115, 116, 118, 121, 127, 128, 129, 135, 136, 138, 140–1, 144, 155, 156, 161, 162, 163, 164, 165, 169, 182, 196, 197, 209, 223
Battambang, 180
Batu Sawar, 119
Bencoolen, 124, 125, 141, 142, 143, 144, 155, 175, 177
Bengal, Bengalis, 26, 29, 51, 63, 64, 115, 151, 178
Bengkalis, 119, 142
Best, Thomas, 98
Bhadravarman, King, 15
Bhamo, 196
Billiton, 118, 164, 177, 191, 193, 209, 223
Bintang, 79, 80, 118, 119
Bombay, 106, 148, 162
Borneo, ix, 10, 12, 15, 16, 20, 47, 48, 62, 63, 93, 142, 143, 164, 192, 196, 205, 209, 222, 223, 226, 256, 259
Borobodur, 27, 35
Bort, B., 117, 118, 125
Both, Pieter, 96

PRINTED BY PURNELL AND SONS, LTD.
PAULTON (SOMERSET) AND LONDON